Translated Texts for H

300–800 AD is the time of late antiquity and the early middle ages: the transformation of the classical world, the beginnings of Europe and of Islam, and the evolution of Byzantium. TTH makes available sources translated from Greek, Latin, Syriac, Coptic, Arabic, Georgian, Gothic and Armenian. Each volume provides an expert scholarly translation, with an introduction setting texts and authors in context, and with notes on content, interpretation and debates.

A full list of published titles in the **Translated Texts for Historians** series is available on request. The most recently published are shown below.

Two Early Lives of Severos, Patriarch of Antioch
Translated with an introduction and notes by SEBASTIAN BROCK and BRIAN FITZGERALD
Volume 59, 175pp., 2013, ISBN 978-1-84631-882-5 cased, 978-1-84631-883-2 limp

The Funerary Speech for John Chrysostom
Translated with an introduction and notes by TIMOTHY D. BARNES and GEORGE BEVAN
Volume 60, 193pp., ISBN 978-1-84631-887-0 cased, 978-1-84631-888-7 limp

The Acts of the Lateran Synod of 649
Translated with notes by RICHARD PRICE, with contributions by PHIL BOOTH and CATHERINE CUBITT
Volume 61, 476pp., ISBN 978-1-78138-039-0 cased

Macarius, *Apocriticus*
Translated with introduction and commentary by JEREMY M. SCHOTT and MARK J. EDWARDS
Volume 62, 476pp., ISBN 978 1 78138 129 8 cased, ISBN 978 1 78138 130 4 limp

Khalifa ibn Khayyat's *History* **on the Umayyad Dynasty (660–750)**
Translated with introduction and commentary by CARL WURTZEL
and prepared for publication by ROBERT G. HOYLAND
Volume 63, 332pp., ISBN 978 1 78138 174 8 cased, 978 1 78138 175 5 limp

Between City and School: Selected Orations of Libanius
RAFFAELLA CRIBIORE
Volume 65, 272pp, ISBN 978 1 78138 252 3 cased, 978 1 78138 253 0 limp

Isidore of Seville *On the Nature of Things*
Translated with introduction, notes, and commentary by
CALVIN B. KENDALL and FAITH WALLIS
Volume 66, 328pp., ISBN 978 1 78138 293 6 cased, ISBN 978 1 78138 294 3 limp

Imperial Invectives against Constantius II: Athanasius of Alexandria, *History of the Arians*, **Hilary of Poitiers,** *Against Constantius* **and Lucifer of Cagliari,** *The Necessity of Dying for the Son of God*
Translated with introduction and commentary by RICHARD FLOWER
Volume 67, 240pp., ISBN 978 1 78138 327 8 cased, 978 1 78138 328 5 limp

The Acts of the Second Council of Nicaea (787)
Translated with an introduction and notes by RICHARD PRICE
Volume 68, 760pp., ISBN 978 1 78694 127 5 cased

For full details of **Translated Texts for Historians**, including prices and ordering information, please write to the following: **All countries, except the USA and Canada:** Liverpool University Press, 4 Cambridge Street, Liverpool, L69 7ZU, UK (*Tel* +44-[0]151-794 2233, *Fax* +44-[0]151-794 2235, Email janmar@liv.ac.uk, http://www.liverpooluniversitypress.co.uk). **USA and Canada:** Turpin Distribution, www.turpin-distribution.com.

Translated Texts for Historians
Volume 69

The 'History of the Kings of the Persians' in Three Arabic Chronicles

The Transmission of the Iranian Past from Late Antiquity to Early Islam

Translated with introduction and notes

by ROBERT G. HOYLAND

Liverpool
University
Press

First published 2018
Liverpool University Press
4 Cambridge Street
Liverpool, L69 7ZU

British Library Cataloguing-in-Publication Data
A British Library CIP Record is available.

ISBN 978 1 78694 146 6 cased
ISBN 978 1 78694 147 3 limp

Typeset by Carnegie Book Production, Lancaster
Printed and bound by CPI Group (UK) Ltd, Croydon, CR0 4YY

CONTENTS

ACKNOWLEDGEMENTS

This book started its life as part of an attempt by me to introduce more Arabic texts into the series Translated Texts for Historians, for which I am a member of the Editorial Committee. I chose Persian-related texts as I was preparing a course on 'Iran from the Sasanids to the Samanids' at St Andrews University at the time and was working on the translation of Bertold Spuler's *Iran in frühislamischer Zeit* (Wiesbaden, 1952; English translation: Leiden, 2015). My long-term passion for historiography was piqued by the question of by what means and in what form material about pre-Islamic Persia was transmitted to Muslim sources, and was enlivened by discussions with my student Michael Jackson Bonner, who wrote a doctoral dissertation (Oxford, 2011–14) on Ahmad al-Dinawari, one of the earliest extant Muslim authors on Persian history.

For academic assistance I am immensely grateful to my friends and colleagues Khodadad Rezakhani, who patiently answered my many Persian language queries, Adam Silverstein, who offered an encouraging and constructive reading of the final draft, Mary Whitby, who offered both positive feedback and useful criticism, and Tim Greenwood and Philip Wood, who kindly discussed their ideas on late antique historiography with me. I should also like to acknowledge Koken Ishii (NYU) for his excellent work on the tables and maps of this book, and my students Charles Mercer and Edward Zychowicz-Coghill (Oxford) for their contribution to an early stage of this project. For succour of a different kind I am truly thankful to Linda and Roger, who provided a peaceful and loving New Mexico retreat in the course of 2017, which allowed me to complete this book in a shorter time than would otherwise have been possible. To Sarah I as always owe everything, both for her thoughtful suggestions and revisions and for her love and support. And to Moss I can, in retrospect, say thank you for the frequent distractions and diversions, which meant that I didn't lose touch with reality.

Abu Dhabi, November 2017.

ABBREVIATIONS

b. = *ibn*, meaning 'son (of)' in Arabic

bt. = *bint* meaning 'daughter (of)' in Arabic

CHIr = *The Cambridge History of Iran*, 7 volumes (Cambridge, 1968–91)

EI = *The Encyclopedia of Islam*, 3 editions (Leiden, 1913–36, 1954–2005, 2007–)

EIr = *Encyclopedia Iranica* (Columbia University, New York, 1982–)

MP = Middle Persian (= Arsacid and Sasanid period)

NP = New Persian (= Islamic period)

OP = Old Persian (= Achaemenid period)

CONVENTIONS

Proper names

One finds considerable diversity in the rendering of pre-Islamic Persian names in modern literature. This reflects the fact that the Persian language has a long history and names have changed their forms over time and that Persian and Arabic have been transliterated into English in different ways by modern scholars. Since my three authors are writing in Arabic and since the transliteration of Arabic into English had been more standardised than that of Persian into English, I have chosen to give the form of the names as they appear in Arabic. If the Persian form substantially differs from the Arabic form I give it in a footnote so that readers can still find it in reference works that, like the *Encyclopaedia Iranica*, favour the Persian form of names. Where names have a well-known English form (e.g. Zoroaster), I have used that rather than the Persian or Arabic form.

Orthography of foreign words

In accordance with TTH conventions I have minimised the use of diacritical marks and the Arabic definite article al-, including them only for little known or uncertain proper names and for words and phrases in the original Persian, Aramaic and Arabic.

References to persons and places

Many persons are mentioned by my three authors, most of whom have their own entries in either the *Encyclopaedia Iranica* (available free online at http://www.iranicaonline.org/) or the *Encyclopaedia of Islam* (available via Brill online), or both. I will give basic information about them, but readers should consult these two encyclopaedias if they wish to know more. The same goes for places, although I have appended a gazetteer and maps to this book so that readers can locate them.

Use of parentheses in the translations

[ ] = information inserted: page numbers, subheadings, numbers to distinguish homonymous kings.
() = words inserted: words missing in the original, words needed to complete the sense or for clarification, words in the original language.

INTRODUCTION

AIMS OF THE PRESENT STUDY

The 'History[1] of the Kings of the Persians'[2] is a title applied to a number of works that were produced in the first century of the Abbasid dynasty (750–850), which governed the Islamic Caliphate from its base in Baghdad. They purport to narrate the career of the Persian[3] Empire (equating approximately, at its height, to modern Iraq, Iran, Turkmenistan and Afghanistan) from its beginnings until its demise in the year 651–52. The basic outline of their narrative is the same in most Muslim accounts: Gayumart, the first man,[4] followed by the four major dynasties of the Pishdadids, Kayanids, Arsacids and Sasanids, the second and fourth of which are brought to a violent end by outsiders, namely the Macedonians under Alexander the Great and the Arabs under the first Muslim caliphs. The account proceeds ruler by ruler in pretty much the same order and comprising mostly the same cast of kings, but there is very considerable variation in the nature and quantity of the information relayed about each

---

1 Two different Arabic words are used for 'History' in this title: either *Ta'rīkh*, which signifies chronologically ordered history, or *Siyar*, which indicates biographically focused history (the singular, *sīra*, refers to the way in which one conducts one's life). In the context of the Persian kings *siyar* may well translate/reflect the Persian word *kār*, denoting the heroic deeds and accomplishments of a person.

2 Two different Arabic words are used for 'Persians' in this title: either *Furs*, which follows Greek and Syriac sources in making the residents of Fars (where the Achaemenids and Sasanids were from) emblematic of the whole people, or *'Ajam*, which simply means non-Arab, but was mostly used to refer to the Persians.

3 I will use the terms 'Persia' and 'Persian' in this book to designate the Empire that was ruled from Seleucia-Ctesiphon (Arabic: Mada'in) and its citizens, simply because that is what our (Greek, Syriac and Arabic) sources do. I will use the terms 'Iran' and 'Iranian' when I am thinking particularly of the land of Iran and its residents. In reality the lands of the Persian Empire comprised very diverse peoples possessing numerous identities.

4 I.e. the first man in Persian tradition (*EIr*, 'Gayomart', 'Gayomard'); when confronted with Biblical history in Islamic times, Persian scholars often identified him with Adam, or sometimes with Gomer, grandson of Noah (see discussion in Tabari, 1.147–49).

one of them.[5] The style and content are of an epic nature, relating the valorous deeds, praiseworthy achievements and tyrannical acts of the sovereigns of Persia and their struggles with enemies at home and abroad. What is the origin of all these works and why do they follow much the same order and recount much the same events, albeit with considerable variation in detail? It has been concluded, reasonably enough, that some common source or sources underlie their shared storyline. Sadly, we have almost no extant historical texts from pre-Islamic Persia, and so it is to Muslim historians that we must turn to investigate this question. The earliest of them are the following:

Abu Hanifa Ahmad al-Dinawari (henceforth Dinawari), d. *ca.* 895

Ahmad ibn Wadih al-Yaʿqubi (henceforth Yaʿqubi), d. *ca.* 910

Muhammad ibn Jarir al-Ṭabari (henceforth Tabari), d. 923

ʾAli ibn Husayn al-Masʿudi (henceforth Masʿudi), d. *ca.* 960

Hamza al-Isfahani (henceforth Hamza[6]), d. *ca.* 960s

The writings of Dinawari and Tabari on Persian history have already been translated and mined for clues about their sources,[7] and so it is the remaining three that I shall treat in this volume: Yaʿqubi, Masʿudi and Hamza. I should make clear at the outset that I am not translating the whole of their works, but only the part that deals with the Persians before Islam, and furthermore I do so with the express aim of trying to understand the transmission of such material. I apologise for this blatantly utilitarian approach, but excuse myself on the grounds that the subject is worthy of the attention of historians and that the translations are useful for illustrating what sort of material we are dealing with. The justification for including them in the Translated Texts for Historians series, which does not usually venture much past 800 AD, is that my authors are taking their accounts from works entitled 'History of the Kings of the Persians' that were composed in the late eighth–early ninth century. To what degree these latter rely on late antique sources will be discussed below.

---

5 For a detailed overview see *CHIr* 3.366–83 (in ch. 10b: 'Iranian National History').

6 Hamza's first name is much rarer than that of Yaʿqubi and Masʿudi, whereas his surname is more common, hence my choice to refer to him by his first name.

7 On Dinawari see Bonner, *Historiographical Study*, and on Tabari see Nöldeke, *Sasaniden*. Bonner provides a translation in the appendix to his work, and Tabari's section on the Persians is translated into German by Nöldeke and into English by C.E. Bosworth (see Bibliography).

HISTORICAL OVERVIEW[8]

Muslim historians give us no concrete information about the first two Persian dynasties, the Pishdadids and the Kayanids, and since they are not mentioned in any other surviving writings or documents we are unable to place them in space or time. They are said to have resided in Balkh, in modern north Afghanistan, and it is possible that they were local east Iranian rulers who escaped the attention of the wider world. The third dynasty, the Arsacids, are real enough, successors to the Seleucids in the East, but their treatment is extremely cursory in our Muslim sources. It is only with the rise of the Sasanid family[9] in AD 224 that we begin to get more extensive coverage and some historical data that match what we find in non-Persian writings, particularly Greco-Roman histories. Under these rulers, the Persian Empire pursued a more centralising and expansionist policy than their Arsacid predecessors, challenging the dominance of the Roman[10] Empire. The Sasanid emperor Shabur I (242–73), for example, launched a series of devastating attacks upon the Roman Empire's eastern flank, achieving numerous victories and even managing to capture the Roman emperor Valerian in AD 260. Only the intervention of the prefect of Palmyra, who rallied an army of townsmen and tribesmen, saved Rome from Shabur's seemingly unstoppable onslaught. Thereafter the two empires came to a grudging acceptance of one another, mostly respecting each other's sovereignty except for occasional skirmishes and forays to extract tribute and captives and to make a show of strength for audiences back home.

Matters changed in the sixth century, which witnessed a sharp escalation in hostilities, culminating in what has been described as the

---

8 This overview is meant only as a brief introduction for the newcomer to this period and region, and so I do not give any references. For more information and suggested reading see, in chronological order of coverage, Wiesehöfer, *Ancient Persia*; Daryaee, *Sasanid Persia*; *id.* and Rezakhani, *Late Antique Iran*; Spuler, *Iran*. The best reference work is the *CHIr*, vols 2 (Medians and Achaemenids), 3 (Seleucids, Parthians and Sasanids) and 4 (early medieval Islamic period).

9 Although 'Sasanian' is now a more common way of referring to the dynasty of the House of Sasan than 'Sasanid', I use the latter here since the Greek -id ending is almost always used for the other major dynasties featuring in this book: Achaemenids, Arsacids, Abbasids and Samanids.

10 I will use the single term 'Roman' in this book for the Empire that was ruled first from Rome and then from Constantinople, in part because that is what our sources do and in part to avoid the messiness of having to decide when to use Roman and when to use Byzantine (which is a modern term not used by the people themselves or their neighbours).

last great military confrontation of antiquity, when the emperor Khusraw II (590–628) waged all-out war against the Romans. The onward march of his forces seemed impossible to check: Syria was captured by 610, Palestine by 614, Egypt by 619 and Anatolia as far as the walls of Constantinople itself by 626. Yet the Roman emperor Heraclius (610–41) launched a desperate and dramatic counterstrike by marching through Armenia and attacking Persia from the north, supported by a large Turkish contingent. Thus he was able to strike at the heart of his enemy's empire, advancing on their capital, sacking royal residences as he went and putting the defeated and disgraced emperor Khusraw to flight. The latter's son, Shirawayh, made peace with Heraclius in 628 and agreed to restore to the Romans all of the lands seized by the Persian troops. Yet he was unable to ensure stability at home. The Persian Empire descended into civil war, rival factions putting up their own candidates for the imperial office. Arab tribes took advantage of the chaos in the Persian sphere and the weakness in the Roman lands to launch major raids right across the Middle East. The Persian capital, which was exposed to the Syrian desert, fell quickly to the Arabs in 638 and thereafter the last Persian emperor, Yazdagird III, remained on the run until his death at the hands of one of his own subjects in the year 651–52.[11]

The first Muslim Arab dynasty, the Umayyad clan of Quraysh (661–750), chose Damascus as its capital and relied on Syrian Arabs for military muscle, and so the lands of the former Persian Empire were relegated to provincial status. However, the 50,000 Arab soldiers who were stationed in the east Iranian city of Merv in the 670s mostly married local women and assimilated to the local culture. When a branch of Quraysh more closely related to the prophet Muhammad's son-in-law, 'Ali, joined forces with a charismatic east Iranian figure by the name of Abu Muslim, they successfully subverted the troops of Merv to their cause of overthrowing the Umayyads. The victors, the Abbasid clan of Quraysh, moved the capital to Iraq and drew heavily on the men of Merv and east Iran more generally, who came to dominate both the army and the bureaucracy. The new imperial headquarters, Baghdad, lay only a short distance from the former Persian capital, and many who ran the new government were of Persian extraction, who now felt confident to celebrate their origins and

---

11 Muslim historians place his death in 31 AH = August 651–August 652 AD, but do not specify the month. The later date used to be favoured, but now it has become common to choose 651.

their culture. Books on Persian wisdom, courtly manners and imperial history began to circulate, in part translated from Persian originals and in part recreated and reimagined for a new age.[12] The eight authors of Persian histories listed by the scholar Hamza al-Isfahani all belong to this wave of new Persians, who came to the fore in the first Abbasid century (750–850).[13]

These pioneers in the creation of an Arabo-Persian imperial culture wrote when the Islamic Empire was booming and Baghdad was a vibrant metropolis, perhaps the biggest in the world at that time. However, the caliph Harun al-Rashid (786–809) unwisely divided the empire between his two sons, Amin and Ma'mun, which led to a civil war that accelerated the centrifugal elements in the vast territories of the Islamic Empire. Since Amin held the west and centre, Ma'mun had to rely on support from even further to the east, including Turkish soldiers. Surprisingly quickly, Turkish generals came to wield enormous power and in the 860s were responsible for the death of four caliphs in quick succession. Large chunks of the empire broke away, ruled by either one of these Turkish warlords or some other strongman. The three chroniclers whose work I translate here all grew up in this fragmented Islamic world. Yet, despite this fragmentation, it was still a culturally vibrant world, for instead of a single large court, based in Baghdad, there were now numerous smaller courts, based in regional capitals, all seeking to demonstrate their cultural credentials. Some of these favoured the Persian language, such as the court of the Samanid dynasty (892–999), headquartered in Bukhara. It was not long before the individual efforts to produce a uniform history of ancient Persia by the scholars of the early Abbasid age led to more directed initiatives by the new Persian-speaking monarchies of the East. The culmination of this was the versified history composed by Firdawsi at the behest of Sultan Mahmud of Ghazna, the energetic ruler of the youthful Ghaznavid Empire, based in modern east Afghanistan, and presented to him in AD 1010. It was entitled the 'Book of Kings' (*Shāh-nāmah*)[14] and was quickly recognised as a monumental achievement that has until this day not been supplanted.

---

12 See Savant, *New Muslims*, for interesting discussion of aspects of this process.
13 See Hamza, 8–9, below.
14 This is the Arabic pronunciation of the name, sometimes written *Shāh-nāma* (the final h is written, but not pronounced); it is also referred to according to the Persian pronunciation: *Shāh-nāmeh/Shāh-nāme*.

HISTORIOGRAPHICAL BACKGROUND:
A SASANID OFFICIAL CHRONICLE?

All Muslim chronicles that take Creation as their starting point recount the histories of three particular pre-Islamic peoples – they may well treat others, but these three always feature. They are the Israelites, included because they were considered part of world religious history and relevant to many stories in the Qur'an; the pre-Islamic Arabs, because they were deemed crucial for explaining where the Muslims came from and for providing a genealogical link to Abraham and Ishmael; and the Persians. The appearance of the latter in the list might seem odd, given that they were, in the pre-Islamic period, dualists, a group condemned in the Qur'an. However, Persian Muslims were so prominent in the intellectual life of the Islamic Empire that they managed to insert their own pre-Islamic past into the Muslim view of antiquity.

The nineteenth-century German Orientalist Theodor Nöldeke noted that this 'Persian history from the first mythic kings to the last Sasanids shows in Tabari and related Arabic texts a certain similarity in conception and representation'.[15] This is undoubtedly true, but how should we explain it? Nöldeke's answer was that there must be 'a uniform underlying source' (*einheitliches Grundwerk*) and that this could only be the 'Book of Lords' (NP: *Khudāy-nāmah*)[16] that Hamza says was 'translated from Persian into Arabic with the title "History of the Kings of the Persians"'.[17] This text was, in Nöldeke's view, 'the most important and comprehensive presentation of Persian history, to which our accounts all go back' and 'the composition of which was initiated by Khusraw Anusharwan (531–79) and then assembled as a complete history under Yazdagird III (632–52)'.[18]

Since no such text has come down to us, how do we know it ever existed? Nöldeke offered four pieces of evidence in support of his contention:[19]

---

15 Nöldeke, *Sasaniden*, xiv.

16 *Ibid*, xiv–xv. In his *Nationalepos*, §13, he says 'its title was almost certainly *Chvatāi-nāmak*, in later pronunciation *Chodhāi-nāme*'; the former (now usually translit-erated as *Khwadāy-nāmag* or *Xwadāy-nāmag*) is a conjectural reconstruction of the MP form working back from the NP form and is nowhere attested in MP sources. Note that the modern term 'Middle Persian' refers to the Persian language of the Seleucid and Sasanid periods, preceded by Old Persian and superseded by New Persian.

17 Arabic: *Ta'rīkh mulūk al-Furs*: Hamza, 16, below, citing Musa al-Kisrawi.

18 Nöldeke, *Sasaniden*, xv.

19 Nöldeke, *Sasaniden*, xiv–xvi; *id.*, *Nationalepos*, §§12, 15; see also Klima, 'Geschichtschreibung', 228.

1. The plea of the deposed and incarcerated King Hurmuz IV in Firdawsi's 'Book of Kings' for 'a book that tells the exploits of our kings so that in hearing I will find relief'.[20]

2. The preface to the copy of Firdawsi's 'Book of Kings' belonging to the Timurid prince Baysonghor, which asserts that Khusraw I collected the historical writings of earlier rulers and that, during the reign of Yazdagird III, a nobleman named Danishwar made this into 'a complete chronicle of Persian kings from Gayomart to Khusraw II'.

3. The substantial overlap in content between the portrayal of ancient Persia in Muslim Arabic histories and that in Firdawsi's Persian 'Book of Kings', which signifies, in Nöldeke's view, that they both rely, independently, on the pre-Islamic 'Book of Lords'.

4. The claim of the late Roman lawyer and historian Agathias (d. *ca.* 580s) to have had access to official Persian records via his friend Sergius the Interpreter.

The first three of these are rather weak. Hurmuz's entreaty in no way implies an authoritative history.[21] Baysonghor's preface is not attested before the fifteenth century, is full of 'inaccuracies and legends' and its statement about Danishwar's chronicle sounds more like an inference from Firdawsi's text than a well-informed report.[22] As regards the third proof, even if we assume that Firdawsi had access to Middle Persian historical texts,[23] it would seem unlikely that these would have remained wholly insulated from the Arabic tradition, given the fact that many texts were translated from Persian to Arabic in early Abbasid period and many senior bureaucrats and scholars were bilingual in Persian and Arabic.[24] A more

20 Firdawsi, 775 (Davis).

21 The same is true of Shahbazi's reference to Bahram Gur's penchant for having books about kings read to him during feasts ('On the Xwadāy-nāmag', 213).

22 Nöldeke, *Sasaniden*, xv (NB 'although this preface to Firdawsi is from the 15th century and tends in the details towards inaccuracies and legends ... , I would take seriously the time of composition specified here'), and *id., Nationalepos*, §§12–13 (where he notes: 'I would no longer put much store by the name of Khusraw, but it goes without saying that by his time records of royal history must have long existed').

23 Davis, 'Ferdowsi's Sources', sees Firdawsi's claim to use ancient texts as a literary ploy. He also proposes that oral sources were primary, which is independently argued by Davidson, *Poet and Hero*. See also Yamimoto, *Oral Background*, and Huyse, 'Late Sasanid Society between Orality and Literacy'.

24 Note that Abu Mansur al-Maʿmari, who compiled a Persian history that is assumed to form the core of Firdawsi's work, lists the same sources as Hamza and gives the same figure for the number of years intervening between Gayumart and Hushang (Minorsky, 'Preface',

plausible explanation of the similarity of Firdawsi's 'Book of Kings' to Muslim Arabic histories of ancient Persia is that they are all drawing on the same corpus of material, which by this point, more than three centuries after the Arab conquest, had been translated, redacted and amplified numerous times. There are differences, but then there are differences between the Arabic versions too, and, moreover, since Firdawsi's 'Book of Kings' was a verse epic intended for a Persophone court audience, it inevitably entailed some liberties with the material. The fourth and final support for Nöldeke's theory is the report of the late Roman lawyer and historian Agathias, which, because of its unassailably pre-Islamic date, is worth considering in detail.

AGATHIAS ON THE PERSIANS

Agathias presents us with an excursus on Sasanid religion and history that he says is based on material found 'among the royal documents'[25] (2.27.5) and translated 'from Persian books' (*ek tōn Persikōn biblōn*, 4.30.2). This was done on his behalf, he says, by a certain Sergius the Interpreter, who went to Persia and 'asked the officials in charge of the royal archives[26] to give him access to the records', which was granted to him; from these writings 'he extracted the names, dates and the most important happenings in their time, and translated all this most skillfully into Greek' (4.30.3–4). Even if we accept this as proof of the compilation and preservation of historical records in the Persian realm, it still does not provide evidence for the existence of a single work of national history. On the contrary, Agathias' text suggests that it was assembled from a variety of texts – 'books', 'documents', 'records' – and that is also implied by his inclusion of

§11). Gutas, *Translation Movement*, mostly focuses on Greek to Arabic, but notes that there were also translations from Pahlavi to Arabic (e.g. *ibid.*, 24–27, 30, 40–50).

25 *En tais basileiois diphtherais*. Cameron, 'Agathias', translates 'royal archives', but *diphthera* just means a piece of prepared hide particularly to be used as writing material. Note that the same phrase is employed by Ctesias of Cnidus (wr. 390s BC), who claimed that he used 'the royal parchments (*basilikōn diphtherōn*) in which the Persians kept their ancient deeds' (Llewellyn-Jones and Robson, *Ctesias*, 58) for his own description of the Persians. *Ibid.*, 58–68, discusses whether such official documents existed and if so what their nature/ contents might have been.

26 *Tous tōn basilikōn apomnēmoneumatōn frouros*; Cameron, 'Agathias', 69, translates 'royal annals', but this implies year-by-year record keeping, whereas the word has the broader meaning of memorials or records (Xenophon's work with this title is usually translated 'Memorabilia').

religious as well as historical data.[27] Moreover, Sergius had apparently to 'extract' the names, dates and events, so presumably they were not easily accessible in a single comprehensive work.

If we strip out from Agathias' account of the first 17 Sasanid kings the notices on Roman matters, which are likely to come from the Latin or Greek sources at his disposal, we will find that he offers only two pieces of concrete information besides length of reign and title. The first is that Shabur II was appointed king while still in his mother's womb and the second is that Firuz I died at the hands of the Hephthalites. Both are indeed recorded in the sections on pre-Islamic Persia in Muslim chronicles, often at great length, but it amounts to surprisingly little historical data from someone who supposedly had, via his friend Sergius, direct access to Persian archives.

Agathias is able to offer more information for the reign of the eighteenth emperor, Qubad I (488–97, 499–531): he knows that he was deposed and imprisoned for his support of the policies of Mazdak, escaped jail with the help of his wife, fled to the Hephthalites to seek their support, returned in triumph and ousted his brother Jamasb from the throne. However, on closer inspection we see that this account is chiefly based on that of his younger and more illustrious contemporary Procopius (d. 565), as Agathias himself notes.[28] He does not claim to use his Persian source for his account of Khusraw, and most of it is in any case taken up with the visit of Uranius and other philosophers to the Persian court and Agathias' own animosity towards Uranius. Given this and the fact that many of his comments about Persian kings are pejorative, Tim Greenwood has concluded that Agathias was using 'an incomplete, hostile summary of Sasanid dynastic history' that he passed off as genuine insider information in order to 'proclaim his superior historical skill' over his older rival Procopius.[29] One might not want to go so far, as there are hints that he had access to some sort of bare chronological text,[30] but at the very least one would have to accept that Agathias does not provide unalloyed testimony for the existence of an official Sasanid history.

27 Cameron claims that the section on Persian religion 'contains little material directly from the Annals', but Agathias insists that both sections are from the same source, i.e. Sergius' notes from the Persian archives.

28 Noted by Cameron, 'Agathias', 158.

29 'Sasanian Echoes', 332–33.

30 He gives reign lengths for all the Persian emperors that are reasonably accurate and, perhaps most telling, he gives the same underestimate of the years of the Arsacids as do Muslim sources (see n. 71 in Translation below).

AN ALTERNATIVE TO NÖLDEKE:
WORKING BACK FROM OUR EXTANT SOURCES

In short, there exists no strong evidence in support of Nöldeke's theory of an officially commissioned Persian history composed in the late Sasanid period.[31] One might think, then, that it should have been dismissed long ago, but such is the conservatism of scholarship on the pre-modern Middle East that it is still widely accepted.[32] Moreover, it is nourished by the portrayal of the emperor Khusraw I as the great reformer of Iran, overhauling its bureaucracy and military, reviving learning and scholarship and championing Zoroastrian orthodoxy after the divisive revolt of the heresiarch Mazdak. Surely, it is assumed, he must have turned his attention to historiography too. 'During the reign of the great Khusraw Anushirwan', claims Klima, 'the idea first arose to compose a History of Iran.'[33] 'By the time of Khusraw Anushirwan', asserts Shahbazi, 'the history of ancient Iran was definitely compiled in a coherent form and kept in the treasury as a national document.' And Howard-Johnston speaks of Khusraw's 'cultural programme' and maintains that the most important component of it was the 'Book of Lords': 'The resulting text was evidently regarded as the official, authorised account of the Iranian past, and was subsequently extended to include the deeds of Khusraw and his successors down to Yazdagird III.'[34]

---

31 When I lectured on this topic at OSU, Stillwater, OK, in April 2017, I was asked why there would be only one authoritative history. It is a good question; Klima's answer is: 'History remained a royal monopoly; its interpretation depended on the king's will, and there were no historians who were private citizens' ('Geschichtsschreibung', 220). However, this view is rank with notions of Oriental despotism and should be treated with caution given our lack of contemporary sources.

32 For example, it informs the most important reference tool for Iranian studies, the *Encyclopedia Iranica*, which states ('Historiography ii'): Khusraw I 'who was interested in history ... resolved to have the Iranian past recorded in a great national history. Scholars at his court compiled such a work and called it *Xwadāy-nāmag* "Book of Lords/Kings"', citing Nöldeke, *Sasaniden*, xiv–xviii, and *id.*, *Nationalepos*, §§12–13.

33 'Geschichtsschreibung', 221; the sources he cites, such as the *Bahman Yasht* and the *Denkard*, mention Khusraw's actions in support only of religion, not of history writing. Klima simply assumes that a great king needs a great history: 'The might of the Persian state reached its peak during the reign of Khusraw I, and for this reason the need for a state chronicle became apparent at this time, which would praise the king and his forefathers ... . Just such a work was the first "Book of Lords"' (p. 224). He also assumes that 'the composition of the great epic (of Firdawsi) allows us to discover in some measure the form of the first "Book of Lords"'.

34 Shahbazi, 'On the Xwadāy-Nāmag', 214, and Howard-Johnston, *Witnesses*, 343, both

Rather than trying to characterise a putative text that does not survive, it would seem better to work backwards from our extant writings. The three authors that I have selected for translation in this volume are particularly helpful in this respect, as they all give indications about their sources. Hamza lists eight works that he consulted and cites two at length.[35] Mas'udi offers details on two of his sources. The first is a book that he saw in Istakhr, which contained biographical notices and portraits of each of the Sasanid emperors and which had been translated from Persian to Arabic for the caliph Hisham (724–43). The second is the 'Book on the History of the Persians', compiled by the Basran scholar Abu 'Ubayda ibn al-Muthanna (d. 825), who was famous for his extensive knowledge of ancient historical traditions.[36] And Ya'qubi has very lengthy entries on the prophet Mani and the noble general and pretender to the Persian throne, Bahram Chobin (d. 591), which plausibly existed as independent biographical accounts.[37]

The Muslim Persian historical tradition begins later than the Muslim Arabic one, but it also gives the impression that it was informed by many and varied earlier sources. Firdawsi tells us in the preface to his work that he had relied substantially on a compilation made by a nobleman who had assembled accounts from aged priests 'about the tales of the kings and the vicissitudes of the world'.[38] This nobleman is commonly identified with a certain Abu Mansur al-Ma'mari, who served the governor of Tus in the 950s and who appears in an early version of the preface attached to Firdawsi's 'Book of Kings'. This preface tells us that Abu Mansur achieved his design not by consulting books after the fashion of his contemporary Hamza but by convening a gathering of men of standing and tasking them with compiling 'books of kings and books about their exploits; the

echoing Nöldeke, *Sasaniden*, xvi: 'In Khusraw I's time there already existed a rather official comprehensive representation (*officielle Gesamtdarstellung*) of Persian history.'

35 Hamza, 8–28, below.

36 Mas'udi, 106–7, below, and *Murūj*, 2.136, 2.237–38. Abu 'Ubayda's text is entitled *Kitāb fī akhbār al-furs*; *akhbār* is another word for 'history' in Arabic (in addition to *ta'rīkh* and *siyar*, see n. 1 above); it is characterised by extended stories and anecdotes employing rhetorical devices for purposes of edification and/or entertainment.

37 Ya'qubi, 180–82, 188–90.

38 Davis, 'Ferdowsi's Sources', 51–53, argues, with some plausibility, that this is just a literary ploy, but it is nevertheless the case that in the tenth century, under Samanid patronage, accounts of the Persian past were being compiled. Bal'ami (d. ca. 963), the Persian redactor of Tabari, gives another example: 'The tales, stories and exploits of these people (i.e the pre-Islamic Persian rulers) are abundant and frequently retold. Abu l-Mu'ayyad (al-Balkhi) has related them all in his *Shāhnāma-yi buzurg*' (*Tārīkh-i Bal'amī*, 1.133).

biography of each one of them, dealing with justice, injustice, calamities, wars and customs during their reigns' with a view to producing a single prose version of the history of Persia before the Arab conquests. One of Abu Mansur's stipulations was that 'it ought to be derived from the statements of the landed gentry (*dihqāns*), for this kingdom was in their hands, and they are the ones who know its strengths and weaknesses, its good and its evil, its want and its plenty'. Four persons of the team are named, and they are all from east Iran and all have Persian Zoroastrian names, such as Mahuyah Khurshid son of Bahram from Nishabur; they were possibly picked because they knew the Persian language of Sasanid times, as well as New Persian and Arabic.[39]

It is also worth noting that narratives about the Persian past were not confined to works of history, but featured also in works of many other genres. Muslim geographers discussed the building and irrigation projects of pre-Islamic Persian kings, Muslim bureaucrats were conversant with the sage administrative practices and refined etiquette of the Persian court,[40] Muslim astrologers matched planetary conjunctions to the deeds perpetrated by and events pertaining to Persian royals[41] and Muslim exegetes linked Biblical characters to ancient Iranian monarchs.[42] In short, material about the Persian past circulated very widely. One of its most popular venues is gnomic literature, which was known as *andarz* in Persian and which consisted of collections of astute advice and prudent actions allegedly conveyed and committed by rulers, administrators and heroes of Persian antiquity. Some of these texts also reveal their sources. A good example is the 'Book of Perennial Wisdom' (*Jāwīdān-khirad*), which the scholar Miskawayh (d. 1030) says he found in the possession of a Zoroastrian priest in Fars and which the bureaucrat Hasan ibn Sahl (d. 850) had apparently

---

39 Minorsky, 'Preface', 266. For more discussion see *ibid.*, 260–64, and Rubin, 'Musa b. 'Isa', 20–23.

40 Particularly important are the works of Ibn Qutayba (d. 889), which frequently cite Persian texts of allegedly pre-Islamic origin; see Appendix 1 below.

41 Early examples are the astrological histories of the Persian Jew Masha'allah b. Athari (d. *ca.* 815) and the Khurasani Muslim Abu Ma'shar al-Balkhi (d. 886). See Kennedy and Pingree, *Astrological History of Masha'allah*, and Pingree, *Thousands of Abu Ma'shar*.

42 One way this was achieved was by positing the Kayanids as rulers of Babylon via vassals who were then linked to Biblical figures, such as Nebuchadnezzar, who attacked the Israelites, and Ahasuerus, who married Esther, allowing Muslim authors to weave the Biblical accounts of these persons into Persian history (thus Tabari, 1.645–655). On Esther in Persian Muslim narratives see Silverstein, *Esther*.

translated from Persian into Arabic. It is presented as a testament of the Pishdadid king Hushang to his descendants, but the aphorisms it contains are attributed principally to the Sasanid monarchs Hurmuz, Qubad and Khusraw, as well as to the latter's vizier Buzurgmihr, with short pieces assigned to the ancient kings Bahman and Jamshid.[43]

WRITINGS ON PRE-ISLAMIC PERSIAN HISTORY
ca. 750–850

Our late ninth- and tenth-century authors suggest, then, that they had access to a considerable variety of different texts on ancient Persia that were being translated, compiled, revised and circulated in the first Abbasid century. Hamza names eight compilers of ancient Persian histories from this period,[44] most of them known for producing translations from Persian to Arabic. One of them, Ibn al-Muqaffaʿ (d. 757), a senior bureaucrat in the Abbasid government, is the person whom Nöldeke and others have deemed principally responsible for translating and transmitting pre-Islamic Persian material to the Muslim world.[45] Yet here he is lined up with seven others who apparently engaged in the same sort of work. Moreover, Hamza lets us know that there were significant differences in content between these eight compositions; he has a whole section, for example, in which he places 'all (the information) that is in the "Book of Lords" that is *not* recounted by either Ibn al-Muqaffaʿ or Ibn al-Jahm'. And for his own outline of Persian history he tells us that he draws on 'epitomes of the Histories of the Kings … and *other books* of theirs'.[46]

One of the eight authors, Musa ibn ʿIsa al-Kisrawi, corroborates this diversity, for he recounts to us how he

examined the book called the 'Book of Lords' (*Khudāy-nāmah*), which was translated from Persian into Arabic with the title 'History of the Kings of the Persians'. Then I looked further at other copies of this book and investigated

---

43 Zakeri, *Persian Wisdom*, 1.73–82.

44 Hamza, 8–9, below.

45 Nöldeke, *Sasaniden*, xx–xxi; *EIr*, 'Ebn al-Moqaffaʿ'. For critical discussion of the idea that Ibn al-Muqaffaʿ's putative translation served as a conduit for later Muslim knowledge of pre-Islamic Persian history see Greenwood, 'Sasanian Echoes', 329; Bonner, *Historiographical Study*, 79–85; Rubin, 'Ibn al-Muqaffaʿ', 67–69; and Appendix 1 below.

46 Hamza, 64–66, 63, below.

them carefully, and I found them to be so different (from one another) that I could not obtain even two copies that were in agreement.[47]

He accounts for such disparity by positing that it 'arose with those translating this book from one language to another'. But are discrepancies in the translation of one single book sufficient to explain the multiplicity of divergent versions and diverse narratives that seem to be circulating in the Muslim world? It seems contradicted by Hamza's reference to two other processes that he says were going on besides translation, namely *jam'*, collecting and combining, and *işlāḥ*, correction and reconciliation. This latter process is attributed to Bahram ibn Mardanshah, who states: 'I collected (*jama'tu*) 20 or so copies of the book called "Book of Lords" and then I correctly reconstructed (*aşlaḥtu*) from them the dates of the kings of the Persians', the implication being that they gave quite different chronological details.[48]

In any case, the picture is again one of diversity, and a trawl through the texts of later chroniclers would seem to confirm this view. There is the aforementioned Abu 'Ubayda ibn al-Muthanna, whose work on Persian historical narratives was used by Mas'udi,[49] and the Zoroastrian priest Abu Ja'far Zaradusht ibn Ahra (fl. 830s), who supplied the Persian materials for the anonymous world chronicle contained in the Berlin manuscript Sprenger 30.[50] Then there is the early collector of antiquarian data, Hisham ibn al-Kalbi (d. 819), on whom Tabari relies for a substantial proportion of his entries on Persian affairs. Evidently a large number of works about ancient Persia entitled 'History of the Kings of the Persians' and the like circulated widely in this period. It seems more reasonable that this reflects the fact that many different types of historical works were available in the late Sasanid period rather than that one official work prevailed, but let us explore this question a little further.

---

47 Hamza, 16–17. For discussion of Musa and his activity see Rosen, 'K Voprosu', and Rubin, 'Musa b. 'Isa'. Biruni, 223, mentions 'al-Kisrawī who conversed with a Zoroastrian priest close to the caliph Mutawakkil (847–61)', but it may not be Musa al-Kisrawi (Hämeen-Anttila, 'Al-Kisrawī', 79–80).

48 Hamza, 24 (Bahram).

49 Mas'udi, *Murūj*, 2.136, 2.237–38. Abu 'Ubayda transmitted his history (*rawāhu*) from 'Umar Kisrā and it described 'their past dynasties, including their histories, speeches, genealogies, the cities they built, the districts they established, the canals they dug, and their noble families and how each group of them ... distinguished themselves'. On 'Umar Kisrā see Hämeen-Anttila, 'Al-Kisrawī', 90–91.

50 Rubin, 'Ibn al-Muqaffa'', 56–57.

SASANID HISTORICAL WRITING

Unfortunately, we have to pretty much skip the whole of the Umayyad period (661–750), as we have no evidence for Persian historiography at that time except for a couple of romances translated by Jabala ibn Salim, who served in the bureaucracy of the caliph Hisham (724–42).[51] We are not much better off when we move into the Sasanid period, for our only surviving historical text from that time[52] is the rather novelistic 'Book of the Exploits of Ardashir'.[53] It has been pointed out, however, that there are some close correspondences between two East Christian texts, the Syriac 'Chronicle of Khuzistan' and the Armenian 'History' of Sebeos, both composed *ca.* 660, and late ninth- and tenth-century Muslim histories, and it has been argued that these might constitute excerpts from the Sasanid 'Book of Lords'.[54] I give here three examples before discussing the question further:

a) Hurmuz IV and Bahram Chobin[55]

'He (Bahram) sent (to Hurmuz) ... a small part of the booty from the enormous treasures acquired from the plunder of the expedition ... (But Hurmuz said to himself) "The feast is exceedingly grand and I acknowledge the token of this portion, but from such great treasures it was not right to send to court merely this much."'

Bahram 'sent to King Hurmuz (some of) what he had plundered from the camp of the (Turkish) king of kings and included with that the (latter's) gold throne. What he had dispatched to him amounted to 300 camel loads. When these

---

51 He translated the books of 'Rustam and Isfandiyar' and 'Bahram Chobin' according to Ibn al-Nadim, 305.

52 Though Muslim texts cite a lot of material claiming to be from the Sasanid period. Bonner, *Three Neglected Sources*, 22–26, gives cautious support for the authenticity of the biography of Khusraw I quoted by Miskawayh (d. 1030), though this emperor loomed so large in the Muslim imagination that much material on him was probably generated in Islamic times. For a survey of other historical texts that may have been composed in Sasanid times see Christensen, *Iran*, 46–53, and Macuch, 'Pahlavi Literature', 172–80.

53 Grenet, *La Geste d'Ardashir*. Bonner, *Historiographical Study*, 91–96, compares this text with Dinawari's entry on Ardashir and shows that there are some correspondences between the two.

54 On the two Christian texts see Hoyland, *Seeing Islam*, 124–32, 182–89. A third Christian text, a tenth-century compilation in Arabic of earlier Syriac materials known as the 'Chronicle of Siirt', is also often cited in this respect, but see Appendix 2 below and Hoyland, *Seeing Islam*, 443–46.

55 Sebeos, 74, and Dinawari, 84–85 (cf. Ya'qubi, 189, below: 'What Bahram had sent to Hurmuz was just a little from a lot').

spoils reached Hurmuz and were set out before him, with his great ministers and governors assembled, Yazdan Gushnas, his chief minister, said: "O King, how great was the banquet whence came this morsel.'"

b) The Persian Capture of Jerusalem[56]
The Persians entered it (Jerusalem), seizing the bishop and the city officials, torturing them for (information on) the wood of the Cross and the contents of the treasury ... . They revealed to them the wood of the Cross, which lay hidden in a vegetable garden.

The Persians came to Jerusalem and seized its bishop, the clergy in it and the rest of the Christians for (information on) the wood of the Cross, which had been put in a golden casket and buried in a garden with vegetables planted over it.

c) A daughter of Khusraw and her chief minister[57]
They installed as queen Boran, Khusraw's daughter, and they appointed as chief minister at court Khorokh Ormizd, who was prince of the region of Azerbaijan. Then this Khorokh sent word to the queen: 'Become my wife.' She agreed, saying: 'Come with a single man at midnight, and I shall fulfil your wish.' Arising at midnight, he went with a single aide. But when he entered the royal palace, the guards of the court fell on him, struck him down and killed him.

Azarmidukht, daughter of Khusraw Abarwiz, reigned for six months. Khurrahurmuz of Azerbaijan ... attended her court and became enamoured of her and wrote asking to meet with her. She agreed upon a night, but ordered the chief of her guard to assassinate him, and this was done.

It is certainly clear that these authors share a source (or sources) and that this must go back to before AD 660, when the 'Chronicle of Khuzistan' and the 'History' of Sebeos were completed. So we do at least have proof for some form of history writing in the Sasanid period. But should we take this as evidence of 'the Christian adoption of Sasanian history' or of 'the penetration of Sasanid historical traditions' into Christian historiography?[58] Is the only explanation of these correspondences that Christian historians were making direct use of an official Persian history?[59] Is it not also

---

56 *Chronicle of Khuzistan*, 25; Tabari, 1.1002.

57 Sebeos, 130; Mas'udi, 103.

58 Wood, 'Christian Reception', 9, and cf. *ibid.*, 15: 'Christian historians ... had begun to adopt the previously alien tradition of the Persian royal annals into their own historical writing'; Greenwood, 'Sasanian Echoes', 346 (also: 'Sebeos preserves an impression of a Pahlavi "Royal History"').

59 Greenwood, 'Sasanian Echoes', 338, says of the 'Royal History' used by Sebeos that there is 'a close connection between that text and a Pahlavi original', pointing to its biographical format and the correspondences between it and Tabari, neither of which

possible that these chronicles were getting their information on Persian affairs from Christian sources?[60] By the late sixth century Christians had become increasingly ensconced within Persian society, even at the level of the court, and this reached its peak in the reign of Khusraw II, who had two Christian wives and a Christian as head of his treasury, and who was, for a time, by virtue of his conquest of Egypt and the Levant, the ruler of more Christians than the Roman emperor. It would not be surprising, then, to find Christians composing histories of the Persian kings. Christians happily produced histories of Muslim Arab caliphs, so why should they not have done the same for Persian emperors?

Probably the most plausible scenario is that our extant sources on Sasanid history reflect a complex blending of narratives from both Christian and Persian traditions. For instance, Tabari has two biographical notices on Hurmuz IV, which seem to come from different perspectives, one anti-aristocrat ('he possessed the intention of benefiting the weak and wretched and opposing the nobles') and one pro-aristocrat (he was 'ill-intentioned – for his Turkish maternal uncles had spoiled him: extirpating the nobles and killing 13,600 of the learned and of the men of ancient ancestry and nobility with the sole aim of winning over and reconciling the lowly').[61] The first notice is attributed to Hisham ibn al-Kalbi, who was a key supplier of Persian materials to Tabari. Hisham tells us at one point that he had access to church archives in Hira, and one could imagine that this town, with its sizeable Christian population and proximity to the former Persian capital, would have been a likely setting for the composition of a history about Persian kings and their wars with Rome.[62] The second notice

necessitates a Pahlavi source. He notes that the 'Royal History' and Tabari portray Khusraw 'as the unsympathetic ruler, contemptuous of the fate of his subjects' (*ibid.*, 345), but that would surely not be the perspective of an official Persian account of Khusraw's reign.

60 Klima, 'Geschichtsschreibung', 229–31, discusses some instances of misspellings in Greek and Arabic texts that he attributes to their reliance on Syriac sources. Since both the 'Chronicle of Khuzistan' and Sebeos start with Hormuz and end with Yazdagird III it is tempting to postulate that they are both using a Christian account of the end of the Persian Empire. Note that they do share a number of common notices that are not found in Muslim Arabic sources, such as that Khusraw II was captured while hiding in the royal gardens (Sebeos, 127; *Chronicle of Khuzistan*, 28), though Ya'qubi, 196, is close when he says he was captured in his orchard.

61 Tabari, 1.988, 990.

62 Hisham says that he 'took the accounts of the Arabs and the genealogies of the clan of Nasr ibn Rabi'a and the lifespans of those who acted as agents for the Persian imperial family and the history of their times from the monasteries of Hira' (Tabari, I.770). See Wood, 'Al-Ḥira and its Histories', for more discussion.

is introduced by a curt and unhelpful 'it is said that' (qīla), which is how the majority of Tabari's reports on the pre-Islamic Persians are presented. It is surprising that this famously scrupulous religious authority, usually careful to name his informants, does not reveal his source(s) for all this material. Is he ashamed of its non-Muslim provenance or of its unscholarly character, or did it circulate anonymously?[63] If we assume that it was ultimately of Persian Zoroastrian origin,[64] one might infer that these two notices on Hurmuz reflect an anti-aristocratic Christian source and a pro-aristocratic Persian one respectively. However, this suggestion remains tentative while so little thought has been paid to the complex realities underlying all this historiographical production.

THE NATURE OF THE EXTANT MATERIAL ABOUT PRE-ISLAMIC PERSIA

It may help to step back a bit and think about what the material about pre-Islamic Persia that has survived in our medieval texts actually looks like. There is an assumption that we are talking about a regular sequential narrative history of the sort familiar to us from the Greco-Roman tradition; 'annals' and 'chronicle' are words that are most often applied to it.[65] But the surviving material suggests a more complex picture. In general, the accounts of many of the rulers are very short, and those that are long are so only because they have been padded out with a story about a specific person or event. For example, the notice about King Tahmurath is largely taken up with a fascinating story about how idolatry was the first religion of mankind. It had begun in the time of this ruler, with people making images

---

63 It may well be that many texts about ancient Persia were simply entitled 'History of the Kings of the Persians' without any mention of the author or else ascribed to some famous/ mythical person of antiquity. Note the vague way that Ibn Qutayba and others say that 'I read in the "biographical histories of the Persians" (siyar al-'ajam) that ...' (see Appendix 1 below).

64 The second notice is close to Sebeos, 73 (he was 'ferocious from his maternal side [he has just said that his mother was the daughter of the Turkish khagan], for he eliminated all the nobles and ancient families from the country of Persia'), but that could support either a Christian or a Persian Zoroastrian provenance.

65 E.g. Klima, 'Geschichtsschreibung', 221, 224 ('Chronik', 'Staatschronik'); Cameron, 'Agathias', 69 ('the Royal Annals', 'annalistic material'); Shahbazi, 'On the Xwadāy-nāmag', 215 ('the official Sasanid chronicle'); Macuch, 'Pahlavi Literature', 172–73 ('an official chronicle').

of people dear to them who had died so that they might remember them, but subsequently they fell to worshipping them. It is closely connected with Budasf, a figure inspired by the Buddha, whose followers practised fasting – initially for want of food, but then as a form of religiosity – and who himself taught the transmigration of souls and the eternity of the world. These idolaters were called Chaldeans in the west and Samaniyya in the east. This terminology then gets an Islamic-period tweak, for it is generally noted that they are now called Sabians or *ḥanīfs*, both words from the Qur'an.[66]

Another example is provided by the reign of King Bishtasb, which is filled out with the tale of the arrival at the royal court of the prophet Zoroaster bringing with him a new religion, which Bishtasb helped to spread throughout his realm 'by force and by treaty'.[67] Zoroaster also brought a Scripture, the Avesta, and devised a special script to write it in. 'It was inscribed on 12,000 skins of oxen with quills of gold in the ancient Persian language', says Mas'udi, echoing various late Sasanid texts.[68] The idea of Zoroastrianism being spread by force and by treaty is also likely to reflect a Sasanid milieu, for we know that a number of Sasanid rulers actively promoted the religion, as is stated proudly by the third-century priest Kardir in his inscriptions. 'I made prominent and revered the Mazda-worshipping religion and priests', he boasts, 'and Jews, Buddhists, Brahmins, Christians, Baptisers and Manichaeans in the empire were smitten, idols destroyed and the storehouses of the demons scattered.'[69]

The notice on the reign of the Arsacid emperor Dara son of Dara (traditionally identified with Darius III) chiefly comprises the tale of his death at the hands of Alexander the Great, who then went on to ransack Iran, and in particular 'he devoted himself to hunting down the books of their religion and sciences and burned them after translating the philosophy, astronomy, medicine and agriculture that they contained from Persian into Greek and Coptic, and sent (those translations) to Alexandria'. Laments about Alexander's theft of Persian learning are recounted in numerous Muslim histories and can be traced back to Sasanid versions, such as that

---

66 Hamza, 30, and Mas'udi, 90–91. For discussion of this tale see Crone, 'Ancient Iranian Paganism'.

67 *Ibid.*, 35.

68 Mas'udi, 91. References and discussion given in Van Bladel, 'Zoroaster's Many Languages', 193–94 and see n. 318 below. Agathias (2.24.6) notes that Zoroaster flourished in the time of Bishtasp (Hystaspes), although he is unaware of the latter's identity.

69 Sprengling, *Sapor and Kartir*, 51. Mazda-worshipping refers to the Zoroastrian beneficent god Ahuramazda.

found in the ninth-century anthology of Zoroastrian texts, the *Denkard*. A counterpart to this sad tale is given in the biography of Ardashir I, the first Sasanid ruler, who attempts to reverse this loss. He sent messengers to China and India to inquire about what books they had there and to have them copied, and he investigated what vestiges of scholarship still survived in Iraq: 'he gathered what had been scattered and harmonized what was at variance'.[70]

As we move into the Sasanid period coverage becomes fuller, but maintains this person-centred and anecdotal approach. We hear, for instance, of the campaigns of Ardashir, the founder of the Sasanid dynasty, against Ardawan, the last Arsacid ruler, and of how the latter's daughter beguiled Ardashir, bearing a son by him who became the second Sasanid emperor, Shabur I, thus ensuring that the Arsacids lived on through the Sasanid line. Then there is the tale of Shabur II's clandestine intelligence-gathering mission in Roman territory, his capture by the Roman emperor Julian (361–63), his subsequent escape and his revenge when he succeeded in seizing Julian and mutilating him.[71] Particularly lengthy are the accounts of the battles of Firuz I (459–84) against the Hephthalite king Akhshunwar, the imprisonment of Qubad I for his support of the heretic Mazdak and his subsequent escape and return to power, the measures of Khusraw I to reform the Persian Empire and his support for the Yemeni prince Sayf ibn Dhi Yazan in his bid to recover his realm from its Ethiopian occupiers.[72] And, as noted above, more than half of the section on ancient Persia in Ya'qubi's 'History' is taken up with the prophet Mani and the general Bahram Chobin, surely drawn from stand-alone biographies of these two characters.[73]

---

70 Hamza, 45 (Alexander). Ibn al-Nadim, 239 (Ardashir), citing Abu Sahl ibn Nawbakht (d. *ca.* 820). Van Bladel, 'Arabic History of Science', 47, concludes, from a comparison with the corresponding section in book 4 of the *Denkard*, that Abu Sahl is probably translating from an MP source.

71 Dinawari, 44–46 (Ardashir); Tabari, 1.841–42 (Shabur II).

72 Appendix 1 below (Firuz), Appendix 2 below (Qubad), Tabari, 1.894–98 and 960–64 (Khusraw), Hamza, 58–60, below (Sayf). An account of the reign of Khusraw I also circulated as an independent text in the Islamic period; see Grignaschi, 'Quelques Spécimens', 4–5, and Bonner, *Three Neglected Sources*, 22–26.

73 Mas'udi, *Murūj*, 2.223, says that 'the Persians have a book devoted to the history of Bahram Chobin and his stratagems in the country of the Turks' and Ibn al-Nadim, 305, lists a 'Book of Bahram Chobin' translated from Persian into Arabic by Jabala ibn Salim (fl. 740s). The account of Ya'qubi on Bahram is so close to that of Dinawari and Tabari (see Ya'qubi, 188–94, below) that they certainly must all have been making use of such a text.

Yet Hamza, who seems to do the most research into Persian histori-ography of all our Muslim sources, focuses chiefly on the Persian kings' reign lengths, titles, regalia and founding of cities. And Agathias, who is the only pre-Islamic author to offer a history of the Sasanid rulers, also gives only reign lengths and titles for the first 17 monarchs of that dynasty, plus occasionally a brief notice on a significant event. One possible explanation is that we have two types of history writing from pre-Islamic Persia: chronological compilations of essential information about kings made by bureaucrats for official purposes (perhaps called the 'Book of Lords') and epic narratives about specific persons, especially kings, and their heroic deeds. If we can judge from the lists of kings given by Hamza at the beginning of his section on the Persians and the complaints of Musa al-Kisrawi and Bahram ibn Mardanshah about discrepancies in reign lengths, it would appear that the chronological compilations still existed in some form in the ninth century.[74] However, it is the epic narratives that were more popular in the Islamic period, such as the 'Book of *Baykār*' (on the wars of Isfandiyar), the 'Book of *Sakīsarān*' (on 'the wondrous tales of the ancient Persians'), the 'Book of the Exploits of Ardashir', the 'Book of Bahram Chobin',[75] the 'Book of Bahram and Narsi' and the 'Life of (Khusraw) Anusharwan'.[76] In the early Abbasid period we also encounter histories that merged these two forms of writing, creating continuous sequential histories that covered the whole span of Persian antiquity and welded the narrative elements to the chronological framework. The first examples that we know of are those by Hisham ibn al-Kalbi (Tabari's main source), Abu ʿUbayda (Masʿudi's main source) and Dinawari, whose history is still extant. With the emergence of Persian dynasties in Iran in the tenth century, these grand historical narratives, presenting a compre-hensive vision of the glorious past of the Persian people, become ever

---

74 One might wonder why, if these chronological compilations were an official production, there would be as much disparity between them as Musa and Bahram claim, but this would be easily explained by the ambiguity of the Pahlavi script, especially since letters were commonly used to represent numerals and Musa and Bahram were particularly interested in reign lengths.

75 Masʿudi, *Murūj*, 2.44 (*Baykār* – the text has b-n-k-sh, but see Masʿudi, 94, below), 2.118–20 (*Sakīsarān*), 2.162 (*al-karnāmaj*; on this still extant work see n. 53 above), 2.223 (Bahram Chobin). Masʿudi says that the first two works were translated into Arabic by Ibn al-Muqaffaʿ, the second of them 'from ancient Persian' (*al-fārisiyya al-ūlā*).

76 These are two out of ten titles that Ibn al-Nadim, 305, lists as examples of 'biographies and true tales about their kings'. On the biography of Khusraw Anusharwan see nn. 52 and 72 above.

more extensive and popular, attaining their zenith with Firdawsi's 'Book of Kings'.[77]

Returning to the Sasanid period, one imagines that the impulse to compose epic narratives came from two directions. The first is royal patronage, as suggested by the following example:

> When Khusraw Abarwiz concluded his wars with Bahram Chobin and consolidated his rule over the empire, he ordered his secretary to write down an account of those wars and related events in full, from the beginning to the end. The secretary complied, but when they read off the narrative to Khusraw, its preface did not please him. Thereupon a young secretary wrote an eloquent and rhetorical prologue to the work and presented it to the king. Abarwiz was delighted with it and ordered the promotion of the young scribe.[78]

The second impetus was likely to be the popularity of reciters and entertainers, as recounted in the entry in Hamza's history below on the reign of Bahram Gur, who is said to have strongly encouraged their employment at all kinds of events. The word that Hamza uses to refer to these performers also occurs in a simile quoted in a Sasanid Manichaean text: 'like a bard (gōshān) who proclaims the worthiness of kings and heroes of old, and himself achieves nothing at all'.[79] Though not very flattering, the simile gives us a hint of the possible role played by these figures in composing and disseminating material about ancient Persia.

CONCLUSION

The theory that I have proposed about two different types of pre-Islamic Persian historical writing does help to explain two features of the material about the Persian past that we encounter in our medieval sources: the homogeneity of the basic chronological framework and the heterogeneity of the narrative details. The first feature belongs to the official king lists, whereas the second pertains to the epic tales and romances. Possibly only the first was referred to as the 'Book of Lords' in the Sasanid period, but in Islamic times it joins with titles such as the 'History of the Kings of the Persians' and the 'Biographical Histories of the Persians' to refer in

---

77 For recent discussion of this see Peacock, *Medieval Islamic Historiography*, 14–47, *id.*, 'Early Persian Historians', and Melville, *Persian Historiography*, chs 1–3.

78 Shahbazi, 'On the Xwadāy-nāmag', 210–11, citing Bayhaqi's *Maḥāsin wa-masāwī*.

79 *EIr*, 'Gōshān'.

general to all historical writing about pre-Islamic Persia.[80] At this stage, my theory is only very tentative, but what I hope to have shown more conclusively here is the weakness of the by now entrenched belief that knowledge about Persians in our extant sources must of necessity derive from a single official text or cluster of closely related texts the production of which was controlled by the royal court, and, on the other hand, the attractiveness of imagining a more diverse picture for Persian historiography.[81] This view has the additional advantage of allowing us to consider Sasanid historical writing on its own terms rather than approaching it in terms of how Sasanid rulers 'brought Iranian culture in line with that of the highly literate Graeco-Roman world'.[82] The genius of Firdawsi's 'Book of Kings' and Persian historiography at large is that it is no pale imitation of Romano-Christian chronography, but very much follows its own distinctive style.

80 'Book of Lords' remains, however, a rare term; besides Hamza, 16, and Mas'udi, 106 (both in the Translation below), we only have a very few references to it: e.g. Ibn al-Nadim, 118, and Maqdisi, 3.197, who recounts the death of Yazdagird on the authority of 'the book *Khudāy-nāmah*'.

81 For a schematic representation of this complex transmission history see Table 4 below.

82 Howard-Johnston, *Witnesses*, 343, strongly advocating the idea that Khusraw had a full-scale 'cultural programme', of which 'the *Khwaday-namag* project should probably be viewed as the single most important element' that constituted 'a radical break with the past'.

TRANSLATIONS

Hamza al-Isfahani (d. *ca.* 960s)

Hamza was a native of Isfahan, where, except for three trips to Baghdad, he spent all of his life.[1] The text from which the section below on the Persians is drawn is his 'History of the Years of the Kings of the Earth and the Prophets'.[2] It is not so much a history as a study of chronologies, specifically those of the Persians, Romans, ancient Greeks, Copts, Israelites and Arabians (subdivided into the tribes of Lakhm, Ghassan, Himyar, Kinda and Quraysh). Some historical outline is provided, but it is particularly dating systems and the durations of reigns and dynasties that capture Hamza's attention. His desire to incorporate non-Muslim chronologies required him to take account of non-Muslim testimonies. For example, he interviewed Zoroastrian priests and an old Greek-speaking man with the help of the latter's Arabic-speaking son, and to help with Israelite matters he interrogated the Jewish rabbi Sidqiya in Babylon on Biblical chronology. He also consulted a considerable number of books that are no longer available to us, such as the chronological work of a certain Pinhas the Hebrew and a 'History of the Greeks' translated into Arabic by Habib ibn Bahriz, bishop of Mosul in the early ninth century.[3] Being a native of Isfahan and proud of his heritage, Hamza puts the Persians first, and, importantly for us, he acknowledges his sources for Persian history. I present Hamza before Mas'udi and Ya'qubi, although he is later chronologically, because his account is fuller and more complete and because he

---

1 The only study of his life and work is by Mittwoch in *EI* and in his article 'Die literarische Tätigkeit Ḥamza al-Iṣbahānīs'; for the 'History' in particular see Pourshariati, 'Ḥamza al-Iṣfahānī'. Most of this section on the Persians was translated by Daudpota, but without annotation, in his 'The Annals of Hamzah al-Isfahani'.

2 I use the edition of J.M. Gottwaldt (Leipzig, 1848), which seems to be the basis of all modern editions. Numbers in bold in the translation below refer to the page numbers of this edition.

3 Adang, 'Ḥamza al-Iṣfahānī', 289 (Pinhas); Hamza, 80 (Habib).

gives fairly equal treatment to all the Persian kings, whereas Masʿudi and Yaʿqubi are less evenhanded.

Translation

[8] CHAPTER 1: Concerning the chronology of the Persian kings according to their four dynasties, with an account of the prophets that appeared in their times from the West, comprising five sections

SECTION I of Chapter 1: A report on the four Persian dynasties set forth without any narrative or biographical data[4] or descriptions

The Persian kings, notwithstanding the long period of their rule and the unity of their power, were divided into four dynasties: the Pishdadids, the Kayanids,[5] the Arsacids[6] and the Sasanids.[7] The chronological information about them is faulty and incorrect, for it has been translated after 150 years from one language into another, and from a script in which the units' digits are of a similar form into another script in which the tens' digits are of a similar form.[8] Therefore, in reporting all that was required for this chapter, I had no recourse but to collect copies (of the 'History of the Persian Kings') that have been differently translated. In all I chanced upon eight copies,[9] which are:

---

4 Arabic: *mujarradan min al-akhbār wa-l-siyar*, i.e. he is just giving the lists of the kings with their reign lengths at this point, leaving out all the accounts of events and deeds that pertain to them.

5 These first two dynasties are not recorded in any of the primary sources that are available to us and their names do not correspond to known rulers, such as the Achaemenids. Possibly they were pre-Parthian east Iranian dynasties.

6 A Parthian dynasty that ruled in Iran from *ca.* 250 BC to AD 226. This period is commonly referred to by early Islamic historians as that of the petty kings (literally 'kings of the parts'/*mulūk al-ṭawā'if*, as they each controlled only a part of Persia). See *EIr*, 'Arsacids'; *EI*, 'Mulūk al-Ṭawā'if (A.) 1. In Pre-Islamic Persia'.

7 The last Persian dynasty before Islam (224–652). See *EIr*, 'Sasanian Dynasty'; *EI*, 'Sasanids'.

8 Arabic: *min khaṭṭ mutashābih ruqūm al-aʿdād ilā khaṭṭ mutashābih ruqūm al-ʿuqūd*. My translation is only a suggestion, as it is not really clear what Hamza means here. *Ruqūm* can mean numerals or diacritical marks.

9 Hamza lists the names of only seven texts here; the eighth is presumably that by Musa b. ʿIsa al-Kisrawi, which Hamza quotes at length below. Hämeen-Anttila, 'Al-Kisrawī', 66–74, shows that the list appears in pretty much the same form in five later sources; plausibly they are all copying Hamza.

'The Biographical History[10] of the Persian Kings' (*Siyar mulūk al-Furs*) translated by Ibn al-Muqaffaʻ;[11]

'The Biographical History of the Persian Kings' translated by Muhammad ibn al-Jahm al-Barmaki;[12]

'The History of the Persian Kings' (*Ta'rīkh mulūk al-Furs*) taken from the library of Maʾmun;[13]

'The Biographical History of the Persian Kings' translated by Zadawayh ibn Shahawayh al-Isfahani;[14]

[9] 'The Biographical History of the Persian Kings' translated or compiled by Muhammad ibn Bahram b. Miṭyar al-Isfahani;

'The History of the Sasanid Kings' (*Ta'rīkh mulūk Banī Sāsān*), translated or compiled by Hisham ibn Qasim al-Isfahani;

'The History of the Sasanid Kings' correctly reconstructed by[15] Bahram ibn Mardanshah,[16] priest[17] of the district of Shabur, in the land of Fars.

10 I translate *Siyar* as biographical history to distinguish it from *ta'rīkh*; the latter conveys a close link with chronology, whereas *siyar* has the sense of history that focuses on a person's deeds. For discussion see the Introduction above and Appendix 1 below.

11 A celebrated Arabic author, translator and senior civil servant of Persian origin, who lived *ca.* 720–57. Ibn al-Nadim, 118, lists some of his translations, placing first the 'Book of Lords' (*Khudāy-nāmah*), which is possibly the same as Hamza's *Siyar mulūk al-Furs*. See further Rubin, 'Ibn al-Muqaffaʻ'.

12 A senior official in the Abbasid caliphate who took an interest in astrology and natural science; he was active in the 820s–30s. Ibn al-Nadim, 245, also mentions him as a translator from Persian into Arabic.

13 The seventh Abbasid caliph, son of Harun al-Rashid and patron of scholarship, who reigned 813–33. The Arabic word for library here is *khizāna*, which means 'storehouse'.

14 Zadawayh (or Zaduyah) is mentioned, along with Muhammad ibn Bahram, Hisham ibn Qasim and Bahram ibn Mardanshah, in a section on 'translators from Persian into Arabic' in Ibn al-Nadim, 245.

15 Arabic: *min iṣlāḥ*, suggesting some form of revision or correction. Hamza uses three different terms for the activities of these eight persons; besides *iṣlāḥ* there is *naql*, 'translation' or 'transmission', and *jamʻ*, 'compilation' or 'collection'.

16 He is quoted by Hamza at length below. As noted by Rubin, 'Musa ibn ʻIsa', 10, the narrow scope suggested by the title of Bahram's work is not borne out by the content, which ranges across Persian history.

17 Arabic: *mūbadh*; MP: *mow-bad*, from OP: *magu-pati*. It refers to a senior figure in the Zoroastrian religious hierarchy. I will follow usual practice and translate it as 'priest' in this book, but it should be borne in mind that they would seem, in the late Sasanid period at least, to have had considerable involvement in legislative and administrative affairs. Cf. Agathias,

When I had brought together these books, I compared them with one another so that I could present this chapter fully and accurately. Abu Ma'shar the Astrologer[18] says that most of the historical dates are confused and corrupt, and this kind of corruption afflicts a nation's history only when it has been eroded by the passage of time and its days have been long. So when that history is copied from one book to another, or from one language to another, errors creep in due to additions and omissions. The same problem affects the Jewish people, whose historians disagree about the number of years that passed between Adam and Noah and the other prophets and peoples of the world whom they tell stories about in their chronicles. So it is too with the dates and histories of the kings of the Persians, which exhibit much confusion and manifest corruption despite the continuity of their rule from the beginning of the world to the passing of their empire. [10] They claim that this is because there have been a number of occasions when the land remained without a king, whether a native one or a foreign one. Thus they allege that the land remained without a king for 170 years or so after the death of Gayumart,[19] the progenitor of mankind, until Hushang Pishdad[20] ruled it. The second occasion was when Afrasiyab the Turk,[21] having ruled the land (of Persia) for 12 years, returned to the land of the Turks for a second time, during which the country of the Aryans[22]

2.23–32: 'The Magi are the objects of extreme awe and veneration, all public business being conducted at their discretion and in accordance with their prognostications, and no litigant or party to a private dispute fails to come under their jurisdiction. Indeed, nothing receives the stamp of legality in the eyes of the Persians unless it is ratified by one of the Magi.' See *EI*, 'Mōbadh'; Shaked, 'Administrative Functions'; Gyselen, *Géographie*, 30–31, 38–40, 121–24 (on seals of the Zoroastrian clergy).

18 A very famous astrologer (d. 886) at the Abbasid court; he was born in Balkh in modern north Afghanistan and was a long-term resident of Baghdad. See *EI*, 'Abū Ma'shar'.

19 Hamza writes Kayumarth, which is a quite accurate rendering of the Persian form of the name; Mas'udi arabises it to Jayumart. Ya'qubi, oddly, has Shaymumarth, but this may be a corruption in the manuscript or a slip of a copyist. I write Gayumart as it is the most popular modern rendering; *EIr* has entries for 'Gayomart' and 'Gayomard'. He is the first human in Iranian mythology and is sometimes regarded as the first king of mankind too.

20 The first king of Iran/the Aryans and the founder of the Pishdadid dynasty. Hamza here renders his name as Hushank, but elsewhere he writes Ushhanj; see *EIr*, 'Hōshang'.

21 The king of the Turan people, who were neighbours and frequent enemies of the Aryan people. The identification of Turan with the Turks, as given here, is a late development, probably connected with the emergence of the Turk Empire in the mid-sixth century.

22 Arabic: *al-aryān*. This term is extremely rare in Arabic texts, where the people of Iran are generally called either *furs* or *'ajam* (meaning non-Arabs in general, but applied to the inhabitants of Iran in particular).

was without a king for an unknown number of years. The third occasion was when Zaw[23] died and the world was thrown into chaos for an unknown but substantial number of years, without any king, until Kay Qubad[24] came to power.

It is also mentioned that from the beginning of the world until their empire passed into the hands of the Arabs, the Persians were several times governed by alien races, which is why there is so much disagreement about the dates of their ancient kings. That happened for the first time in the time of Biyurasb,[25] the second time in the days of Afrasiyab, the third time in the days of Alexander[26] and the fourth time when their empire finally passed into the hands of the Arabs.

Abu Ma'shar says: The Persians also disagree with regard to [11] the reigns of their kings. For instance, some allege that Kay Qubad ruled the land for 120 years, while others assert that he ruled only a little over ten years. Likewise, says Abu Ma'shar, there is just as much disagreement over the chronology of the Greeks as over that of the Persians. This is because their ancient chronology and history were translated from Hebrew, and the Hebrew script is not uniform: the one in vogue with the Samaritans differs from the one commonly used by the Jews. Hence the Greek versions are different just as the Septuagint differs from other (translations of the Hebrew Bible). Furthermore, he says, there exists a lot of difference in the calculation of years from the day of Creation[27] up to the year of the Hijra.[28] The Jews, reporting on the authority of the Torah, arrive at 4,042 years and three months, while the Christians, reporting from the same source, cite a figure of 5,990 years and three months. The Persians, however, derive it from their religious book, which Zoroaster[29] brought and which is named

---

23 Hamza calls him Zab, but Mas'udi and Ya'qubi have Zaw, as does Firdawsi, so I use this latter form here.

24 Persian: Kay Kawad/Kobad, the first of the Kayanid kings, the dynasty that succeeds the Pishdadids.

25 The text has Fiyurasb here, but elsewhere Biyurasf. I follow Mas'udi, 85, who has Biyurasb. This character, one of the key foes of Iran and Zoroastrianism, is often called Dahak/Dahag or Zahak. See *EIr*, 'Aždahā' ('dragon'), the section on Aži Dahāka.

26 That is, Alexander the Great (Arabic: *Iskandar*), king of Macedonia, who reigned 336–323 BC. These three figures constitute the three greatest enemies of ancient Iran.

27 Arabic: *ibtidā' al-tanāsul*, literally 'the beginning of procreation/breeding'.

28 That is, the migration of the prophet Muhammad and his followers from Medina to Mecca in 622, from which year the Muslim calendar begins.

29 Arabic: *Zaradusht*, which is derived from the MP form. I use Zoroaster, because it is the usual English form for the ancient Iranian prophet and founder of Zorastrianism,

the Avesta,[30] and they say that from the time of Gayumart, the progenitor of mankind, up to the year of the accession of Yazdagird[31] (there have elapsed) 4,182 years, 10 months and 19 days.[32]

Yet the astronomers, says Abu Ma'shar, adduce a figure that vastly exceeds that [12] and assert that from the day the planets journeyed from the head of Aries to the day on which (the caliph) Mutawakkil set out for Damascus[33] 12,320,000,000 solar years had elapsed of the lifespan of the earth. And the time that elapsed between the Flood and the morning of the accession of Yazdagird b. Shahriyar, which took place on Tuesday, the day of Hurmuz, in the month of Frawardin,[34] and from the dawn of that day to the dawn of the first day of Muharram 244 AH[35] – which was the first day of Mutawakkil's departure for Damascus[36] and which also occurred in Frawardin on the day of Hurmuz – is (in total) 3,735 years, 10 months and 20 days. This is the lifespan of the earth and from it is derived the sequence of dates of the Persian kings and their beginning. Moreover, all Persians maintain that humans originated from a man whom they call Gayumart, 'King of Clay', which is (in Persian) *Gilshāh*,[37] who lived for 40 years on the earth.

deriving from the Greek form *Zōroastrēs* (possibly based on a folk etymology relating to Greek *astra*, 'stars'). Nietzsche's form Zarathustra in the title of his famous philosophical novel reflects the Avestan form. For full discussion see *EIr*, 'Zoroaster i. The Name'.

30   The Avesta is a collection of ancient texts that survive today only in manuscripts of the thirteenth century AD and later; it is assumed, though, to have been written down and revised already in the Arsacid and Sasanid periods. See *EIr*, 'Avesta'.

31   Yazdagird III b. Shahriyar, the last Sasanid emperor, who reigned from 632 to 651–52.

32   Tabari, 1.1068, records the same figure, though in his account it is measured to the death of Yazdagird.

33   Mutawakkil was the tenth Abbasid caliph (847–61). He apparently went to Damascus to launch a massive campaign against the Romans (Cobb, 'Al-Mutawakkil's Damascus'). Presumably he would have commissioned a horoscope to ascertain the best time to do this and Abu Ma'shar is likely to have been present.

34   The day of Hurmuz (*rūz Hurmuz*) is New Year's Day (*nawrūz*) in the Zoroastrian calendar, and Frawardin is the first month of the year.

35   Tuesday 19 April AD 858. It is confusing that three fixed points are given for this period of 3735 years; perhaps Yazdagird's accession is regarded as a crucial point in the period between the Flood and 244 AH/AD 858.

36   Tabari, 3.1435, gives the date of Mutawakkil's departure as 20th Dhu l-Qa'da 243 AH (Tuesday 8 March AD 858).

37   Hamza writes *Kilshāh*. In some sources he is called 'King of the Mountain'/*Gārshāh*; for discussion see Daryaee, 'Gayōmard: King of Clay or Mountain'.

The First Dynasty: the Pishdadids[38]

There were nine rulers of this dynasty, and the period of their rule, including the years of (Gayumart) *Gilshāh*, extended to 2,470 years.

[13] Hushang Pishdad, who was the first of the kings, ruled the world for 40 years.

Then Tahmurath b. Nawbijahan ruled for 30 years.

Then his brother Jam b. Nawbijahan ruled for 716 years.

Then Biyurasb b. Arwandasb 1,000 years.

Then Afridun b. Athfiyan ruled for 500 years.

Then Manushihr[39] ruled after him for 120 years.

Then Afrasiyab the Turk ruled for 12 years.

Then Zaw b. Tahmasb[40] ruled for three years.

Then Karshasb ruled with Zaw for nine years. And God knows best whether this is correct.

The Second Dynasty: the Kayanids

They numbered 10 and the period of their rule was 778 years.

Then Kay Qubad ruled for 126 years.

Then Kay Kawus ruled for 150 years.

Then Kay Khusraw ruled 80 years.

Then Kay Luhrasb ruled for 120 years.

Then Kay Bishtasb[41] ruled for 120 years.

Then Kay Bahman ruled for 112 years.

Then Khumani[42] Shahrazad ruled for 30 years.

---

38 At this point Hamza just lists Persian kings and their reign lengths (including those of his two main sources, Musa b. 'Isa and Bahram b. Mardanshah), but afterwards he gives information about them, as do Mas'udi and Ya'qubi, so the reader wishing to have biographical details about these rulers should skip the lists.

39 Hamza writes Manujihr, Mas'udi Manushihr, both trying to render the Persian form Manuchihr. I use Mas'udi's form, Manushihr, since it is the most common in Arabic.

40 Hamza writes here Zab b. Sawmasb, but later Zaw b. Tahmasb.

41 His name has two forms: Wishtasb (Greek: Hystaspes; Arabic: Bishtasb) or Goshtasb. Hamza has the latter, but Mas'udi and Ya'qubi have the former, which I will therefore use throughout this book. He is famous for having met Zoroaster and accepted his religion.

42 Hamza gives Humay, as does Firdawsi, so this is presumably the NP form. Mas'udi and Ya'qubi have Khumani, which is the usual Arabic form (thus also in Tabari 1.654, 687–90),

Then her brother, Dara b. Bahman, ruled for 12 years.

Then his son Dara b. Dara[43] ruled for 14 years.

[14] Then Alexander (the Great) ruled for 14 years.

The Third Dynasty: the Arsacids[44]
They number 11, and their rule lasted for 344 years.[45]

Then Ashak b. Ashak[46] ruled for 52 years.

Then his son Shabur b. Ashak ruled for 24 years.

Then his son Gudarz[47] b. Shabur ruled for 50 years.

Then his nephew Wanhan b. Balash b. Shabur ruled for 21 years.

Then his son Gudarz the Younger b. Wanhan ruled for 19 years.

Then his brother Narsi b. Wanhan ruled for 30 years.

Then his uncle Hurmuz b. Balash b. Shabur ruled for 17 years.

Then his son Firuz b. Hurmuz ruled for 12 years.

Then his son Khusraw b. Firuz ruled for 40 years.

Then his brother Balash (b. Khusraw) b. Firuz ruled for 24 years.

Then his son Ardawan b. Balash b. Firuz[48] ruled for 55 years.

which I will therefore use throughout this book. She was daughter, wife and successor of Bahman.

43 The last king of the Kayanid dynasty, often identified with the last Achaemenid king, Darius III (336–330 BC), simply because Alexander the Great is known to have defeated Darius III; but the latter, whose birth name was Artashta, was the son of Arsames, not of Dara/Darius. In Arabic the name is written with long 'a's, Dārā.

44 Arabic: al-Ashghānīya, which conveys Persian: Ashkāniyān. This dynasty is known from historical sources; it held power from approximately 250 BC to AD 224. Because of the decentralised nature of their rule the kings of this dynasty, along with other more minor and less long-lived dynasties, were referred to by Muslim authors as mulūk al-ṭawā'if, literally: 'kings of the parts'.

45 The actual figure is around 475 years and there were some 30 rulers, not 11. Tabari, 1.706 and 708, gives 266 years, but lists the same number of rulers (with the same names, except that he has Bizan instead of Wanhan and Ardawan instead of Firuz), though on pages 709 and 710 he gives two more lists, which include some additional rulers.

46 This corresponds to the Greek form Arsaces; he was the eponymous founder of the dynasty, who seized power from a Seleucid satrap of north-east Iran ca. 247 BC.

47 Hamza has Kudarz, Mas'udi Judarz (Ya'qubi omits the Arsacid kings), both trying to represent Persian Gudarz.

48 He is presumably Artabanus/Ardawan IV, the last Arsacid king, who ruled ca. AD 208–24.

The Fourth Dynasty: the Sasanids[49]
There were 28 of them and their rule lasted for 429 years, three months and 18 days.[50] Ardashir [I] b. Babak ruled for 14 years and six months.

Then **[15]** Shabur [I] b. Ardashir ruled 30 years and 28 days.

Then Hurmuz[51] [I] b. Shabur ruled for a year and 10 months.

Then Bahram [I] b. Hurmuz ruled for three years, three months and three days.

Then Bahram [II] b. Bahram ruled for 17 years.

Then Bahram [III] b. Bahram b. Bahram ruled for 13 years and four months.

Then his brother Narsi b. Bahram ruled for nine years.

Then Hurmuz [II] b. Narsi ruled for seven years and five months.

Then Shabur [II] b. Hurmuz ruled for 72 years.

Then his brother Ardashir [II] b. Hurmuz ruled for four years.

Then Shabur [III] b. Shabur ruled for five years and four months.

Then Bahram [IV] b. Shabur ruled for 11 years.

Then Yazdagird [I] the Sinner[52] b. Bahram ruled for 21 years, five months and 16 days.

Then Bahram [V] Gur b. Yazdagird ruled for 23 years.

Then Yazdagird [II] b. Bahram Gur ruled for 18 years, four months and 18 days.

Then Firuz[53] [I] b. Yazdagird ruled for 27 years and one day.

Then Balash b. Firuz[54] ruled for four years.

---

49 A dynasty that arose in Fars in AD 224 and held power until ousted by the Arabs in 651–52. For a good recent account of their history and rule see Daryaee, *Sasanian Persia*. For the family tree and reign lengths of this dynasty see Table 3 below.

50 Though, when adding up the individual reigns given by Hamza, the total is 449 years, 10 months and 16 days.

51 The usual Persian form of the name is Hormizd.

52 Yazdagird I earned this negative epithet for his harsh treatment of Iranian nobles, but he was sometimes popular with Christians and Jews for his generally favourable policies towards them. For discussion see McDonough, 'A Second Constantine?', and Daryaee, 'Epithets', 12–13.

53 The usual Persian form of the name is Peroz. Hurmuz III briefly ruled after his father Yazdagird II, but he was quickly ousted by his brother Firuz, who had Hephthalite support (see Tabari, 1.872, and Ya'qubi, 184, below).

54 Balash was actually a brother of Firuz, not his son, as pre-Islamic sources make clear

Then Qubad[55] [I] b. Firuz ruled for 43 years.

Then Khusraw[56] [I] Anusharwan[57] b. Qubad ruled for 47 **[16]** years and seven months.

Then Hurmuz [IV] b. Khusraw ruled for 11 years, seven months and 10 days.

Then Khusraw [II] Abarwiz[58] b. Hurmuz ruled for 38 years.

Then Shirawayh[59] b. Khusraw ruled for eight months.

Then Ardashir [III] b. Shirawayh ruled for a year and six months.

Then Buran Dukht bt. Khusraw ruled for a year and four months.

Then Jushnashbandah, who was not of the royal line,[60] ruled for two months.

Then Azarmidukht bt. Abarwiz, ruled for a year and four months.

Then Khurrazad Khusraw ruled for a month.

Then Yazdagird [III] b. Shahriyar (b.) Abarwiz ruled for 20 years.

Thus the entire period covered by all the Persians kings is 4,071 years, 10 months and 19 days, during which 60 kings reigned.[61]

(e.g. Ps-Joshua, 248; Procopius, 1.5.2; Agathias, 4.27.5); this mistake is repeated by Mas'udi and Ya'qubi and, indeed, by all Muslim authors.

55 Hamza always writes Qubad, which I follow in this book, but Mas'udi and Ya'qubi write Qubadh. The usual Persian form of the name is Kawad/Kawadh.

56 Hamza uses the form Kisrā for this ruler and the next but one ruler, but elsewhere he uses the form Khusraw, which is closer to the Persian form of the name. For this reason and because it is the form most commonly used in modern literature, I will write Khusraw throughout this book.

57 Meaning 'of immortal soul' in Persian (MP: *anūshag-ruwān*).

58 Meaning 'victorious' in Persian (MP: *abarwēz*, NP: *parwēz*).

59 This is the Arabic form of the name; one could also read it as NP Shiruyah (MP = Shiroi, rendered as Siroes in Greek sources).

60 If he is the same as the Jushnasdih of Tabari, 1.1064, then he was a distant relative of Khusraw II's paternal uncle.

61 Actually Hamza has listed 58 rulers, whose combined reigns add up to 4,039 years, 10 months and 16 days, which is 32 years and 3 days less than the total that Hamza gives.

SECTION II of Chapter 1: Review of some of the chronology
covered in section I together with a commentary on it in the book
of Musa b. ʿIsa al-Kisrawi[62]

Musa says: I examined the book called the 'Book of Lords',[63] which was
translated from Persian into Arabic with the title 'History of the Kings
of the Persians'. Then I looked further at other copies of this book and
investigated them carefully, [17] and I found them to be so different (from
one another) that I could not obtain even two copies that were in agreement.
This confusion arose with those translating this book from one language to
another. I met with Hasan b. ʿAli al-Hamadani, who made (astronomical)
calculations[64] in Maragha[65] for its headman al-ʿAlaʾ b. Ahmad[66] and who was
the most knowledgeable person in this field that I have ever encountered.
We compared the years of the third and fourth dynasties of Persian kings
that ruled after Alexander (the Great), namely the Arsacids and Sasanids,
with the dating of Alexander, which has been accurately determined by the
calculations of the astronomers in their handbooks.[67] Then we sought (to
work out the length of time) between the years of Alexander and the Hijra
in order to make it the foundation (of our chronology). We found that figure
corroborated in the observatory handbook[68] exactly as I shall recount here.
Thus the astronomers maintain that the interval between the Alexandrian
era and the Hijra, from the noon of Monday, the first day of Tishrin I, to the
noon of Thursday of Muharram,[69] comprises 340,901 days, which are equal
to 961 lunar years and 154 days, and in Chaldean (solar) years, each [18] of

---

62 Ibn al-Nadim, 128, mentions him in his section (3.2) on 'kings, secretaries, orators,
correspondents and bureaucrats'. For his floruit (mid-ninth century) and biography see
Rubin, 'Musa b. ʿIsa', and Hämeen-Anttila, 'Al-Kisrawī'.

63 NP: *Khudāy-nāmah*.

64 Arabic: *al-raqqām*. This can mean either someone who counts/makes calculations or
someone who can do ornate writing. The context would seem to favour the former sense.

65 An ancient city of the province of Azerbaijan, in modern north-west Iran. The Mongol
leader Hulagu made it his capital and inaugurated an observatory there in 1259; possibly it
had some connection with astronomy before this date.

66 Al-ʿAlaʾ was later appointed governor of Azerbaijan and died in 874 (Tabari, 3.1886).

67 Arabic: *al-zījāt*, singular: *zīj*. This word, which almost certainly derives from Persian,
signifies a handbook or manual of astronomical tables giving calculations for positions and
conjunctions of the sun, moon, stars and planets. It is on the basis of these that astrologers
then made their predictions.

68 Arabic: *zīj al-raṣd*. The latter word could refer to an observatory (short for *bayt
al-raṣd*) or could just mean 'observation, lookout'.

69 Tishrin is the first month of the old Syro-Mesopotamian solar calendar, coinciding

365¼ days, amount to 932 years and 289 days or nine months and 19 days. To these we added the years between the beginning of the Hijra and the fall of the Persian Empire; their (last) king, Yazdagird, died in the year 40,[70] and so the total period amounted to 972 years and 289 days. From these we deducted the period of rule of the Arsacids, that is, 266 years,[71] and so this gives for the period of rule of the Sasanids, from the accession of Ardashir to the death of Yazdagird, 786 years[72] and 289 days.

Now that we have verified the total number of years of the rule of the Sasanids, we shall move on to the details regarding the number of their kings, their names, and the length of each one's reign. We shall also add three names which have not been mentioned by the transmitters, who were led astray by the identical phrasing of their names; for example, there are two Yazdagirds and two Bahrams. Thus Yazdagird the Sinner, father of Bahram Gur, was son of Yazdagird b. Bahram b. Shabur, and this Yazdagird, whom the transmitters forgot about and omitted his name, was more illustrious than his son Yazdagird the Sinner. **[19]** It was he who was a friend of Sharwin of Dastan[73] and not (Yazdagird) the Sinner. Moreover, he governed with kindness, mercy and compassion, unlike his son. As an example of his fidelity it is recounted that one of the kings of the Romans, at the time when death approached him, entrusted his young son to Yazdagird (asking) that he dispatch from his statesmen a steward who could keep a check on his son and his actions until he reached manhood. Yazdagird sent Sharwin Barniyan, head of the district of Dastan, and appointed him to the land of the Romans, which he kept in order for 20 years. After that Yazdagird fulfilled his trust by returning the kingdom of the Romans to

with October in the Roman calendar. Muharram is the first month of the Muslim lunar calendar.

70   This is incorrect: Yazdagird was assassinated in year 31 (651–52) of the Hijra.

71   Tabari, 1.706 and 708, gives the same figure, and it is strikingly close to the figure of 268 years given by Mas'udi below and of 270 years given by Agathias, 2.26.1. Since the latter is writing in the mid-sixth century, this (erroneous) computation of the duration of the Arsacid dynasty evidently already circulated in the Sasanid period.

72   Or rather 706 years (972 minus 266). The correct figure is about 428 years (ca. AD 224–652); the problem here is a huge underestimate of the period between Alexander's death and the Sasanids' inception, which is actually 535 years (312 BC–AD 224).

73   His story is narrated by Hamza below and is confirmed by Greek sources, which call him Antiochus and tell us that the Roman emperor in question was Arcadius and his son was named Theodosius. But the Greek sources tell us that the Persian ruler at the time was Yazdagird I. The latter was despised by some and praised by others (see McDonough, 'A Second Constantine?'), and it is possible that these differing assessments misled Musa into making two persons out of Yazdagird I.

the boy and recalling Sharwin, who had established a city there, naming it Bashirwan, which, in its Arabised form, is called Bajarwan.[74]

Transmitters have omitted two other names on account of their identical pronunciation: Bahram b. Bahram b. Bahram, and another Bahram: Bahram b. Yazdagird b. Bahram Gur, the father of Firuz.[75] I will now list the years of the kings of the Sasanids in order to make clear, if God Almighty and Most Holy wishes it, the deficiency of the (extant) versions:

In the name of God the Protector the Most High

Ardashir [I] b. Babak ruled for 19 years and six months.

Then his son Shabur [I] of the Armies[76] ruled [20] for 32 years and four months.

Then his son Hurmuz [I] b. Shabur ruled for one year and 10 months.

Then his son Bahram [I] b. Hurmuz ruled for nine years and three months.

Then Bahram [II] b. Bahram ruled for 23 years, and others say he ruled 17 years.

Then Bahram [III] b. Bahram b. Bahram ruled for 13 years and four months.

Then his brother Narsi b. Bahram b. Bahram ruled for nine years.

Then Hurmuz [II] b. Narsi ruled for 13 years.

Then Shabur [II], the Lord of the Shoulders,[77] b. Hurmuz ruled for 72 years.

Then Ardashir [II] b. Hurmuz ruled for four years until his (Shabur II's) son had attained puberty and left behind childhood.

Then Shabur [III] b. Shabur, who was crowned while still in his mother's womb,[78] ruled for 82 years.

---

74 Near Raqqa and south of Resh'aina in northern Syria.

75 The first Bahram given here is Bahram III and is usually included in lists of Sasanid rulers, but the second Bahram, Musa's Bahram VI, is not commonly included. For discussion of the differences between Musa's and Hamza's lists of Sasanid kings see Rubin, 'Musa ibn 'Isa', 11.

76 Arabic: *Shābūr al-Junūd.* The nickname presumably refers to the fact that he conducted many successful military campaigns.

77 He is nicknamed 'Lord of the Shoulders' (*Dhū l-Aktāf*) by Muslim historians, because he allegedly pierced the shoulders of eastern Arabian leaders. See also nn. 209–10 below.

78 This applies to Shabur II, not Shabur III. Also, the latter is usually assigned a reign of only five years.

Then his son Bahram [IV] b. Shabur b. Shabur ruled for 12 years.

Then his son Yazdagird [I] the Gentle[79] b. Bahram b. Shabur, companion of Sharwin of Dastan, ruled for 82 years.

Then his son Yazdagird the Rough[80] b. Yazdagird ruled for 22 years.

Then his son Bahram Gur [V] b. Yazdagird ruled for 23 years.

Then his son Yazdagird [II] b. Bahram Gur ruled for 18 years [21] and five months.

Then his son Bahram [VI] b. Yazdagird ruled for 26 years and a month.

Then his son Firuz [I] b. Bahram ruled for 29 years and one day.

Then his son Balash b. Firuz ruled for three years.

Then his brother Qubad [I] b. Firuz ruled for 68 years according to the 'Great (book of) Biographical History' and 43 years according to the 'Small (book of) Biographical History'.[81]

Then his son Khusraw [I] Anusharwan ruled for 47 years, seven months and some days.

Then his son Hurmuz [IV] b. Khusraw ruled for 23 years, and some say 13 years.

Then his son Khusraw [II] Abarwiz b. Hurmuz ruled for 38 years.

Then his son Shirawayh b. Khusraw ruled for eight months.

Then his son Ardashir [III] b. Shirawayh ruled for one year.

Then Shahrbaraz,[82] who was not of the royal line, ruled for 38 days.

---

79 Arabic: *al-layyin*. This is Musa's extra Yazdagird that he mentioned above, not generally included by other Muslim historians. The epithet 'the gentle' is usually applied to Yazdagird II.

80 Arabic: *al-khashin*. This is presumably the Yazdagird that other Muslim historians call Yazdagird the Sinner.

81 Arabic: (*kitāb*) *al-siyar al-kabīr* and *al-siyar al-ṣaghīr*. It is not clear what texts Musa is referring to here.

82 The text has Shahrīzad, which looks very similar in Arabic to Shahrbaraz, the honorary title (meaning 'boar of the realm') of this famous Persian general, who had achieved many victories against the Romans for Khusraw II. Sebeos, 129–30, recounts how he came to power with the support of the Roman emperor Heraclius and had Ardashir assassinated. *Chronicle of Siirt*, 236, which calls him Shahriyūn, says that 'he was living in the land of the Romans serving King Heraclius' but went back to Persia at the request of a faction opposed to Ardashir and with military support from Heraclius, who evidently seized the opportunity to have a pro-Roman leader on the Persian throne. *Chronicle of Khuzistan*, 29–30, calls him by his personal name, Farrukhan, and assigns him 40 days of rule.

Then Buran Dukht bt. Khusraw Abarwiz, who returned the Cross of Christ[83] to the Catholicos, ruled for a year and a few days.

Then after her Jushnashbandah, who was not of the royal line, ruled for two months.

Then Khusraw [III] b. Qubad[84] b. Hurmuz b. Anusharwan ruled for 10 months.

Then Firuz [II],[85] who was descended from Ardashir b. Babak, ruled for [22] two months.

Then Azarmidukht bt. Khusraw [II] Abarwiz ruled for four months.

Then Farrukh b. Khusraw[86] Abarwiz ruled for a month and some days.

Then Yazdagird [III] b. Shahriyar ruled for 20 years.

Thus there were a total of eight rulers after Khusraw Abarwiz in a period of only four years and six months, and Yazdagird b. Shahriyar was the ninth of them.[87] These are all the reigns of the Sasanids of the kings of Persia, which I investigated very thoroughly until I had put them in proper order as set out above.

83 Arabic: *khashabat al-masīḥ*. This is the fragment of the 'True Cross' that was taken by the Persians from Jerusalem in 614 to Iraq and then was returned by them to Emperor Heraclius (an action usually ascribed to Shahrbaraz, not Buran Dukht, though *Chronicle of Khurasan*, 30, does have Buran send peace ambassadors to Heraclius). The latter then restored it to its original place in Jerusalem in Easter 630; see Zuckerman, 'Return of the Holy Cross'.

84 The text has '-b/m-ā-d, but one should read Qubad with Mas'udi, 102 (below). He may be the 'Khusraw of the family of Sasan' mentioned by Sebeos, 130.

85 Tabari, 1.1066, says that he was a great-grandchild of Khusraw I and that he was killed after only a few days on the throne because certain nobles viewed as inauspicious the tightness of his crown. Hamza, 28 (below), citing Bahram b. Mardanshah, speaks of 'Firuz called Jushnasbandah'.

86 This is presumably the same as Khurrazad Khusraw, listed by Hamza, 16, above and 28, below. Mas'udi, 103 (below), Ya'qubi, 198 (below) and Tabari, 1.1066, call him Farrukhzad Khusraw. Sebeos, 130, only knows of a ruler called Hormizd between Azarmidukht and Yazdagird.

87 He has just listed nine rulers, with Yazdagird making ten. Some of these rulers would not have been universally recognised; cf. *Chronicle of Siirt*, 259–60: 'When matters had been placed on a firm basis (by envoys of Queen Buran) between the Romans and the Persians, internal discord broke out among the Persians. Firuz, the commander of the Persian army, plotted against Buran and strangled her; the length of her reign was 16 months. Opinions were now divided in the army: those who were in Khurasan gave allegiance to a boy of royal descent named Mihr Khusraw; those in Mada'in to Azarmidukht, daughter of Shirin, wife of Khusraw; and those in Istakhr and the districts of Fars to Yazdagird son of Shahriyar son of Khusraw.'

As regards the reigns of the kings of the Arsacids, who preceded the Sasanids, I have not concerned myself with them because of the disasters that occurred in the days of those kings. That was because Alexander, when he appropriated the land of Babylon and subjugated its people, envied them for all the learning that they had amassed and that no other nation possessed, and so he burnt all the books that he could get hold of. Then he proceeded to kill all their priests and clerics,[88] scholars, sages and those who preserved for them (the Arsacids) their histories in the course of their studies until he had destroyed them all. This he did after he had had translated all of their knowledge that he needed into the Greek language. Thereafter the Persians no longer knew the length of the days of the Arsacids, who were called the Petty Kings [23] and who had none among them who revived learning or took an interest in wisdom. (This continued) until their empire was restored to them upon the rise of Ardashir. Yet, when he had taken control of the kingdom, he dated events only according to the years of his own reign. This practice led to confusion in their dates, whereas the Arab kings did well to establish the dates of the years of their days (by counting) in continuous succession from the beginning of the Hijra up to whatever was the sum total of years (at the relevant point in time).

(Hamza:) This is all that al-Kisrawi has recounted and he noted that he had investigated the matter deeply until he had managed to make the years of the House of Sasan correspond with the Alexandrian era. Yet what al-Kisrawi has recorded and has claimed to have taken care to correct is also wrong and inconsistent with the Alexandrian era, for he set out in detail the years (of Sasanid rule) as amounting to 696 years and nine days.[89] Thus between the calculation that I have come up with, according to the (aforementioned) astronomical table, and that of al-Kisrawi there is (a discrepancy of) 90 years, nine months and 10 days.[90]

---

88 Arabic: *al-mawābidha wa-l-harābidha.* These were the two main categories of the Zoroastrian religious establishment; the latter (singular: *hirbadh*) would seem to have had some responsibility for religious instruction and possibly some connection with fire-temples (see Ya'qubi, 202, below).

89 This is actually about right (it is difficult to be exact, as Musa sometimes just says 'some days') if, on the three occasions that Musa gives two options for a king's reign length, one always take the higher figure.

90 Hamza is referring to his calculation on page 18 above of 786 years for the years of the Sasanid rule, although, as we noted there, the result of his calculation (972 minus 266) should have been 706 years.

SECTION III of Chapter 1: Review of everything that has been covered in Section I together with a commentary on it done by Bahram **[24]** b. Mardanshah, priest of the district of Shabur in the region of Fars

Bahram the priest said: I collected 20 or so copies of the book called the 'Book of Lords' and then correctly reconstructed from them the dates of the kings of the Persians from the time of Gayumart, the father of mankind, to the end of their days with the transfer of their rule to the Arabs. The first person to live on the face of the earth was a man whom the Persians called Gayumart *Gilshāh*, that is 'the King of Clay', for his sovereignty was over clay alone (and it lasted) 30 years. He left behind a son and a daughter, called Masha and Mashyana.[91] They passed 70 years without bearing children and then 18 children, male and female, were born to them in a space of 50 years. This couple died and the world remained without government for 94 years and eight months. Thus the entire period without government from the reign of Gayumart to the beginning of the reign of Hushang Pishdad is 294 years and eight months. Then Hushang b. Firwal b. Siyamak b. Masha b. Gayumart ruled for 40 years. Then Tahmurath b. Nawbijahan b. Aywankahdh b. Hawankahdh b. Hushang ruled over the seven climes[92] for 30 years. Then his brother Jam b. **[25]** Nawbijahan ruled the seven climes for 616 years. Then he remained on the run from Biyurasb for 100 years. Then Biyurasb ruled over the seven climes for 1,000 years. Then Afridun b. Athfiyan ruled over the clime of Hunayra[93] for 500 years. After him Manushihr ruled for 120 years, during (some of) which time Afrasiyab the Turk took possession of his kingdom by force and conquest. Then Zaw b. Tahmasb ruled for four years, although in his days Karshasb held some regions.

So that is the entirety of the period of the first dynasty of the kings of the Persians, comprising nine reigns and 2,734 years and six months.[94]

91 Also recorded in Tabari, 1.154. They are the first human couple according to the *Bundahishn*, the Persian book of creation.

92 Arabic: *iqlīm*, from Greek *klima*, meaning region or zone. In Greco-Roman geography the world was divided up into a certain number of *klima*s/climes; Ptolemy stipulated seven and this number became standard in late antique and early Islamic geographical thinking.

93 This corresponds to MP *khwanirah*, which designates the clime at the centre of the seven climes.

94 The reign lengths that Hamza gives for the Pishdadids do not seem to add up to more than 2704 years, even taking into account the 294 years without government and the 100 years when Jam was on the run.

The Second Dynasty [Kayanids][95]

Then Kay Qubad ruled for 100 years.

Then Kay Kawus b. Kay Qubad ruled for 150 years.

Then Kay Khusraw b. Siyawush b. Kay Kawus ruled for 60 years.

Then Kay Luhrasb ruled for 120 years.

Then Kay Bishtasb b. Kay Luhrasb ruled for 120 years.

Then Kay Ardashir b. Isfandiyar (b.) Bishtasb, also called Bahman, ruled for 112 years. Then Khumani Shahrazad bt. Bahman b. Isfandiyar, who was mother of Dara b. Bahman, ruled for 30 years.

Then Dara b. Bahman ruled for 12 years.

Then Dara b. [26] Dara b. Bahman ruled for 14 years.

That is all the kings of the second dynasty, comprising 718 years. Afterwards the country was ruled by Alexander the Greek for 14 years, and then by a number of governors of the Greeks together with Persian ministers for 54 years, making 68 years, though God knows best.

The Third Dynasty [Arsacids]

And after them Ashak b. Dara b. Dara[96] ruled for 10 years.

Then Ashak b. Ashak ruled for 20 years.

Then Shabur b. Ashak ruled for 60 years.

Then Bahram b. Shabur ruled for 11 years.

Then Balash b. Bahram ruled for 11 years.

Then Hurmuz b. Balash ruled for 19 years.

Then Narsi b. Balash ruled for 40 years.

Then Firuz b. Hurmuz ruled for 17 years.

Then Balash b. Firuz ruled for 12 years.

Then Khusraw b. Malad ruled for 40 years.

Then Balash ruled for 24 years.

Then Ardawan b. Balash ruled for 13 years.

---

95 Subheadings in square brackets are not in the text, but are added by me for clarification.

96 This figure appears in some lists of the Arsacid kings, either instead of or as well as Ashak b. Ashak; one imagines that he is invented to give a clear genealogical link to the Kayanids, being portrayed as a son of the last Kayanid king.

Then Ardawan the Elder b. Ashak ruled for 23 years.

Then Khusraw b. Ashak ruled for 20 years.

Then Bihafarid b. Ashak ruled for 15 years.

Then Balash b. Ashak ruled for 22 [27] years.

Then Gudarz b. Ashak ruled for 30 years.

Then Narsi b. Ashak ruled for 20 years.

Then the other Ardawan, who is called Afdam in Persian, ruled for 31 years.

That is the entire period of the third dynasty, which comprised, including Alexander, 20 kings (who reigned for) 463 years,[97] as found in the books.

The Fourth Dynasty [Sasanids]
Then Ardashir b Babak ruled for 14 years and 10 months, having spent 30 years at war with the Petty Kings.

Then Shabur [I] b. Ardashir ruled for 30 years and 15 days.

Then Hurmuz [I] b. Shabur ruled for two years.

Then Bahram [I] b. Hurmuz ruled for three years and three months.

Then Bahram [II] b. Bahram ruled for 17 years.

Then Bahram [III] b. Bahram b. Bahram ruled for 40 years and four months.

Then Narsi b. Bahram [I], brother of Bahram [II], ruled for nine years.

Then Hurmuz [II] b. Narsi ruled for seven years.

Then Shabur [II] b. Hurmuz ruled for 72 years.

Then Ardashir [II], brother of Shabur, ruled for four years.

Then Shabur [III] ruled for five years.

Then Bahram [IV] b. Shabur Kirmanshah[98] ruled for 11 years.

Then Yazdagird [I] the Sinner b. Bahram [28] ruled for 21 years, five months and 18 days.

---

97 Actually 452 years, including Alexander's 14. Note that Bahram b. Mardanshah's list of Arsacid kings is quite different from that of Hamza/Musa.

98 So-called because he had been made governor of Kirman during his father's reign and had built a city there.

Then Bahram [V] Gur b. Yazdagird ruled for 19 years and 11 months.

Then Yazdagird [II] b. Bahram Gur ruled for four years, four months and 18 days.

Then Firuz [I] b. Yazdagird ruled for 17 years.

Then Balash b. Firuz ruled for four years.

Then Qubad [I] b. Firuz ruled for 41 years.

Then Khusraw [I Anusharwan] b. Qubad ruled for 48 years.

Then Hurmuz [IV] b. Khusraw ruled for 12 years.

Then Khusraw [II] Abarwiz b. Hurmuz b. Khusraw ruled for 38 years.

Then Qubad [II] b. Khusraw son of[99] Shirawayh ruled for eight months.

Then Ardashir [III] b. Shirawayh ruled for a year and six months.

Then Buran Dukht bt. Khusraw ruled for a year and four months.

Then Firuz, called Jushnashbandah,[100] ruled for some days.

Then Azarmidukht bt. Abarwiz, including the days of Jushnashbandah, ruled for six months.

Then Khurrazad Khusraw b. Abarwiz ruled for one year.

Then Yazdagird [III] b. Shahriyar ruled for 20 years.

That is the entire period of the fourth dynasty, which comprised 28 kings who ruled, excluding the 30 years **[29]** of Ardashir b. Babak's war with the Petty Kings, for 456 years, a month and 22 days.[101] And the total from the time of the beginning of Creation up to the last days of the kings of the Persians was 66 kings (who ruled) for 4,409 years, nine months and 22 days.

---

99 Perhaps this should read 'known as', since the names Qubad and Shirawayh belong to the same person, who was son of Khusraw II.

100 This conflation of Firuz and Jushnasbandah is also found in Mas'udi, 103, below. Tabari, 1.1066, speaks of 'Firuz son of Mihran Jushnas, who was also called Jushnasdih', so possibly Jushnasdih equates to/is a mistake for Jushnasbandah. If so, then the statement of Hamza, 16 and 22, that Jushnasbandah was 'not of the royal line', may just mean that he was not in the direct line of succession, though still belonging to the House of Sasan.

101 Actually 445 years, 4 months and 21 days.

SECTION IV of Chapter 1: A brief account of the history of the Persian kings as fits with the aforementioned chronological sequence and in conformity with what is in the biographical histories[102]

[Pishdadids]

Hushang Pishdad

He was the first of the kings of the Persians. The meaning of Pishdad is 'the First Law-giver',[103] because he was the first to give judgements in the kingdom. He was crowned at Istakhr, and for that reason Istakhr was called (in Persian) *Būm Shāh*, that is, 'Country of the King'. The Persians claim that he and his brother Wikart were prophets. One of his innovations was that he mined iron and devised a means to make (from it) weapons and manufacturing tools. Also he ordered people to hunt down wild animals and kill them.[104]

Tahmurath Zīnāwand

The meaning of Zīnāwand is 'the Sharp-Weaponed'.[105] He built the city of Babylon (in Iraq) and the citadel of Merv. In some copies (it is said) that he built Kardīndād, which is one of the seven cities of Mada'in.[106] I think that it should be (written) Kardābād,[107] about which a (famous) story

102 Arabic: *kutub al-siyar*. This title, and related ones such as *siyar al-'ajam* and *siyar al-mulūk*, seems to be a common way of referring to histories recounting the lives of Persian kings and heroes. See further the introduction above and Appendix 1 below.

103 This is a possible interpretation, in that MP *pēsh* means 'first' and *dād* could relate to the root *da-*, 'to give', but perhaps more likely is 'first given' or 'first created'; see *EIr*, 'Hōšang'.

104 Tabari, 1.171, also mentions his working of iron and decree about killing animals, specifying that it was for food and skins.

105 The text has *zyb'wnd*, which should be emended to *zyn'wnd*: (b and n are the same in Arabic except for the placement of the dot): MP *zīn* (*zyn*) 'weapon, sword' + *āwand* (suffix indicating quality), which corresponds well to Arabic *shākk al-silāḥ*.

106 Mada'in, which just means 'cities' in Arabic, is the name applied in Islamic times to the cluster of royal settlements (the two largest being Seleucia and Ctesiphon) that lie on either side of the River Tigris south of Baghdad and that served as the capital of the Persian Empire for the Arsacids and Sasanids.

107 Hamza presumably did not think that the second part of the name, i.e. *īndad*, sounded right, and so he opted for *ābād*, meaning 'settlement', which appears as the second element in numerous place-names. The correct name is Kardbandād (reading 'b' for 'y', the two being distinguishable in Arabic only by a dot).

(is told),[108] **[30]** but it was obscured and misread as Kardīndād. He also erected two grand buildings in Isfahan, one of them called Mahrin and the other Sarawayh.[109] As regards Mahrin, it became thereafter the name for the village below this edifice, which had beforehand been called Kuk. As regards Sarawayh, he had it enclosed within the walls of the city of Gay[110] after thousands of years (during which it had been unprotected). The remains of both of them are still standing.

In his time arose the worship and fashioning of idols. The reason for this was that many people suffered the loss of their loved ones and they adopted effigies after their image so that they could console themselves by looking at them. Much time passed by until worship of them suggested itself to them, and they worshipped them turning to (the idea) that they were intermediaries between themselves and God, who would bring them nearer to Him in rank.[111] Also in his time fasting took off; the instigators of it were some poor people, who followed a man named Budasf.[112] (Obtaining) food became difficult (for them), and so they planned to go hungry during the day and then drink enough water to sustain the spark of life. They practised that for a time and they came to consider it a religion and a way of worshipping God. These groups were called the Chaldeans,[113] and in the time of the rule of Islam they called themselves Sabians.[114] In reality

108 Hamza uses the Persian word *dastān*, meaning 'story, romance, fable'.

109 On this building see Appendix 3 below.

110 This is the MP form of Arabic *Jay*; it is identified with ancient Gabae, which hosted an Achaemenid royal palace, according to Strabo, and was very close to Isfahan.

111 This phrase echoes Qur'an 34:36 ('neither your wealth nor your children are what will draw you nearer to Us in rank'). On this account of the origins of paganism in Iran see Crone, 'Ancient Iranian Paganism'.

112 Here written Yudasf, which is the Persian form of the name. The Arabic form, Budasf (or Budhasf, Budasb etc.), presumably derives from the term bodhisattva, a term for the Buddha, on whose life this text is loosely based. See Toral-Niehoff, 'Legende', and Crone, 'Ancient Iranian Paganism'.

113 Earlier (on page 5 of the Arabic text) Hamza had explained that humans used to all follow the same (pagan) religion; in the east they were called Samīniyūn (Samaniyūn or Samanīya in most Arabic texts, ultimately deriving from *Sramana/Samana*, the Sanskrit/Pali word for an ascetic) and in the west Chaldeans. Historically, Chaldean refers to a people prominent in southern Iraq in the first half of the first millennium BC.

114 The Sabians are mentioned in the Qur'an, along with Jews and Christians, as believers in God and the Last Day, for which they merited protection. Presumably the Chaldeans, as ancient pagans, claimed to be Sabians so as to acquire this protection. It is unclear who the Sabians of the Qur'an really were, though the Mandaeans of southern Iraq have been seen as a possibility and that could be what Hamza is thinking of here. See further Van Bladel, *Arabic Hermes*, 115–18.

the latter were a Christian sect, who lived between the desert [31] and the flood plains (of southern Iraq), in opposition to the majority of Christians, and were counted among their heretics. People say that Tahmurath would declare: 'Every group likes its own creed, so do not bother them.' This rite still exists in the land of India.

Jamshid

Shīd means 'light' (in Persian) and so sunlight is called *khwarshīd*.[115] They maintain that Jamshid was only called this because light emanated from him. He is (to give him his full name) Jam b. Finwanhkan[116] b. Hawankahdh b. Aywankahdh[117] b. Hushang Pishdad. The biographical histories are full of examples of his achievements, but I have omitted mention of them lest the narration of this section be too long. Among the marvels that he accomplished was an arched bridge that he had erected over the Tigris. It stood for a long time until it was destroyed by Alexander. (Later) kings sought to rebuild it, but they were unable to do so, and instead they placed arches over the arches of the (original) bridge. The traces of this bridge still remain in the excavated parts of the Tigris, by the western crossing-point of the two (main) cities of Mada'in, and so sailors turn away from it when the water is low. It was he who laid out the city of Ctesiphon, which is the biggest of the seven cities that make up Mada'in.

Biyurasb Dahak

The derivation of Dahak is *dah*, which is the (Persian) word for ten, and *ak*, which is the (Persian) word for disaster.[118] So the meaning is that he is the one responsible for ten disasters that he introduced into the world, though this is not the place to mention them. [32] This is a most terrible nickname, but when they rendered it in Arabic it became very beautiful, for Dahak when Arabicised is turned into *Daḥḥāk* ('laughing'), and thus he is referred to in Arabic texts. (His full name is) Biyurasb b. Arwandasb

---

115 This is a compound of MP *khwar* (sun) and *shīd* (light, radiance).
116 The Arabic name here is trying to represent the MP form Vivanghan, a solar deity. On Hamza, 24, above, Jam is made son of Nawbijahan, like his brother Tahmurath, but here we have an allusion to the mythical Jam.
117 I have slightly modified the transliteration of these two names to make them conform to how they appear on Hamza, 24, above.
118 This is a folk etymology, though quite an ingenious one. This person is called *aži dahak* in Persian creation myth and the whole phrase may mean something like snake-man (*aži* = 'serpent').

b. Rikawan b. Madah-Surrah b. Taj b. Firwal b. Siyamak b. Masha b. Gayumart. Taj, his grandfather, was the ancestor of the Arabs, wherefore they are called Tajiyan.[119] Biyurasb used to stay in Babylon and so he made there a residence in the form of a crane[120] and named it Kangdiz,[121] which the people called Daman Ḥit.[122]

Afridun[123]

Afridun b. Athfiyan ruled the clime of Hunayra for 500 years. At the beginning of the thirtieth year of his reign there appeared Abraham, the Friend of God and prophet, peace be upon him – or so they say. And in the time of Manushihr, Moses appeared and took the sons of Israel out of the land of Egypt. In the days of Kay Khusraw, Solomon ruled over the Israelites, and in the days of Luhrasb, Nebuchadnezzar[124] headed for the western lands and destroyed Jerusalem, the city of the Jews, and he brought them as captives to the lands of the east. He shared them out amongst its cities according to their professions. Zoroaster appeared in the time of Bishtasb, and Alexander conquered the western lands in the time of Dara b. Dara. Christ[125] appeared in the time of Shabur b. Ashak, [33] Mani in the time of Shabur b. Ardashir, and Mazdak in the time of Qubad.[126]

119 Arabic: *tājiyān*, or perhaps this should read *tāziyān*. This term for Arabs is thought to derive ultimately from the name of the tribe of Tayyiʾ, which lived on the western borders of the Sasanid Empire, and for that reason their name became used as a generic term for all pastoralist tribes and tribesmen of the Arabian/Syrian deserts by the East Syrian Christians (Syriac: *ṭayyāyā*) and by the Persians (MP: *tāzīk*, NP: *tāzi*). See *EIr*, 'Tajik I'.
120 Meaning the bird of this name; compare the statement in the biography of Shabur I below that 'they used (at that time) to build cities according to the representation of certain things'.
121 Hamza has *klnk dīs*, but this must be the mythical fortress (MP: *dīz*) of Kang, which appears frequently in Iranian literature; see *EIr*, 'Kangdez'.
122 Hamza does not explain this name and its meaning is unclear.
123 Hamza writes Faridun here, but elsewhere he writes Afridun, which is the more usual form in Arabic texts. Faridun is, however, closer to MP Frēdōn.
124 Arabic: Bukht al-Naṣr. He ruled Babylon *ca.* 605–562 BC and his destruction of Jerusalem is usually placed in 587.
125 Arabic: *al-masīḥ*, 'the anointed one', which is the epithet of Jesus son of Mary in the Qurʾan.
126 Mani (d. 276) and Mazdak (d. *ca.* 530) were two religious missionaries who flourished in Iran in the third and early sixth centuries respectively. Both have attracted much scholarly attention; for a recent discussion with citation of earlier literature see Bausani, 'Two Unsuccessful Prophets: Mani and Mazdak', and Daryaee, *Sasanian Persia*, 72–75 (Mani), 86–90 (Mazdak).

Afridun divided his kingdom among his three sons: Salm, Tuj and Iraj. He made over Iraq and its dependent territories, along with the lands of the west and the land of India, to Iraj, the youngest of his sons, and designated for him the crown and the throne. He assigned the land of the Romans as far as the country of the Franks, along with the lands of the west, to Salm, the eldest of his sons. To Tuj, his middle son, he gave Tibet, China and the lands of the east. Tuj and Salm both became jealous of Iraj and they embarked upon his assassination.

Afridun invented incantations and created an antidote from the body of snakes. He founded the science of medicine and showed which plants would repel diseases from animate beings. He bred asses with horses in order to produce mules, combining the strength of asses and the swiftness of horses. He used to reside at Babylon, but God knows best.

Manushihr

Manushihr was one of the sons of Iraj b. Afridun. It was he who dug the River Euphrates and the River Mihran,[127] which is bigger than the Euphrates, and he diverted several large canals from the Euphrates and Tigris. In the sixtieth year of his reign Moses, peace be upon him, led the Israelites out of the land of Egypt and remained in the wilderness known as Tih regulating the affairs of the sons [34] of Israel for 40 years, during which he wrote the Torah for them. It was also during his (Manushihr's) reign that his (Moses') deputy, Joshua, brought the Israelites to Palestine. Manushihr transplanted odiferous plants from the mountains to the open plains and put a wall around them. When their fragrance had spread, he named these enclosures *bustān*, a word meaning mines of scent and perfume.[128]

During his reign Afrasiyab the Turk gained control over the regions of his realm for 12 years, drove Manushihr from the throne of his kingdom and confined him to the forests of Tabaristan. During the years of his control over the kingdom of Iran, Afrasiyab went on destroying cities, razing forts, stopping up rivers, filling up canals (with earth) and blocking up springs. In year five of the years of his control the people were afflicted by drought[129] and remained so until the end of his days. The waters dried

---

127 The Indus River, which is indeed longer than the Euphrates. Tabari, 1.436, only has him dig the Euphrates.

128 The Persian word *bustān* does effectively mean 'place of scent' and so a garden.

129 *Yadfunu l-anhār wa-yaṭummu al-qunīy ... wa-fī sanat khams min sinī ghalbatihi qaḥaṭa l-nās*; cf. Tabari, 1.529: *dafana l-anhār wa-l-qunīy wa- qaḥaṭa l-nās fī sanat khams min mulkih*. Similar wording (as opposed to general closeness in content) in two accounts

up, the lands became barren and the crops failed until God restrained him. Afrasiyab built (the part) of the wall of Merv that is between the citadel and the bend near the Gate of Niq. God knows best about what is manifest and what is secret.

Zaw b. Tahmasb
When Zaw came to the throne, he ordered the restoration of the cities and forts that Afrasiyab had ruined, the clearing of the waterways that he had blocked up. He removed from the people [35] the taxes and duties (that Afrasiyab had imposed) whereupon the country prospered and returned to the best of how it had been. He dug two water channels in the land of the Sawad called the two Zabs,[130] and by means of them sweetened the water of the Tigris. In his reign arose Kay Qubad, father of the Kayanid kings, and also in the days of Zaw's dominion Karshasb held power.[131]

[Kayanids]

Kay Qubad
When Kay Qubad reigned, people began to cultivate the land and paid the tithe on their crops, and he directed it towards the maintenance of the army, the securing of the borders and defending the country against enemies. Isfahan was formed of only one district, like Rayy,[132] but Kay Qubad added another district to it and called it the county of Iran-winārd-Kawad;[133] this is the district which in the days of al-Rashid[134] contained the cantons placed under the authority of the prefecture of Qum.[135]

---

from the Muslim tradition is rare for the period of the first three Persian dynasties, though it is common for accounts of the Sasanid dynasty (see Appendices 1–2 below).

130   The Sawad, literally meaning 'blackness' in Arabic, refers to the dark alluvial plains of southern Iraq. It is not clear whether this is a mythic explanation of how the two Zab rivers (greater and lesser Zab) in the north of Iraq were formed, or a reference to the digging of two canals with the same name as the rivers, perhaps flowing in or out of them.

131   Tabari, 1.533, says that Karshasb was Zaw's vizier, though he notes that others say he shared the rule with Zaw.

132   Ancient Rhages, the ruins of which lie to the south of modern Tehran.

133   Meaning 'Kawad has ordered Iran'. This is the corrected reading of Ryka Gyselen, who linked it with a seal and literary reference ('Toponyme Sasanide').

134   Harun al-Rashid, the fifth Abbasid caliph, who reigned 786–809.

135   The four administrative divisions given in this sentence are *kūra* (which I translate as district), *ūstān* (county), *rustāq* (canton) and *'amal* (prefecture).

Kay Kawus

He resided at Balkh, and I have read in some books of biographical histories[136] that he initiated (many things) in Babylon; (for example) he built an edifice that towered high into the air. I reckon that it is the building behind Baghdad that is called ʿAqarqūf,[137] for it is one of the marvels of that land. Some transmitters say that this edifice was called al-ṣarḥ. There may be some truth to this, for there are two words for 'castle' in the language of the Nabaṭ of Iraq and the Jaramiqa of Syria:[138] sarḥā and maʿdalā, which when Arabicised are pronounced sarḥ and maʿdal.[139]

Kay Khusraw

The Persians claim [36] that he was a prophet and it is noted that he resided at Balkh. Their histories say that he was once informed that between the end of (the territory of) Fars and the beginning of (that of) Isfahan there was a red mountain, named Kūshīd, and that in it was a dragon that had put an end to ploughing and procreation.[140] He marched towards it, mustered all the men (who lived) around the summit of the mountain, attacked the dragon from below and finally killed it. He then erected by the side of the mountain the fire-temple known as the fire-temple of Kūshīd.

Kay Luhrasb

Luhrasb was the deputy of Kay Khusraw over his kingdom and his cousin, for Luhrasb was the son of Kay Ujan b. Kay Manush b. Kay Fasin b. Kay Abiweh. He was the first to establish a register for the army.[141] He

136 Arabic: kutub al-siyar. See n. 102 above and Appendix 1 below.

137 This refers to some ruins west of Baghdad commonly associated with the story of Nimrod. See EI, 'Aḳarḳuf', and Sarre and Herzfeld, Archäologische Reise, II.96–102.

138 This is how Arabic sources designate the Aramaic-speaking people of Iraq and the Levant respectively. See EI, 'Nabaṭ', 'Djarāmiqa'. I have not rendered Nabaṭ (pl. anbāṭ) as Nabataean, though this is common practice, because this term is mainly used in modern scholarship for the Nabataeans who had a kingdom based in Petra, in modern south Jordan, which flourished ca. 300 BC–AD 100, but who are almost unknown to Muslim historians. Whether the Greek term for this people (Nabataioi) is related at all to the Arabic Nabaṭ is unclear.

139 In Nabataean Aramaic ṣarīḥ means a vaulted structure, but it is likely that this is an Arabism rather than that Arabic ṣarḥ is an Aramaicism. As for maʿdalā, this is presumably a mistake for/derivation from magdalā, which means tower in many Aramaic dialects.

140 I.e. had put an end to all human activity.

141 Arabic: dīwān al-jund. This is the term used to refer to the register allegedly introduced by the caliph ʿUmar I (634–44) to keep a record of all the soldiers enrolled in the army, along with their dependents, affiliation and stipends. See EI, 'Diwan'.

instituted thrones for the governors[142] and decorated them with bracelets, and he embraced the use of pavilions. In the sixtieth year of his reign Nebuchadnezzar b. Wiw b. Gudarz invaded Palestine and destroyed Jerusalem.[143] He took captive the Jews in it and made them servants and slaves of the people of the regions of his kingdom. Before Nebuchadnezzar, Sennacherib of Nineveh had sent (troops) against them, but he achieved no victory over them. Luhrasb left his kingdom to his son while still alive.

Kay Kushtasb
Kushtasb was in the thirtieth year of his reign and the fiftieth of his life when Zoroaster came to him in Azerbaijan, offering him [37] his religion. Kushtasb believed in him and sent envoys on his behalf to the Romans and called on them to (accept) it (Zoroaster's religion). However, they (the Romans) brought out to them (the envoys) a treaty from Afridun (guaranteeing) peace on the basis that they might practise any religion that they wished. Kushtasb therefore left them alone, disliking to violate (the treaty) that they possessed.[144] He built in the district of Darabgird in the province of Fars a triangular city and named it Rām Washnāsqān, which is the city of Fasa. Later a man from there, called Āzādmard Kāmkār, who was the governor of Fars on behalf of Hajjaj b. Yusuf,[145] breached its walls and rendered its triangular shape into a circular one. Also in the time of the reign of Kushtasb, his son Isfandiyar built a 20 leagues-long barrier opposite the Turks and beyond Samarkand. Finally, Kushtasb erected a fire-temple in Mamnūr, a village situated in the canton of Ānārabād, in the district of Isfahan, and endowed upon it (the revenues of) an estate of the district (for its upkeep).

142 Arabic: *al-marāziba*, the plural form of *marzbān*, literally 'border-guard' (see Mas'udi, 104, below). It was a title given to military governors of frontier provinces in the Sasanid Empire.
143 Tabari, 1.645–47, says that Luhrasb sent Nebuchadnezzar 'against the Israelites' and presents him as subject to Luhrasb rather than as an independent ruler of the Babylonian kingdom.
144 Tabari, 1.648, says that Bishtasb forced his subjects to adopt the new faith and massacred those who did not. This point is discussed in Crone, 'Ancient Iranian Paganism', 35–37.
145 Viceroy of the East for the Umayyad caliphs 'Abd al-Malik and al-Walid for the years 694–714.

Kay (Bahman) Ardashir

He is Bahman b. Isfandiyar b. Bishtasb, and was called long-armed[146] on account of his far-reaching campaigns. It is said that he reached on his raids as far as al-Rumiyya[147] and that to the south he invaded Zabulistan and took captive many of its people. In the land of the Sawad he built a city which he named, after his own name, Ābād[148] Ardashir; it is the one called Hamaniya[149] in Nabaṭi (Aramaic) and is situated in the sub-district of the Upper Zab (river). Also in the land of Maysan he built [38] a city and again called it after his own name, Bahman Ardashir; this city is (now) called Furat al-Basra.[150] The Israelites maintain that Bahman is (the same as the one) named Cyrus[151] in the history books (written) in their language. He built in (the vicinity of) Isfahan three fire-temples in the course of a single day, one at the rising of the sun, one as it attained the middle of the sky and one at its setting. Of these the fire-temple of Shahr Ardashir was erected near the castle of Mārīn; Shahr means 'twilight'[152] and Ardashir is the (regnal) name of Bahman. The second was the fire-temple of Dharwān Ardashir erected in Dārak, a village in the canton of Khuwār; and the third fire-temple was Mihr Ardashir, erected in the village of Ardistān.[153]

146 Arabic: *al-ṭawīl al-bā'*; the general sense is powerful, mighty. Because of this epithet he is commonly identified with the Achaemenid ruler Artaxerxes I (465–425 BC), who bears a similar epithet in Greek and Latin sources (*macrocheir/longimanus*); see *EIr*, 'Bahman (2) son of Esfandiar'.

147 In Arabic this usually refers to the city near Madaʾin founded by the Sasanid ruler Khusraw I, but perhaps here it just means Roman territory.

148 This means thriving or populous in MP, and so often designates a population centre or residential settlement.

149 Arabic: *hamāniyā*; Tabari, 1.687, has *humayniyā* (in De Goeje's vocalisation) and does not say it is of Nabati (Aramaic) origin. It may well rather be connected with the name Bahman (i.e. perhaps Bahmaniya).

150 Tabari, 1.687, calls it Ubulla, ancient Apologos, now within the modern city of Basra in southern Iraq.

151 Arabic: *Kūrush*, presumably Cyrus the Great, the founder of the Achaemenid Empire, who lived *ca.* 600–530 BC.

152 *Shahr* means land or country in Persian and month in Arabic; possibly we should read *sahr* (removing the dots from the first letter), which means 'evening' in Arabic.

153 Yaqut says that Khuwār is a city in one of the districts of Rayy and Ardistān is a city between Qashan (modern Kashan) and Isfahan.

Khumani Shahrazad[154]

She was Shamiran bt. Bahman, and Khumani was her sobriquet. She used to reside in Balkh. She sent one of her armies to raid the land of the Romans and they took many captives, among them skilful artisans. She engaged the builders among them in the construction of the buildings called (in Arabic) 'the strongholds of Istakhr' and in Persian *hazār sitūn*.[155] These were a trio of buildings in three sites: one beside Istakhr, the second along the road leading to the district of Darabgird and the third along the main road to Khurasan.[156] She also established in Isfahan, in a canton called Taymara, a pleasant city [39] of wonderful design, which she named Ḥamhīn, but which Alexander subsequently destroyed.

Dara b. Bahman

He was the first king to establish postal routes and along them he prescribed the stabling of docked-tail horses, and so it was called 'the tail post' (*barīd dhanab*). Then they Arabicised the term and elided the latter half, and so they said *barīd*.[157] And he built in the last district of the province of Fars (going eastwards) a city and called it Darabgird (meaning) 'what Dara had founded'. It gave its name to the district, which before that was known as Istān Farkān, but God knows best.

Dara b. Dara

It was during his reign that Alexander (the Great) became active in the land of the west. At that time the kings of the Persians received tribute from the Egyptians and the Berbers in the west, the Romans and Slavs in the north and the Jaramiqa and Jarajima of Syria and Palestine. When Alexander gained control of the kingdom (of the west) and (envoys) came on behalf of Dara demanding the tribute, he replied: 'Tell him that the hen which has until now laid eggs is no longer laying.'[158] This was the reason for the

---

154 She is also called Khumani in Arabic sources. The epithet Shahrazad, 'of noble countenance', is here spelled with an initial 'j', but Shahrazad is the more usual form.

155 This means 'a thousand columns'.

156 Thus also Tabari, 1.690, who says the second and third buildings were one farsakh and four farsakhs away from Istakhr respectively (*ca.* 3 and 12 miles).

157 The word is derived from the Greek *beredos* and Latin *veredus*, meaning 'post horse', but the invention of the institution is often attributed to Dara. See *EI*, 'Barid'; *EIr*, 'Dara(b) (1), i. Dara(b) I'.

158 The same story is told in Tabari, 1.700, who says that Alexander's father used to pay tribute to the Persians in the form of 'golden eggs', but that Alexander, when asked for that tribute, replied: 'I have slaughtered that hen which laid those eggs and ate its meat'.

flaring up of the troubles between Dara and Alexander which resulted in the death of Dara. He built above Nisibis a city and he called it Dārā-Ān, which exists still now and is known as Dāriyā.[159]

Alexander

When Alexander had finished with killing Dara and had won control of **[40]** the province of Fars, he started behaving badly and was immoderate in the shedding of blood. In his camp 7000 prisoners taken from the leading men and nobles of the Persians were assembled bound in chains and every day they would call for 21 out of these to be killed until he reached Kashgar.[160] There he resided for a while before marching back to Babylon. When he reached Qumis, he fell ill; along the way his ailment became protracted and he died before arriving at Babylon, which he had previously reduced to a mound of dust. According to the reports that story tellers have put about, Alexander built 12 cities in the land of Iran, all of which he named Alexandria: one in Isfahan, one in Herat, one in Merv, one in Samarkand, one in Soghdia, one in Babylon, one in Maysan and four in the Sawad. However, this report is baseless, for Alexander was a destroyer rather than a builder.[161]

The Arsacid Kings

When Alexander had finished with slaying the nobles and dignitaries of Persia, accomplished the destruction of cities and forts and attained all that he sought, he wrote to Aristotle: 'I have persecuted all the people of the east by killing their kings and razing their strongholds and forts. I now fear that after me they may join forces to attack the lands of the west. I am therefore thinking of **[41]** pursuing the sons of the kings whom I killed, bringing them together and joinng them to their fathers (in death), but what is your opinion?' Aristotle replied to him: 'If you kill the sons of the kings,

---

159 Tabari, 1.694, has 'Dāranwā, which is today called Dārā'. The city of Dara of Hamza's day was built by the Emperor Anastasius in 505, but possibly on top of or near to the Persian city. See *EIr*, 'Dara(b) (1), ii. Dara(b) II'; Dara (city)'.

160 A city now in east China, near the border with Kyrgyzstan and Tajikistan.

161 This negative view of Alexander reflects one of two strands in Sasanid tradition. The first, as here, portrays him as the wrecker of Persian culture, while the second, generally known as the Alexander romance, casts him as an intrepid hero. See *EIr*, 'Alexander the Great, ii. In Zoroastrian Tradition'; 'Eskandar-Nama'; *EI*, 'Iskandar Nama'. Tabari, 1.702, also asserts that Alexander built 12 cities.

the rule will pass to the low and the base. And if the low become kings, they will have power; if they have power, they will be tyrannical, unjust, oppressive and aggressive; and what is to be feared from their foulness (i.e. its consequences) could be even more terrible. I think therefore that you should assemble the sons of the kings and appoint each one of them to a city òr a district in their country. Then if any one of them envies another for what he possesses, enmity and hatred will arise among them, and thus preoccupied with their own affairs they will be distracted from the people of the west, who are far away from them.'[162] Accordingly Alexander distributed the eastern lands to the kings of (its various) parts, and he took away from their country to the land of the west the sciences of astronomy, medicine, philosophy and agriculture, after having them translated into Greek and Egyptian.[163]

When Alexander perished and the country fell into the hands of the Petty Kings, they ended all warfare and contention between themselves. Instead they would outdo one another only in (solving) abstruse problems. It was in their days that books found in the hands of people (today) were composed, such as the Book of Maruk, the Book of Sindbad, the Book of Barsnas, the Book [42] of Shimas and similar books, the number of which reaches about 70.[164] In this way they continued until more than 20 of them had ruled, and some of them aspired to go out on campaign. There were in all 90 of these Petty Kings, and they honoured the king who ruled over Iraq and resided at Ctesiphon,[165] which is Mada'in. Whenever he corresponded with them, he began with his own name.

Shabur b. Ashak

Among those who readied themselves for campaigning was Shabur b. Ashak b. Udhran b. Ashghan. It was in his time that Christ appeared, peace

---

162 This exchange between Alexander and Aristotle is found in a number of Muslim sources, and with very similar wording in Dinawari, 40–41.

163 See Introduction, above, for discussion of and references to Alexander's theft of Persian learning.

164 The book of Sindbad is an edifying narrative about a wise man who educates a prince (nothing to do with the sailor), and one assumes that the others listed here are similar in nature. The same list appears in other sources, sometimes with more titles; for discussion see Zakeri, *Persian Wisdom*, 116–17.

165 Presumably meaning the Arsacid king, though this dynasty did not make Ctesiphon their main base until 141 BC. Note that Hamza does not include an entry for the first member of this dynasty, Ashak (Arsaces in Greek sources), who starts raiding Seleucid territory in north-east Iran (Parthia) around 250 BC and is crowned king shortly thereafter.

be upon him. He raided Roman territory at the time when it was ruled by Antiochus;[166] he was the third king after Alexander and he is the one who founded the city of Antioch.[167] Shabur inflicted killing and imprisonment on them, gathered their children into boats and drowned them, exclaiming: 'O for the vengeance of Dara'. He regained much of what Alexander had removed from the country of the Persians and restored it to his kingdom. He expended some of it on digging a canal in Iraq, called in Arabic 'the Canal of the King'.[168]

Gudarz b. Ashak[169]

Among them was Gudarz b. Ashak, who fought against the sons of Israel, and this took place after the death of John (the Baptist) son of Zakariah, on them both be peace. He destroyed their city Jerusalem for the second time and put the people to the sword; [43] he was excessive in his killing of Jews and captured a multitude of them. Before that the Roman king Titus b. Isfiyanus had attacked the Jews, killing and enslaving them, some 40 years after the ascension of Jesus.[170]

---

166 If this is meant to be the son of Ashak, Arsaces II (it is not self-evident, since Ashak/ Arsaces became the epithet for all the rulers of this dynasty), then the chronology is very awry, for he obviously ruled long before Christ. He did fight against Antiochus III (222–187) *ca.* 210 BC, which could be what lies behind the claim that he raided Roman territory. Otherwise one could identify this Shabur with Artabanus III (AD 1–38), who was in power during much of Christ's lifetime and who had to contend with the Romans. It is more likely, however, that elements from different royal biographies have become confused, and in any case no Arsacid ruler appears to have borne the name Shabur. Tabari, 1.711 and 719, says that whereas the Christians reckon 303 years between the death of Alexander the Great and the birth of John the Baptist and Jesus, the Zoroastrians allow for only 51 years, which is much too short and in part explains why this period of Persian history is so compressed in Muslim sources.

167 It was actually Seleucus Nicator (305–281) who founded Antioch, but named it after his son Antiochus I Soter, who succeeded him.

168 This is the modern Yusifiyah canal, south of Baghdad, a major watercourse that draws from the Euphrates to serve numerous settlements.

169 This may be the Gotarzes II (AD 40–51) of the Roman sources, which portray him as a tyrant, although he is not known to have persecuted Jews and certainly not to have sacked Jerusalem. Tabari, 1.713–23, has a very long account of this second onslaught on Jerusalem and the Jews, which he connects with Qur'an 17:4–8, which narrates how the Israelites, in return for 'causing corruption in the land twice', are punished twice by an external enemy sent by the Lord.

170 Titus son of Vespasian commanded the recapture of Jerusalem in AD 70 (subsequently emperor, 79–81), which is 'about 40 years after the ascension of Jesus'.

Balash[171] b. Khusraw

Among them also was Balash b. Khusraw. He was informed that the Romans intended to invade Persia. He therefore wrote to the neighbouring Petty Kings and sought their help. Every king sent to him as much manpower and money as they could. When he received the reinforcements he paraded them and placed in charge of them the ruler of Hatra, one of the Petty Kings neighbouring the Roman provinces.[172] He reached the camp of the Romans as they were assembling and making ready; he slew their king, plundered their camp and returned with the booty to Iraq, making over a fifth of it to Balash. This campaign was the reason for the Romans paying out for the cost of building a fortified city, and they moved the royal residence from Rome to there so that the imperial capital would be nearer to the territory of the Persian ruler. They fixed their choice on a patch of land (called) Constantinople, on which they erected (many) buildings and to which they transferred (the seat of) the kingship. At the time of its construction their king was Constantine b. Nayrun, and they derived the name of the city from his name.[173] He was the first king of the Romans who converted to the faith [44] of Christianity and he summoned to it the people of his kingdom. Then he sought to expel the sons of Israel from the holy city of Jerusalem, and after that until today none of them remained living there.

171 Or Vologases, a name borne by at least five Arsacid kings between 51 and 208. It is not possible to say which one, since the events recounted are difficult to identify. The Romans and Arsacids frequently clashed, and no Hatran ruler killed a Roman emperor.

172 Hatra is a fortified city in the north Syrian steppe, lying about 70 miles south-west of Mosul. It had its own king during the Arsacid period and remained independent until it fell to Shabur I in 241. The Hatran episode recounted here (and also in Tabari, 1.705) could be a confused recollection of the failed sieges of that city by Trajan (in 116–17) and Septimius Severus (in 198–99), though neither emperor was killed by the Persians or their allies.

173 The mention of conversion to Christianity and the building of Constantinople make it certain that Constantine the Great is meant here, but his reign (306–37) occurred after the Arsacid period. In addition, he was the son of Valerius Constantius, which does not obviously relate to Hamza's Nayrun. Note that the account in Tabari, 1.705–6, is very close to the one here.

[The Sasanids][174]

Ardashir [I] b. Babak

When Ardashir arose, he first of all conquered the city of Istakhr. He received the support of its people and with their help he seized all the districts of Fars from the Petty Kings. When he had control of them, he fixed the crown on his head and looked to the affairs of the people. He saw that the number of kings around him was small and that the territory of each of them was of minor consequence and limited extent, and their impositions on their subjects were great. He did not like the diversity that was manifest in their realms despite the unity of their religion. He knew that only a previous state of union could have bound them together in one religion, and so he asked those men in his entourage who were well informed about matters of religion and circumstances of state the reason for (the discord) that he found among the kings of his age. They informed him that the affairs of the first kings were always well ordered, there never being more than one king, for that single (incumbent ruler) would unite his subjects in loyalty to him and they would follow his command. In consequence their religion was strong, their country prosperous and their enemies subdued. However, when the kingship devolved to Dara b. Dara, **[45]** his subjects all came to dislike him, to find his rule burdensome and to reject his reign, and so they desisted from fighting their common enemy and abandoned their concern for the borders, and fell to quarrelling and fighting amongst themselves.

Alexander then marched from the land of the west to their land while they were in this situation; he found things much as he had hoped and was encouraged to wage war with Dara. However, it happened that one of the bodyguards attacked Dara, shot him from behind and slew him. Thereupon Alexander took charge of the Persian kingdom, inflicted widespread killing upon the magnates and nobles, butchered its great men and nobles and extended destruction to all the cities and fortresses. Then he devoted himself to hunting down the books of their religion and sciences and burned them after translating the philosophy, astronomy,

---

174 Hamza now moves on to the Sasanids without even mentioning the last Arsacid ruler, Ardawan or Artabanus V (208–24). The same is true of Tabari, although he deals with Ardawan's demise in his entry on Ardashir.

medicine and agriculture that they contained from Persian into Greek and Coptic, and sent (those translations) to Alexandria.[175]

On hearing this, Ardashir realised that he would not succeed to disseminate justice among the people and regulate them by the art of politics until they had a single king, and that he should be the one to unite their hearts and to aid them to a state of well-being. So he set about issuing letters to the neighbouring Petty Kings; this was the first step of his policy. Then [46] he continued to constantly renew his policy as it suited him until he had purged the realm of the land of Iran[176] of the Petty Kings, killing 90 of them.

Ardashir established a number of cities, such as Ardashir Khurrah, Bih Ardashir, Bahman Ardashir, Ansha'a Ardashir, Ram Ardashir, Ramhurmuz Ardashir, Hurmuz Ardashir, Bud Ardashir, Wahisht Ardashir and Batn Ardashir.[177] As regards Ardashir Khurrah, it is the city of Firuzabad, situated in the land of Fars, and was called Gur; *gūr* and *gār*[178] are two nouns meaning a pit or a trench, not a grave or a tomb, for Persians did not have burial places, but disposed of their dead in charnel houses or sarcophagi. It was 'Ali b. Buwayh[179] who changed its name to Firuzabad. As regards Bih Ardashir, it is the name of two cities, one in Iraq and the other in Kirman. The one in Iraq was one of the seven cities of Mada'in and stood on the western bank of the Tigris; its name was Arabicised to Bihrasir, while the other one in Kirman was Arabicised in a different way and they pronounced it Bardashir. As regards Bahman Ardashir, it is the name of a city on the bank of the One-Eyed Tigris[180] in Maysan, and the people of Basra call it by two names, Bahmanshir and Furat Maysan. As regards Ansha'a Ardashir, [47] it is the name of a city on the bank of the

---

175 See introduction above for discussion of and references to Alexander's theft of Persian learning.

176 Arabic: *mamlakat Īrān shahr*; literally: 'the kingdom of the country of Iran'. See *EIr*, 'Ēran, Ēranšahr'.

177 Tabari, 1.820, lists eight cities said to have been founded by Ardashir, rather than the ten listed here by Hamza. All these cities are on the western side of the Persian Empire, from northern Iraq to south-west Iran.

178 Written with initial 'k' in the Arabic to convey the Persian 'g'. *Gūr* does mean grave/pit, but *gār* is not attested; possibly, though, the two forms are just offered as approximations to MP *gōr*.

179 Or, in the Persian rendering, Buyah. His regnal name was 'Imad al-Dawla (934–49), the eldest of the three Daylami brothers who became the founders of the Buyid dynasty that ruled Iraq and Iran from 934 to 1062.

180 Arabic: *Dijlat al-'Awrā'*, the name given to the waterway which ran from the marshes to the Persian Gulf.

(River) Karun[181] and is also called Karkh Maysan.[182] As regards Ram Ardashir, I do not know its location.[183] As regards Riw Ardashir,[184] it is called Rishahr by the people of today.

As regards Ramhurmuz Ardashir, it is one of the cities of Khuzistan. Since its name consists of so many letters, people left out the last word from it (and it is simply called Ramhurmuz). As regards Hurmuz Ardashir, it is the name of two cities. When Ardashir planned these two, he called each one of them by a name constructed from his own name and that of God the Mighty and Majestic. He settled in one of them common people and in the other grandees and nobles. The city of common people gained another name, Hūjistān Wājār, which was rendered into Arabic as Suq al-Ahwaz;[185] the name of the other city was Arabicised as Hurmushir. When the Arabs reached Khuzistan, they destroyed the city of the aristocrats, but spared the city of the common people. Afterwards, during the war of Hajjaj with the Qurrā',[186] they also destroyed two other cities of Khuzistan, one of them called Rustam Kawad,[187] which was Arabicised into Rustaqabad,[188] and the other Jawastad. As regards Bud Ardashir, it is one of the cities of Mosul.[189] As regards Wahisht Ardashir,[190] I do not know its location.

---

181 Arabic: *Dujayl*, literally 'the Little Tigris'. It flows from its source in the Zagros Mountains, in west Iran, for 450 miles before emptying into the Persian Gulf near Basra.

182 Ancient Charax Spasinou, on the east side of the Tigris to the north of Basra. Tabari calls it Astabadh Ardashir, which is a more likely rendering than Hamza's Ansha'a Ardashir (*ansha'a* means 'he founded' in Arabic, which might be appropriate, but presumably Ardashir would have used a Persian word).

183 Tabari, 1.820, includes it among the cities that Ardashir built in Fars.

184 Hamza (or a copyist) accidentally writes Ram Ardashir again, but Riw Ardashir must be correct since it is what Tabari has (and the two accounts are very close here) and it was indeed the earlier name of Rishahr. Its ruins lie near modern Bushehr on the south-west coast of Iran.

185 I.e. the market of Khuzistan/the Khuzi people. The Persian term is oddly rendered; one would expect Khūzistān Wāzār.

186 A name used in the sources to refer to a group from Iraq who rose up against the Umayyads, having earlier rebelled against 'Uthman and 'Ali. The nature and grounds for their dissent and the significance of their name are disputed. See *EI*, 'Ḳurra''.

187 Or perhaps Rustaq Kawad. It is medieval 'Askar Mukram (see *EI* and *EIr*, s.v.), modern Band-e Qir.

188 Emending the third letter from y (how it appears in the edition) to t, which only requires a change in dots.

189 Tabari, 1.820, specifies that it is Hazza, modern Heza, south-west of Erbil, in the ancient province known as Adiabene.

190 Literally: 'Paradise of Ardashir'. The cities founded (or often just refounded, with a

As regards Batan Ardashir, it is one of the cities of Bahrain. It was called [48] Batan Ardashir only because its walls were built on the corpses of its inhabitants who had thrown off their allegiance to Ardashir and disobeyed his authority. He made one layer of the walls with bricks and the other with corpses. For this reason he called it Batan Ardashir.[191] He distributed the waters of the valley of Isfahan by the agency of Mihr b. Wardan.[192] He also distributed the waters of the valley of Khuzistan and dug canals for its water, one of them being the Mashruqān, which in Persian bore the name of 'that of Ardashir'.[193]

In the book 'The Portraits of the Kings of the Sasanids',[194] the vest of Ardashir is speckled with gold, his trousers are azure and his crown is green on gold; in his hand is a lance and he is standing.

Shabur [I] b. Ardashir

He built the *shādhurwān* dam of Tustar,[195] which is one of the marvels of the East. He founded many cities, such as Nishabur, Bishabur, Shad Shabur, Bih-Az-Andiyu Shabur, Shabur Khwast, Balash Shabur and Firuz Shabur.[196] As regards Nishabur, it is one of the cities of the district of Abarshahr, which is a district of Khurasan. As regards Bishabur, it is one of the cities of Fars and it is also the name of the district (in which it is situated). In Arabic the name of this city is abbreviated, the first word being elided, and it is referred to as 'Shabur'. And Shabur erected this city seeking to restore again a city built by Tahmurath and subsequently destroyed

new name and a new building/some restoration work) by the Sasanid emperors tend to be accorded grandiose names connected with the ruler or deity; e.g. Ardashir Khurra means 'Fortune of Ardashir', and so on.

191 This presumably has to do with the Persian word *tan*, which means body or person; thus *tan ba-tan* means 'man by man'.

192 No explanation given; presumably some relevant authority figure.

193 Here rendered as *ardashīrkān*, representing MP *ardashīragān*. On early Sasanid irrigation works in Khuzistan, including the Mashruqān canal, see Christensen, *Decline of Iranshahr*, 107–10.

194 Arabic: *Kitāb ṣuwar mulūk Banī Sāsān*. Hamza is now using a new source, which would appear to be the same as, or at least related to, that described by Mas'udi, 106, below. The latter cites the book for the regalia of Ardashir and it is extremely close to what Hamza has here.

195 *Shādhurwān* is a Persian word meaning a barrier or platform for controlling water. The one of Tustar is celebrated by most Muslim geographers for its solid construction in stone, iron and lead (e.g. Ibn al-Faqih (Beirut), 397, and Istakhri, 89).

196 For Shabur's building activities see *EIr*, s.v. 'Shabur I, i. History'.

by Alexander, but its original name has been forgotten. As regards Shad Shabur, it is the name of a city in Maysan [49] that was called Wabhā in Aramaic.[197] As regards Firuz Shabur, it is the name of one of the cities of Iraq and is called Anbar in Arabic.

As regards Bih-Az-Andiyu Shabur, it is one of the cities of Khuzistan and it is the one that when Arabicised is pronounced Jundishabur. As for its derivation in Persian, Andiyu is the name of Antioch, *bih* is the word for better, and so the meaning (of the whole name) is 'Better than Antioch'.[198] The layout of this city is in the form of a chess-board, with eight roads in the middle crossing eight other roads. They used (at that time) to build cities according to the representation of certain things. In that style is Susa, which is in the form of a hawk, and Tustar, which is in the form of a horse.

According to 'The Book of the Portraits of the Kings of the Sasanids' his vest is azure, his trousers of red embroidered cloth and his crown red on green; he is standing with a lance in his hand.

Hurmuz (I) b. Shabur

He was like his grandfather Ardashir in appearance and size, and extremely strong, powerful and brave-hearted, but as regards clarity of thinking he was not so accomplished. His mother was Kardzad, in whose name a (famous) story[199] circulates. He inaugurated the building which is in the royal (estate of) Daskara.[200]

His vest, according to 'The Book of the Portraits', is red and embroidered, his trousers green and his crown [50] also green (set) in gold. He has a lance in his right hand and a shield in his left hand and he is riding a lion.

197 Tabari, 1.830, has Dima or Rima, also noting that this is its Aramaic name. Shad Shabar means 'joy of Shabur' in Persian.

198 I.e. the better-than-Antioch (city of) Shabur; thus also in Tabari, 1.831, who gives an extended account of the city's founding. *Bih* is the NP form of the word 'better, good'; the MP form is *weh/wyh*.

199 Again Hamza uses the Persian word *dastān*; see n. 108 above.

200 Arabic: *Daskarat al-malik*, also known as Dastagird. This is the most important of the royal residences of the Sasanid emperors, situated *ca.* 60 miles north-east of Mada'in. Herzfeld visited the site in the early twentieth century and drew the one surviving fired-brick wall, which was 500m long with 16 round towers (Sarre and Herzfeld, *Reise*, II.76–93, IV-plates 127–28).

Bahram (I) b. Hurmuz

In his days Mani, the propagandist of the Manichaeans,[201] was captured after he had been on the run for two years and in hiding. He (Bahram) gathered scholars to dispute with him (Mani) and they compelled him to accept the arguments of the heads of the assembly. Then Bahram ordered him to be killed and for his skin to be flayed and stuffed with hay and hung up on one of the gates of the city of Jundishabur.

In 'The Book of the Portraits' his vest and trousers are red, his crown sky-blue, with two crests and a gilded moon of gold.[202] He is standing with a lance in his right hand and a sword in his left, resting on it. Such is his portrait, but (God) knows best.

Bahram (II) b. Bahram

His vest is red and embroidered, his trousers are green and his crown is sky-blue between two crests and a crescent of gold. He is sitting on his throne, with a strung bow in his right hand and three arrows in his left. (God) knows best.

Bahram (III) b. Bahram b. Bahram

He was (also) called Bahram b. Bahram. His title was Sakan Shah.[203] The reason for this title and those like it is that when a king of the Persians appointed a son or a brother of his as his heir-apparent, he designated him the shah of a particular principality, and he was addressed by this title throughout the lifetime of his father.[204] If the rule passed **[51]** to him he

201 Arabic: *al-zanādiqa*. For more on Mani's life see the account in Ya'qubi, 180–82, below.

202 Arabic: *m'zrj dhahab*. The first word is Persian: *māhzarrag*, which is a compound of moon (*m'h*) and gold (*zrr*). It is mentioned in connection with only Bahram I, III and IV, and presumably relates to some specific moon-like feature on their crowns. Hamza adds in Arabic that it was 'of gold' (*dhahab*), seeming not to realise that the word already contained the sense of 'golden'.

203 I.e. 'the king of the Sakas', who are the people of Sakastan/Sagastan (Arabic: Sijistan) in south-east Iran.

204 Cf. Agathias, 4.24.6–8: 'He was given the title Saghanshah, which he received not, I think, idly or without good reason, but in accordance with an ancient ancestral custom. When the Persian kings make war on some neighbouring people of considerable size and importance and reduce them to submission, they do not kill the vanquished inhabitants but impose a tribute on them all and allow them to dwell in and cultivate the conquered territory. However, they consign the former leaders of the nation to a most pitiful fate and assign the title of ruler to their own sons, presumably in order to preserve the proud memory of their victory. Now since the Segestani were subdued by his father Bahram II it was only

was then called Shahanshah.[205] This is how it was for King Bahram (IV), who bore the title Kirmanshah. And Anusharwan, during the lifetime of his father Qubad, bore the title Yaqarsajān Karshah while he was in command of Tabaristan, for *yaqar* means 'mountain', *sajān*[206] means plain and slopes, and *kar* means hills and uprisings.[207] And (going back to the title of Bahram) *sakān* is a name for Sijistan.

The vest of Bahram b. Bahraman is sky-blue and embroidered, his trousers are red and he is sitting on his throne with his hand resting on his sword. His crown is green and has two crests and a gilded moon of gold.

Narsi b. Bahram

His vest is of red embroidered cloth, his trousers are sky-blue and embroidered and he is standing with both hands resting on his sword. His crown is red. (God) knows best the secrets.

Hurmuz [II] b. Narsi

He established in Khuzistan, in the province of Ramhurmuz, a canton named Wahisht Hurmuz, also known as Kurank. It is next to Idhaj,[208] which is also situated in the province of Ramhurmuz.

His vest is of red embroidered cloth, his trousers are embroidered and sky-blue, his crown is green, and he is standing with both hands resting on his sword. [God] knows best.

Shabur [II], Lord of the Shoulders

They named Shabur *hūyah sunbā*,[209] *hūyah* meaning 'shoulder' and *sunbā* meaning piercer. [52] He was called that because whenever he raided the Arabs, he used to pierce their shoulders and he would join together the two shoulder-blades of a man by means of a ring. So the Persians gave him this

natural that the son should be given the title Saghanshah, which is Persian for "king of the Segestani'".

205 This title literally means 'king of kings'.

206 *Qadsajān* is written here, but the *qad* is not in the title *yaqarsajān* that Hamza is explaining. Possibly behind this latter word is the term for the mountain range south of the Caspian Sea that bounded Tabaristan, namely *padishkhwār*.

207 *Kar* or *gar* does indeed mean mountain, so Karshah/Garshah literally means 'mountain king'.

208 Idhaj is ancient Ayapir, modern Izeh, about 90 miles north-east of Ahwaz.

209 This would appear to be the MP form, so it may well be the origin of the Arabic epithet 'Lord of the Shoulders'.

name and the Arabs named him 'Lord of the Shoulders'.[210] Shabur was the one whose father died while he was still a foetus and so they affixed the crown to the abdomen of his mother. And he was the one who entered the land of the Romans in disguise and visited some of their churches, whereupon they took him prisoner.[211] He remained as king for 72 years, of which he stayed from his birth until the completion of his thirtieth year in Jundishabur and then he relocated to Mada'in, which was his place of residence for the rest of his life. When he defeated the king of the Romans, he required that the latter renovate all that he had destroyed and that he renovate what had been in mud brick and clay with baked brick and lime. Thus the walls of the city of Jundishabur were half in mud brick and half in baked brick.

His vest is rosy and embroidered, his trousers are red and embroidered, and he is sitting on the throne with a battle-axe in his hand. His crown is sky-blue, coloured gold around the edges and in its centre two crests and a crescent of gold.

He built a number of cities, including Buzurg[212] Shabur, which is 'Ukbara, Khurra Shabur, which is Susa, and another city next to it.[213] He sent elephants to trample one of them, for its inhabitants had disobeyed him. [53] Then he brought many captives from Roman territory and settled them in the new city. The remaining prisoners he dispersed[214] throughout

---

210 Tabari, 1.843–44, says that he was called this because he 'tore out' (*laza'a*) the shoulders of the chiefs of the Arabs in retaliation for their raids in south-west Iran. Nöldeke, *Sasaniden*, 52 n. 1, suggests that the nickname must originally have been positive, perhaps 'broad-shouldered' in the sense of able to bear well the burden of government, but was given a negative spin in later Arabic folkloric tales, though Nöldeke did not take account of the Persian derivation given by Hamza.

211 This story of Shabur's clandestine intelligence-gathering mission into Roman territory is recounted at length in a number of Arabic sources (e.g. Tabari, 1.844–45). It results in Shabur's capture by the Roman emperor, his subsequent escape and his revenge when he succeeded in capturing the emperor and mutilating him. Possibly this story is connected with the Syriac Julian Romance, which recounts Emperor Julian's persecution of Christians and his ill-fated campaign of AD 363 into Persian territory (Wood, *No King but Christ*, 133–40).

212 Not *barzakh*, as read by the editor; cf. Tabari, 1.839. It is on the east bank of the Tigris north of Mada'in.

213 This may refer to Iran-Shahr-Shabur (= Arabic: al-Karkh; Syriac: Karka d-Ledan), which is given by Tabari, 1.840, and is indeed next to Susa. Tabari continues by saying that Susa was built 'next to' a fortress containing the sarcophagus of the prophet Daniel. Hamza has possibly contracted/corrupted the original report that is given more fully in Tabari.

214 Reading *badhara* rather than *badara*. On Shabur's deportations, see *EIr*, s.v. 'Deportations, ii. In the Parthian and Sasanid Periods'.

the country. He erected in the village of Ḥarwān, in the canton of Jay, a fire-temple, which he named Surūsh Ādarān,[215] and endowed it with the revenue of the villages of Yawān and Jājāh of the canton of Najjān. In his time lived Azadyard,[216] on whose chest molten brass was poured.

Ardashir [II] b. (correctly, brother of) Shabur
His vest is embroidered and speckled in sky-blue, his trousers are embroidered in red, his crown is green, and he is holding a lance in his right hand and leaning upon his sword with his left. [God] knows best.

Shabur [III] b. Shabur
His vest is red and embroidered, his trousers are sky-blue, under his vest there is another vest of yellow, and his crown is green on red with two crests and a crescent of gold. He is standing; in his (right) hand is an iron staff that has on its top the head of a bird and his left hand is resting on the hilt of his sword.

Bahram [IV] b. Shabur
He was called Kirmanshah.[217] He was coarse and conceited. He never read a story throughout his reign or looked into the wrongs of people. At his death, all the letters coming to him from the provinces were found with their seals still unbroken. He ordered that there should be inscribed on his tomb (the words): 'We know that this body will be placed in this structure, where it will be neither benefited by the advice of a sympathiser nor harmed by the scorn of a foe.'

His vest **[54]** is embroidered and sky-blue, his trousers are red and embroidered, and his crown is set amidst three crests and a gilded moon of gold. He is standing with a lance in his right hand and resting his left hand on his sword. [God] knows best.

---

215 Written here *Ādhar*, but Hamza, 56, below, has *Ādar*; both are possible forms of the NP word for fire (MP: *ādur* ['dwr]); *surūsh* refers to the deity of obedience, but came to mean an angel; so one might translate here angel-fires.

216 This presumably intends Adarbad-i Mahrspandan, high priest for Shabur II, who collated the Avesta and sought to demonstrate the accuracy of his work by subjecting himself to the molten brass ordeal (if, when poured on the chest, it leaves no mark, then the person is proved right/innocent). See Daryaee, *Sasanian Persia*, 85–86.

217 King of (the province of) Kirman. Hamza is negative about him, but Tabari, 1.847, and Ya'qubi, 183, below, both characterise him very positively.

Yazdagird [I] b. Bahram, the Sinner[218]

He was called the Criminal, the Sinner and also the Ruffian, and in Persian the Outcast[219] and the Sinner.[220] His vest is red, his trousers are sky-blue, his crown is also sky-blue, and he is standing with a lance in his hand.

Bahram [V] Gur b. Yazdagird[221]

Many tales are told about him among the Turks, Romans and Indians. He arrived in the land of India in disguise. He urged his people to work for half of every day and then to rest and devote themselves to eating, drinking and playing, and in particular to drink to the accompaniment of minstrels[222] and foods. Therefore musicians acquired great prestige and the fee for a performance of minstrels reached a hundred dirhams. One day he passed by a group of people drinking without entertainers and he said to them: 'Have I not forbidden you to do without entertainers (when drinking)?' Thereupon they went to prostrate before him and said: 'We sought them (offering) more than a hundred dirhams, but we were not successful.' He at once requested inkwell and parchment and wrote to the king of India appealing for entertainers. The latter sent to him 12,000, whom he distributed in the lands of his kingdom. Here they begat children, who still remain, **[55]** though they are few, and they are the Zuṭṭ.[223] He had written on his tomb: 'Once we had been granted power in the world, we impressed upon it enduring and praiseworthy deeds. Now we are confined to this place and we are certain of our remaining here.'

218 See nn. 52 and 73 above.
219 Text has *dafr*, though Nöldeke, *Sasaniden*, 72 n. 4, suggests reading *dabz*, meaning 'rough' or 'harsh' in Persian, which would then correspond better to 'Ruffian' (Arabic: *faẓẓ*).
220 The text has *bazahkard*, but presumably MP *bazahkar/bazahgar* is meant (Nöldeke, *Sasaniden*, 72 n. 4).
221 Hamza's account of Bahram focuses on the matter of entertainers, but the repertoire of traditions about him is very diverse, including his upbringing at the Lakhmid Arab court at Hira and his victories in the East. See *EIr*, 'Bahram (2), vi. Bahram V Gōr in Persian Legend and Literature'.
222 The text has *ḥwshyh*. One could relate this to Arabic *ḥāshiya* (pl. *ḥawāshin*), meaning retinue or dependents, but it would perhaps be better to connect it, as I have done, with the Persian word *gws'n*, 'poet-musician' (so reading the first letter of the Arabic word as a 'j/g' not a 'ḥ').
223 Thaʿalabi, 567, who recounts this anecdote with similar wording, says that the Indian king sent 'black Luris'. Both terms are assumed to refer to the Jat people of the Indus Valley, who in turn are regarded as ancestors of the Roma in Europe; for discussion see Marsh, 'Firdawsī Legend'.

His vest is sky-blue, his trousers are green and embroidered, and his crown is sky-blue. He is sitting on the throne with a mace in his hand.

Yazdagird [II] the Gentle[224] b. Bahram

His vest is green, his trousers are embroiderd, black with gold brocade and his crown is sky-blue. He is sitting on the throne, and leaning on his sword. [God] knows best.

Firuz [I] b. Yazdagird

His vest is red, his trousers sky-blue and embroidered in gold, and his crown is also sky-blue. He is sitting on the throne, holding a lance in his hand.

He built several cities: one of them in India, another on the borders of India, another in the region of Rayy, another in the region of Gurgan and another in the region of Azerbaijan. He called them all by names derived from his own name. Thus he called one of the cities in India Ram Firuz and another Rushi Firuz.[225] He built a wall beyond the river (Oxus) between the realm of Iran and the land of the Turks.[226] He placed the completion of the city wall of Jay and the locking of its gates in the hands of Adharshabur b. Adhar Manan al-Isfahani, and for that he granted him the document known as [56] al-ḥafna.[227] He ordered half of the Jews of Isfahan to be put to death and their children to be surrendered as slaves to the fire-temple of Surūsh Ādarān in the village of Ḥarwān, for they had flayed the skin from the backs of two Magian priests, joined them together and used them for tanning.

224 Arabic: al-layyin. This reflects his positive image in histories of Sasanid Persia as someone who promoted justice and wellbeing in his realm; see McDonough, 'Question of Faith'.

225 Tabari, 1.874, also specifies three cities in the regions of Rayy (= Ram Firuz), Gurgan (= Rushan Firuz, presumably equivalent to Hamza's Rushi Firuz) and Azerbaijan (= Shahram Firuz).

226 This may refer to the wall protecting Bukhara, though Mas'udi, 65, says it was built by a king of Soghdia. Otherwise Hamza may intend the Gurgan wall (see Nokandeh, *Great Wall of Gorgan*), though this is not beyond a major river. Reference to the Turks is anachronistic here and one should understand Hephthalites; Firuz's wars against this people are recounted in a number of Muslim histories (e.g. Tabari, 1.873–80); see also Ya'qubi, 184–85, and Appendix 1 below.

227 It is unclear what this refers to; in Arabic the word means a handful or a hollow. Adharshabur's surname, al-Isfahani, tells us that he was, like Hamza, a native of Isfahan, and possibly his name lived on in that city and this document, perhaps granting him authority or possession of some locations, was part of his fame.

Balash b. Firuz

His robe is green, his trousers are red and embroidered in black and white, and his crown is sky-blue. He is standing with a lance in his hand. He built two cities, one of them by the throughfare of Mada'in, which he called Balashabad, and the other beside Hulwan, which he called Balashfarr.[228]

Qubad [I] b. Firuz

He was also called Kawad the protector of evil custom.[229] During his days the country was ruled by his brother, Jamasb b. Firuz, who, however, was not regarded as a king because he ruled during the rebellion of Mazdak. Then Qubad was restored to his position and they inserted him (Jamasb) within the years of Qubad.[230]

Qubad's vest is sky-blue and embroidered in white and black, his trousers are red and his crown is green. He is leaning upon his sword and sitting on his throne.

He built several cities: one of them between Hulwan and Shahrazur, which he called Iran Shad Kawad; another between Jājān and Abarshahr, which he called Shahrabad Kawad;[231] another in Fars, which he called Bih-Az-Amid Kawad, namely Arrajan, and which he made into a provincial city [57] – its name means 'Better than Amid'.[232] He also built a city next to Mada'in and called it Hanbu Shabur, though the people of Baghdad

---

228 The name of Balashabad, which acted as the port of Mada'in, goes back to the Arsacid king Vologases I (*ca.* AD 51–79) and not to the Sasanid Balash; see *EIr*, s.v 'Balaš: Balaš, Sasanid King of Kings' and Nöldeke, *Sasaniden*, 139 n. 4, who also points out that the reading of Balash'azz in the edition of Hamza is a mistake for Balashfarr.

229 *Pryz' 'yn dsh*, which Daryaee, 'Epithets', 13, argues is an attempt to render MP *pahrēz-i ēwēn-dush*, a clear reference to Qubad's support for Mazdak's doctrine.

230 Agathias, 4.28, says that a group of nobles, angry at Qubad's support for the heretic Mazdak, deposed and imprisoned him in his eleventh year (498) and crowned Jamasb, but that Qubad escaped from prison and sought refuge with the Hephthalite king. With the latter's aid he returned to power after a four-year absence. Agathias' narrative is very similar in its outlines to that of Tabari, 1.885–87, except that the latter places Qubad's deposition in his tenth year and his return after an absence of six years. See further Appendix 2 below.

231 This wording seems close to that of Yaqut for his entry on 'Shahr Qubad', which he locates in Fars between Arrajan (perhaps Hamza's Jājān) and Abarshahr; the latter is a district of Khurasan, but maybe there was a place of the same name in Fars.

232 I.e. 'better than (the Roman city of) Amida', which Qubad had successfully besieged in 502–3. Arrajan is in south-west Iran, just above the north-east tip of the Persian Gulf. Note that Hamza uses the Persian form Kawad for the names of these cities, except for Izad Qubad Kard.

say Janbu Shabur; another which he called Walashgird;[233] another, next to Mosul, which he called Khabur Kawad; and another in the Sawad, calling it Īzad Qubad Kard. He appointed Harith b. ʿAmr b. Hujr al-Kindi as a king over the Arabs.[234]

Khusraw [I] Anusharwan b. Qubad

His vest is white and embroidered in variegated colours and his trousers are sky-blue. He is sitting on his throne and resting on his sword.

He built a number of cities. Among them was one that became included in the seven cities that made up Madaʾin and he called it Bih-Az-Andiyu Khusraw – it is the one now named Rumiyyat al-Madaʾin and the meaning of Bih-Az-Andiyu is 'Better than Antioch'.[235] He also built Khusraw Shabur and other cities. He built the barrier of Darband, which is (also called) Bab al-Abwab.[236] The length of this barrier from the sea to the mountain is 20 *farsakhs*.[237] He settled at each end a commander with a regiment assigned to him and he provisioned them from (the produce of) neighbouring farms, which he afterwards gave as an endowment to their children. Thus the descendants of those (first commanders) have become custodians of the lands around the wall. Khusraw bestowed upon each commander, on the day he despatched him **[58]** to defend the aforementioned frontier, a robe of silk brocade decorated with a particular figurative design, and he gave to each commander so empowered a title relevant to that figurative design. So they had names like Baghran-Shah, Shirwan-Shah, Filan-Shah and Alan-Shah.[238] He singled out one of them (to receive) a silver throne, and so

---

233 This is likely to be modern Velashgerd, between Kermanshah and Hamadan in west Iran.

234 On Harith see Smith, 'Arabia', 446–47. Tabari, 1.888–90, presents relations between Harith and Qubad as more combative.

235 Tabari, 1.898, tells how Khusraw conquered Roman Antioch in 540 and brought numerous captives from it to a new city that he had built near Madaʾin on the exact model of the Roman city, calling it al-Rumiyya, 'the Roman (city)'.

236 Literally: the Gate of Gates. Its foundation is traditionally ascribed to Khusraw I; e.g. Baladhuri, 194, and Masʿudi, *Murūj*, 2.3 (ch. 17), who both also state that Khusraw settled people there.

237 Approximately 120 kilometres, though there is substantial variation in the value ascribed to this measure. Note that Baladhuri, 194, has Qubad build a mudbrick barrier (*sadd al-lubn*) in the same region, between Sharwan and the Alan gates (the Dariel pass north of Tblisi), though other authors attribute the construction to Khusraw.

238 Some of these names relate to an animal (*baghrān* = boar, *shīr* = lion, *fīl* = elephant), so Hamza may mean that these animals featured on the robes, though Ālān is just the name of a people. Similar accounts are given in Baladhuri, 196–97 ('Anusharwan crowned kings,

he was called *sarīr shāh*, which in Arabic means 'the Throne King' – *sarīr* is not an Arabic word but is a Persian word applied to a small seat.[239]

Among the great victories achieved by Khusraw Anusharwan were the conquest of the city of Sarandib,[240] the conquest of the city of Constantinople[241] and the conquest of the lands of Yemen.[242] What happened to him in the case of the conquest of Yemen is something the like of which has only ever happened to prophets. He sent only 600 of his cavalry against 30,000 men and they killed them all so that none got away except for those who sought refuge from the heat of the sword in the water of the sea and so drowned themselves. The cause of this was that the Abyssinians had crossed the sea to Yemen, expelled all the men and devoted themselves to bedding the women. The Yemeni king Sayf b. Dhi Yazan[243] went to Anusharwan and stood for seven years at his gate until he gained access to him. He raised with him the affair of the Abyssinians and what had been done by them to the women. **[59]** Anusharwan felt very solicitous for him and took pity on him, and so said: 'I shall look into your affair.' Then he thought about it and said: 'It is not possible in my religion for me to risk my army by dispatching them across the sea to aid someone who is not of my religion. However, in my prisons there are those who

ranked them and assigned to each man shah-ship of a region [then lists them]'), and Masʿudi, *Murūj*, 2.4 ('he assigned to them ranks, conferred on them titles and defined for them borders [then lists them]').

239 It is not clear why Hamza would think *sarīr* is a Persian word.

240 This was the name given to the island of Sri Lanka in Arabic. We have no contemporary record of such a conquest and it may well be that it is given here just as an example of the extent of Khusraw's power.

241 Khusraw achieved notable victories against the Romans, especially the capture of Antioch and Dara, but he did not get near to Constantinople.

242 The account of the conquest of Yemen by Khusraw's emissary Wahriz on behalf of the Yemeni prince Sayf is related in many Muslim histories, such as Ibn Hisham, 41–43; Dinawari, 64–66 (though he places the incident in the reign of Firuz); Tabari, 1.946–58; and Maqdisi, 3.188–95. The latter has Wahriz speak some words in New Persian, from which Hämeen-Anttila, 'Maqdisi', 158, concludes that he 'is quoting from the Persian original of the text which the others used in Arabic translation'. This is not impossible, but the reverse could also be true: that Maqdisi is using a Persian version of this story based on the original Arabic text (note that Maqdisi's version is more florid and accords more space to Sayf at the court of Khusraw), or, more simply, that he, a native of east Iran and a regular at the Samanid court, decides to attribute a few words in Persian to Wahriz.

243 Sayf was a noble of Himyar, the south Arabian tribe that had governed Yemen from *ca.* 280 until the Ethiopians conquered it *ca.* 525. His reign fell somewhere between 558 (last dated inscription of Abraha, the Ethiopian ruler of Yemen, though he was succeeded by at least one of his sons) and 579 (the death of Khusraw, to whom Sayf appeals).

deserve to be killed, and so it would be fitting to send them out to fight this enemy (of yours). If they are victorious I shall make over that land to them as a means of subsistence, but if they perish I shall have done no wrong.' He therefore ordered the prisoners (to be released), and their number amounted to 809, most of them being descendants of Sasan and Bahman b. Isfandiyar. He appointed over them Wahriz, a descendant of Bihafaridun b. Sasan b. Bahman b. Isfandiyar.[244] Thereupon Sayf b. Dhi Yazan said to him: 'O King of Kings! How do these measure up against those whom I have left behind?' Khusraw replied: 'A little fire is a match for a lot of firewood.' They set off in eight ships, out of which two sank and the six arrived safely.[245] They disembarked from the boats and Wahriz ordered his men to eat, which they did. Then he took hold of the remaining provisions and plunged them into the sea. His men complained: 'You have taken our supplies and fed them to the fish.' He replied: 'If you live, you will eat the fish, but if you do not live you will not grieve for the lack of food (for you will also have to contend) with the destruction of your souls!' Then he went over to their boats [60] and burned them. Then he addressed his men: 'You must choose for yourselves either victory by fighting these people or perdition by falling short.'[246] Then he attacked the Abyssinians and he made the name of God, the Mighty and Glorious, and the name of the king his battle-cry, and he defeated them with God's permission.[247] He killed them all to the last man within five hours of the same day and news of this victory travelled among the kings of the nations.

The birth of the Prophet, may God pray for him and his family and grant him peace, occurred in his days, after 41 years of his rule.[248] When

244 The tale of this figure's exploits in Yemen features in several Arabic sources, each of which ascribes to him noble birth. *Wahriz* may be a title rather than a personal name: Procopius, 1.12.10, describes an expedition sent by Qubad I, the commander of which held the title Ourazēs, which possibly equates to the Arabic Wahriz.

245 Tabari, 1.945–58, has two accounts of Wahriz's campaign, one from Ibn Ishaq (d. 767) and one from Hisham ibn al-Kalbi (d. 819). They are, however, very close, and both have this detail of eight ships setting out and two sinking on the way.

246 Wahriz's pep talk and destruction of the food and boats is only in the Hisham ibn al-Kalbi account, not in the Ibn Ishaq version (Tabari, 1.954).

247 Hamza omits the detail that is given in most Muslim accounts, that Wahriz killed the Ethiopian king Masruq with an arrow between the eyes (e.g. Dinawari, 65; Tabari, 1.949 and 955). Note the Islamicising trend here: saying that victory was achieved 'with God's permission' is a trope of the Muslim conquest narratives.

248 I.e. year 41 of Khusraw, which would be 572–73; the prophet Muhammad's birth is usually placed in either 570 or 573.

death approached him (Khusraw), he ordered to be written on his tomb: 'Whatever good we have advanced is with Him Who is not slow to reward; and whatever evil we have accomplished is with Him Who is not impotent to punish.'

Hurmuz b. Khusraw

His vest is red and embroidered, his trousers are sky-blue and embroidered and his crown is green. He is sitting on the throne with a mace in his right hand and resting the left hand on his sword. [God] knows best.

Khusraw [II] Abarwiz b. Hurmuz

His vest is pink and embroidered, his trousers are sky-blue and his crown is red. He is holding a lance in his hand.

He acquired in his palace 3000 free women and 12,000 female slaves for music, amusement and various kinds of service, and in his bodyguard he employed 6000 [61] men. In his stable there were 8500 horses for him to ride, excluding those of his retinue, 960 elephants, 12,000 mules for his luggage and 20,000 Bactrian camels.[249] He became angry with Nuʿman b. Mundhir and had him killed in the desert and his dead body trampled under the feet of elephants.[250] He allowed his property, wives and children to be captured and ordered that they be sold at the lowest price. He erected a fire-temple in al-Bārmīn, a village in the district of Kirman, and endowed it with (the revenue from) the villages in its vicinity.

[Qubad II] Shirawayh b. Khusraw

His vest is embroidered red, his trousers are sky-blue and his crown is green. He is standing with an unsheathed sword in his right hand.

He suspected an uprising by his brothers, and so killed 18 of them and several of their children. The names of these brothers were: Shahriyar, Mardanshah, Kuranshah, Firuzshah, Afrudshah, Shadman, Zadabzudshah,

---

249 Tabari, 1.1041, gives two versions of this enumeration of Khusraw's wealth (one from Hisham Ibn al-Kalbi and one from 'not Hisham'): 12,000 concubines, 999 elephants, 50,000 riding animals; 3000 concubines, 3000 male servants, 760 elephants, 8500 riding animals, 12,000 mules.

250 Nuʿman III b. Mundhir IV (d. ca. 602), the last ruler of the Arab Lakhmid dynasty that served as vassals of the Sasanids. *Chronicle of Khuzistan*, 20 (written ca. 660), says that Khusraw had him poisoned in revenge for his refusal to marry his daughter to him. Tabari, 1.1025–29, also says that Nuʿman fell foul of Khusraw because of his refusal to give him a woman from his household. This is one of a number of points of contact between the two texts that suggest a common late Sasanid source (see introduction above).

Shadzik, Arwandzik, Qas Dil, Qas Bih, Khurra, Mardkhurra, Zadan Khurra, Shirzad, Jawanshir and Jahan Bakht.[251]

Ardashir [III] b. Shirawayh
His vest is ornamented and sky-blue, his crown is red and he is standing with a lance in his right hand and resting his left hand on his sword.

When it reached [62] Shahrbaraz, the commander of the western frontier, that they had crowned a boy, he marched towards him, entered his palace and killed him.

Buran Dukht bt. Abarwiz
Her vest is embroidered green, her trousers are sky-blue and her crown is also sky-blue. She is sitting on the throne with a battle-axe in her hand.

It is she who returned the wood (of the Cross) to the Catholicos.[252] Her mother was Maria, daughter of Heraclius,[253] the king of the Romans. She came to the throne only because Shirawayh had wiped out all the male children of his father and so they were compelled to enthrone women.

Azarmidukht bt. Abarwiz
Her vest is red and embroidered in various colours, her trousers are variegated and sky-blue and her crown is green. She is sitting on the throne with a battle-axe in her right hand and resting her left hand on a sword.

She was strong and fair. She built a fire-temple in Qarṭmān, a village in the canton of Abkhāz.[254] [God] knows best.

Yazdagird [III] b. Shahriyar
His vest is green and embroidered, his trousers are sky-blue and embroidered

251 Though he specifies 18 brothers, Hamza names only 17. The number of these brothers varies in the sources between 16 and 18. Hamza gives 17 here; Tabari, 1.1060, specifies 17, but does not name them.
252 This is the title of the leader of the largest Christian sect in Sasanid Persia. See n. 83 above regarding Buran.
253 The *Chronicle of 1234* says that she was the daughter of Emperor Maurice (Hoyland, *Theophilus*, 52).
254 This is the usual Arabic term for Abkhazia/the Abkhazians in the north-east Caucasus, but it is unclear whether this is what is meant here. If the Caucasus is intended, one could possibly assume that Qarṭmān is an Arabic rendering of Gardman, the district to the east of Ganja in modern Azerbaijan.

and his crown is red. His shoes, like all of them,[255] are red. He has a lance in his hand and is resting upon his sword.

The reason for his escape from death at the hands of Shirawayh was that a family member contrived to get him out of Mada'in and taken to a remote place and hid him there. **[63]** After being made king he never ceased (to be involved) in wars for 16 years until he was killed in Merv in 31 AH, the eighth year of the caliphate of 'Uthman.[256] When Yazdagird travelled[257] from Iraq, he brought as many jewels and vessels of gold and silver as he could together with his children, women and retinue. Among those who left with him were 1000 cooks, 1000 minstrels,[258] 1000 lynx-trainers and 1000 falconers. Also Khurrazad b. Khurra Hurmuz,[259] brother of Rustam, the commander of (the battle of) Qadisiyya, departed with him and brought him to Isfahan, then to Kirman and then to Merv, where he handed him over to Mahawayh, the governor of Merv. The latter wrote for him an acknowledgement of his delivery of the king to him, then Khurrazad left him to go to Azerbaijan. At that point the king of the Hephthalites[260] intended to make war against Yazdagird and so Mahawayh made common cause with him to kill Yazdagird, and (hence) his descendants are up to this day called in Merv and its regions 'king-killers'.[261] Finally Yazdagird was killed in a mill.

255 The Arabic just says 'all their shoes are red' without explanation; presumably it means Sasanid rulers always wore red shoes.

256 Since 'Uthman became caliph at the beginning of 24 AH, his eighth year corresponds exactly to 31 AH, August AD 651–August AD 652.

257 Text has *istaqalla*; read *intaqala*, 'transfer, travel, relocate'.

258 The text has *hwsy'n*, which should probably be identified with the *hwšyh* who feature in the entry on Bahram Gur above, both a mistake for the Persian word *gws'n*, 'poet-musician'. See n. 222 above.

259 Sebeos, 137 and 132, confirms that Khurrazad (Armenian: Khorokhazat) helped Yazdagird evacuate Mada'in and that his (and Rustam's) father was called Khurra Hurmuz (Armenian: Khorokh-Ormizd), as also does Mas'udi, 103, below: 'Khurra Hurmuz the Azeri was commander of Khurasan and the father of Rustam'. Tabari, 1.1065, is confused, calling him here Rustam b. Farrukh-Hurmuz and, further on, when relating the battle of Qadisiyya, Rustam b. Farrukhzad the Armenian (*ibid.*, 1.2235).

260 The Hephthalites, also called the White Huns by modern scholars, were a Central Asian people who dominated the region *ca.* 450–550 from their base in modern north Afghanistan. They were ousted by the Turks in the mid-sixth century, so the latter are probably meant here, though it is possible that some Hephthalite groups survived. Tabari, 1.2878, calls this king Nizak Tarkhan; on his identity and affiliation see Esin, 'Tarkhan Nizak'. Note that Tabari, 1.2872–2883, cites many subtly differing versions of the last days of Yazdagird, though all involve his death in a mill near Merv at the instigation of Mahawayh.

261 Hamza here uses the Persian expression *khudāh kushān*, literally 'lord-killers'.

This (material), with which I have filled out this section, is from epitomes of the 'History of the Kings' and only a small amount of it is to be found in books of chronological histories and biographical histories,[262] and the rest is from other books of theirs. As regards their correspondence, bequests and the like, such as are found in history books, I have excluded them from this book.

SECTION V of Chapter 1: **[64]** concerning the report of all that is in the 'Book of Lords' that is not recounted by either Ibn al-Muqaffaʿ or Ibn al-Jahm

I have put these (accounts) at the end of this chapter so that the reader may treat them in the same way as the tales of Luqman b. ʿAd[263] among the Arabs and of Uj[264] and Buluqiya[265] among the Israelites and so that he understands that.

I have read in a book copied from their scripture, the Avesta, that God the Almighty and Glorious determined that the lifespan of the world, from the beginning of Creation up to the Day of Separation (of the virtuous from the evil) and the end of trials, should be 12,000 years. The world remained on high, without disease or disaster, for 3000 years. Then it was brought down low, where it remained without disease or disaster ' for a further period of 3000 years. At that point Ahriman[266] came against it and there appeared maladies and mayhem, and evil became mixed with good, after 6000 years without the interference of evil. This adulteration began at the start of the seventh millennium (known as) the alloyed (millennium). The first creatures of the earth that God made, without the pairing of male

---

262 'History of the Kings': *akhbār al-mulūk*; chronological histories: *al-tawārīkh*, biographical histories: *siyar*. Hamza seems to be making a distinction between *akhbār al-mulūk* (usually *akhbār* implies anecdotal narration) on the one hand and the *tawārīkh* and *siyar* on the other; one might relate this to my proposed distinction in the Introduction between narrative histories and chronological compilations, but the terminology Hamza uses here is too vague.

263 Luqman is a legendary sage of pre-Islamic Arabia after whom chapter 31 of the Qurʾan is named, and the ʿAd are considered one of the seven or eight ancient indigenous peoples of Arabia.

264 The Arabic name for the Biblical ʿOg, the giant king of Bashan (Deuteronomy 3:11).

265 A character from the 'Thousand and One Nights', often said to be an ancient Israelite prince, who goes on a long journey to find the herb of immortality, encountering many fantastic places along the way.

266 The evil deity who is the opponent of the good god Ohrmazd in Zoroastrian cosmology.

and female, were a man and a bull. The man was called Gayumart[267] and the bull Abu Dhād.[268] Gayumart means living, rational and mortal, and his title is *Gilshāh*, that is, the 'King of Clay'. [65] This man became the founding ancestor of mankind and he spent 30 years in the world. When he died a drop of semen issued from his loins and soaked into the earth, and it remained in the womb of the Earth for 40 years. Then there grew two sprouts resembling two rhubarbs[269] and became transformed from the plant species to the human species, one male and the other female. They emerged with the same size and shape, and their names were Masha and Mashyana. After 50 years Masha coupled with Mashyana and they begot children. From the time of their begetting children until Hushang Pishdad ruled the earth was 93 years and six months.

I have read much the same thing in another book with different wording and more explanation in the narrative, namely that the first thing that God the Mighty and Glorious created were a man and a bull and they remained in the folds of the heavens and the centre of the highest regions for 3000 years, without any disease or disaster. These were the three millennia of Aries, Taurus and Gemini. Then they were brought down to the earth, where they remained free from any disease or disaster for the three millennia of Cancer, Leo and Virgo. When this came to an end and the millennium of Libra began, antagonism arose and Gayumart ruled over the land, the sea, the bovines [66] and the plants for the first 30 years of the millennium of Libra. The Ascendant at the commencement of this millennium was Cancer with Jupiter in it, when the sun was in Aries, the moon in Taurus, Saturn in Libra, Mars in Capricorn, Venus in Pisces and Mercury also in Pisces. The planets started from these signs of the zodiac in the month of Frawardin, on the day of Hurmuz, the day of Nawruz, and the night became distinguished from the day by the revolution of the sphere.

---

267 Here written Kahumarth rather than Hamza's usual form of Kayumarth.

268 Abu Dhād derives from the epithet 'sole-created'/*ēw-dād*, which is applied to the primordial bovine in Zoroastrian cosmology, the fifth of the six original creations of Ohrmazd, Gayumart being the sixth and last.

269 Arabic: *rībāsatayn*, which is *rheum ribes*, Syrian or currant-fruited rhubarb, and which grows in mountainous areas of the Middle East as far east as Afghanistan.

ʿAli al-Masʿudi

Masʿudi (d. *ca.* 960) effectively wrote a whole series of historical works. Of the two that are extant, one – 'The Meadows of Gold and Mines of Gems' (*Murūj al-dhahab wa-maʿādin al-jawhar*) – is intended to be comprehensive – and the other – 'The Instructive Overview' (*al-Tanbīh wa-l-ishrāf*)[270] – is more of a selection of highlights of world history with a geographical introduction.[271] Both contain numerous digressions on an amazing variety of topics, for Masʿudi had an insatiable curiosity about human societies, past and present. He spent much of his life travelling and took great pride in the fact that he had personally witnessed and investigated many of the things that he wrote about. The excerpt below is taken from the shorter work, which includes in its pre-Islamic section a survey of the seven most important peoples of antiquity, 'their languages, their beliefs, the places they inhabited, what distinguishes them one from another' and salient points in their history.[272] Being of Persian ancestry himself, it is not unexpected that Masʿudi begins with a section on the Persians, and this is what I translate here.[273] One of the reasons for choosing this excerpt is that it gives us lots of interesting snippets of information on Persian literature and language that are not found elsewhere, such as his description of a book containing exquisitely drawn portraits of the Sasanid kings that he saw himself in Istakhr, and his observations about the different scripts used to write the Persian language.

---

270 *Tanbīh* is the verbal noun of the verb *nabbaha*, 'to call attention to, instruct', and *ishrāf* is the verbal noun of the verb *ashrafa*, 'to look upon from above' (in the sense of 'have an overview of' or 'have oversight of', i.e. supervise, direct). So the work is intended as an overview (of history) that is instructive.

271 On his life and works see Shboul, *Al-Masʿudi*, and the useful entry by Michael Cooperson in *EIr*.

272 The section on the Persians in the *Murūj* is 135 pages long, and so it is partly for practical reasons that I translate from the more manageable 26-page section in the *Tanbīh*, but also because the *Murūj* mainly gives a straightforward account of the history of the Persian kings, whereas the *Tanbīh* offers lots of observations on Persian language and texts, which are more pertinent to the aims of this book.

273 I translate from the M.J. de Goeje edition (Leiden, 1894); numbers in bold in the translation below refer to the page numbers of this edition. This is the first English translation of this section; for a French version see Carra de Vaux, *Avertissement*, 123–37.

Translation

[77] We shall now mention the seven nations that those concerned with the history of ancient peoples and their realms believe to be the most illustrious of them and the most important. They were the seven in antiquity that stood out (above the rest) for three things: their natural disposition, their innate character and their languages. (First are) the Persians, a nation that included within its borders the Jibal-Mahat region,[274] Azerbaijan to the land of Arminiya, Arran and Baylaqan to Darband, which is (known in Arabic as) the Gate of Gates, Rayy, [78] Tabaristan, Masqat, Shabaran, Gurgan, Abarshahr, which is Nishabur, Herat, Merv and the other cities of Khurasan, Sijistan, Kirman, Fars, Ahwaz and the adjoining parts that at this time belong to the land of the Persians.[275] All these regions once constituted a single kingdom with one king and one language, though there were some slight distinctions in the language. Yet a language may be said to be one if the letters in which it is written are the same and the way the letters are joined is the same, even if there are differences in other respects, as is the case with Pahlavi,[276] Dari,[277] Azeri[278] and other Persian dialects … .[279]

274 Arabic: *al-jibāl min al-māhāt wa-ghayruhā*. *Al-māhāt* is a late form, with Arabic plural ending, of OP: Mada, i.e. Media, which corresponds to the Muslim province of the Jibal (literally 'the mountains'), dominated by the Zagros mountain range of modern west Iran.

275 In this list Mas'udi is proceeding clockwise from west/north-west Iran (Jibal, Azerbaijan etc.), to the north (Tabaristan etc.), to the east (Khurasan etc.), and to south-west Iran (Fars and Ahwaz).

276 Arabic: *fahlawiyya*, i.e. Pahlavi. It is described as 'the first Persian' or 'ancient Persian' by many authors (thus Ibn Taghribirdi, 1.61, citing Mas'udi). The geographer Istakhri, 137, specifies that it is the language 'in which are the history books of the Persians and the writings of the Zoroastrians amongst themselves', adding that 'it needs explanation for (modern) Persians to understand it'. It seems, then, to correspond pretty much to what modern scholars refer to as Pahlavi/Middle Persian.

277 Arabic: *dariyya*. It literally means language of the court (*dar*). In Mas'udi's day the courts that used Persian were in the East, especially Khurasan and Transoxania, and this is where geographers locate the heartland of *dariyya* (e.g. Muqaddasi, 335: 'the language of the Bukharans … is *dariyya*, and whatever is like it is called *dariyya* because the letters of the ruler are written in it and stories recounted to him in it'; Istakhri, 363: the language of Soghdia is *dariyya*).

278 Arabic: *ādhariyya*, the Persian dialect prevalent in Azerbaijan before Turks arrived there in the medieval period.

279 Mas'udi now introduces the rest of the seven most prominent ancient nations: the Chaldaeans, Greeks, Libyans (which includes Egypt), Turks, Indians and Chinese.

[85] Mention of the Kings of Persia according to their dynasties from Gayumart, who was the first of their kings, to Yazdagird b. Shahriyar, the last of them, with the number of years they reigned

... The sum of the years of the kings of the first Persians according to their dynasties, the Petty Kings, and those of the second Persians, who were the Sasanids, is 4,140 years and five months and a half. Many who have concerned themselves with the history of Persia, its kings and dynasties, are of the opinion that there were interregnums in the sovereignty of the first Persians amounting to 331 years, namely an interregnum of 223 years between the kings Gayumart and Hushang, and another of 108 years between the kings Hushang and Tahmurath. If the years of these interregna are added to the number of years we mentioned, the total comes to 4,471 years and five months and a half.

Mention of the first order[280] of the kings of the first Persians

The first of these kings was Gayumart *Gilshāh*, which means 'King of Clay'.[281] It is to him that the Persians trace their lineages, since he is for them (the equivalent of) Adam, the father of mankind and the fount of all human progeny. He reigned for 40 years, or some say 30, during the first millennium[282] after the (beginning of mankind's) procreation, and he dwelt in Istakhr in Fars. Next, Hushang ruled for 40 years, Tahmurath ruled for 30 years, Jam ruled for 700 years and three months, and Biyurasb, who is Dahak, ruled for 1,000 years. The Persians speak a lot about this latter, [86] and one of the tales they relate is that on his shoulders were two serpents that afflicted him and were only calmed by (being fed) human brains. They also say that this king was a sorcerer, whom the jinn and men would obey, and that he ruled over the seven climes.

When his tyranny waxed and his arrogance increased and after he had exterminated a great number of the people of his realm, there arose a man from the common people, of those who possessed piety, and an inhabitant of Isfahan, a shoemaker by the name of Kabi. He raised a banner of leather

---

280 Instead of the usual division of the pre-Islamic Persian kings into four dynasties, Mas'udi divides them into the First Persians and the Second Persians, and then further into five subdivisions or orders. The First Persians are the Pishdadids (split into two orders), Kayanids (order 3) and Arsacids (order 4), and the Second Persians are the Sasanids (order 5). He does the same in his section on the Persians in his *Murūj* (2.105–241, chs 21–24), though at the end of that he gives the usual ordering of four dynasties, citing Abu 'Ubayda b. al-Muthanna.

281 But see n. 37 above for a possible interpretation of this title as 'King of the Mountain'.

282 Using the Persian word *hazārīkah* (MP: *hazārag*).

as his emblem and he called upon the populace to depose and kill Dahak and to enthrone Afridun. The commoners and many of the elite followed him, marched against Dahak and captured him. Afridun dispatched him to the very top of Mount Dabawand,[283] between Rayy and Tabaristan, and deposited him there. He is still alive to this day, bound in chains in the same place; about him there are stories[284] that it would take long to recount and that we have set out in our book 'The Meadows of Gold and Mines of Gems'. The people were greatly cheered by what befell Dahak for his injustice and wicked government, and they regarded that standard as propitious, calling it *dirafsh kābiyān*,[285] linking it with its owner, Kabi. *Dirafsh* in ancient Persian means banner, whereas in this (modern) Persian it means the awl of the cobbler.[286] It was decorated with gold and all kinds of precious jewels, and was only brought out for important battles, spread over the head of the king or the heir apparent or whoever was taking his place.

This banner continued to be venerated by all their kings up until the time when Yazdagird b. Shahriyar, the last of the kings of the Sasanid Persians, sent it with Rustam the Azeri[287] for the battle against the Arabs at Qadisiyya in the year 16, though there is some disagreement over that. When the Persians had been defeated and Rustam killed, this banner fell to Dirar b. al-Khattab al-Fihri.[288] Its value was estimated at two million dinars. It is also said that it was seized **[87]** on the day of the conquest of Mada'in, or that of Nihawand, which was in either the year 19 or the year 21. It was because of what Kabi and his companions had accomplished against Dahak that, in his will, Ardashir frequently warned the kings who

283 Or, more commonly, Damawand. At 5609m high, Mount Damawand is the highest mountain in Iran and indeed in the whole Middle East, and plays an important role in Iranian mythology.

284 Emending *fī akhbār yaṭūlu dhikruhā* to *fīhi akhbār yaṭūlu dhikruhā*.

285 The banner of Kabi/Kawah is the legendary royal standard of the Sasanid kings; see *EIr*, 'Derafš-e kavian' and Daryaee, 'Kāve the Blacksmith'. Tabari, 1.207, has much the same account, adding the detail that Kabi was spurred to act by the fact that his sons were about to be fed to Dahak's serpents.

286 Emending *kharz* to *kharrāz*. Mas'udi contrasts the first/original/ancient Persian (*al-fārisiyya al-ūlā*) with 'this Persian' (*hādhihi l-fārisiyya*), presumably meaning the contemporary form of the language.

287 Rustam b. Khurra Hurmuz, the Persian general who was vanquished at Qadisiyya. He is called the Azeri (*al-Ādharī*) in reference to the fact that his family lands were substantially based in the north-west Iranian province of Azerbaijan (MP: *Ādurbādagān*; Arabic: *Adharbayjān*). See also n. 259 above.

288 A poet of Mecca and chief of the Qurayshi clan of Muharib ibn Fihr; he played a major role at the Arab siege of Mada'in.

would succeed him against disparaging the ability of the cleverest and most pious of the men of the people to rally and lead (an opposition). If that were neglected and reached a head, it could lead to a transfer of power or the demise of traditions. Aristotle did likewise in his warnings to Alexander in several of his epistles, as did others knowledgeable in the government of religion and the state.

The Yemeni Arabs claim Dahak (as one of them) and assert that he is from (the tribe of) al-Azd. The poets of Islam mention him, and he is cited with pride by Abu Nuwas Hasan b. Hani',[289] freedman of the family of Hakam b. Sa'd al-'Ashira b. Malik b. Udad b. Zayd b. Yashjub b. 'Arib b. Zayd b. Kahlan b. Saba b. Yashjub b. Ya'rub b. Qahtan, in his poem where he satirises all the tribes of Nizar and boasts about Qahtan and its tribes.[290] It is the famous piece for which he was long held captive and harshly punished by (the caliph) al-Rashid. It begins:

> I can find no interest in an encampment effaced and transformed by the double blows of the wind and the rain.

He speaks in praise of Yemen in it and also mentions Dahak:

> We are the masters of Na'it and to us is San'a' which has musk in its palaces; Dahak was one of us, he who was obeyed by the demons and birds in their flight.

And in it he spoke mockingly of Nizar:

> Disparage (the tribe of) Nizar, rend its skin and (thereby) expose its shortcomings.

Many of those who belonged to Nizar responded to this poem of his, one of whom was a man of the descendants of Rabi'a b. Nizar, who spoke mentioning Nizar and its merits and Yemen and its vices in a poem that begins: [88]

> Cease praising those of our men who have passed away. Is the age of Ma'add then over, as its detractors claim?[291]

---

289 A very famous poet of the early Abbasid period, who died in 813. Since the family to which he was attached descended ultimately from the southern Arabian tribe of Qahtan (allegedly, anyway), Abu Nuwas could be expected to support the southerners' claim that Dahak was one of theirs.

290 Nizar and Qahtan are the putative common ancestors of the northern and southern Arabian tribes respectively.

291 Ma'add was the father of Nizar and his name is frequently used to refer to all the north

He further said:

> Praise Ma'add, and boast of its high birth which is above that of other men. Expose the men of Yemen, sons of Qahtan, and do not fear them.

Abu Tammam[292] mentioned Dahak in a poem praising the Afshin, whom he compares to Afridun, and in which he speaks of Babak, comparing him to Dahak.[293] This poem begins:

> The two-edged sword has conquered the fortress of Badhdh,[294] now buried in dust; only the wild beasts still live in it.

It goes on to say:

> He (Babak) resembled Dahak who tyrannised the world whereas you (Afshin) were Afridun.

Many versed in the history of ancient nations and their kings believe that Dahak was one of the early kings of the Nabaṭi Chaldeans of southern Iraq. Afridun reigned for 500 years.

Mention of the second order of the kings of the first Persians, named Balān,[295] which means those on high
The first was Manushihr, who reigned 120 years. The Persians have high regard for him and celebrate him for various deeds they have commemorated and marvels they have recounted. Between him and Afridun are 13 generations; he himself was the son of Iraj b. Afridun and had seven children, to whom most of the peoples of Persia and the remaining dynasties of its kings can trace back their lineages. He is like the tree trunk for the ancestry of the Persians, just as the Kurds,[296] in the reckoning of the Persians, are the offspring of Kurd b. Isfandiyar b. Manushihr.[297] Belonging

Arabian tribes. The point being made here is that the age of Ma'add is certainly not at an end, so one should continue to celebrate it.

292 A celebrated Abbasid poet and literary anthologist who died in 845.

293 Afshin was the title (of Central Asian origin) borne by the military commander who succeeded in crushing the lengthy revolt of Babak (816–37), a Zoroastrian revolutionary active in north-west Iran/southern Caucasus. A comparison is being drawn here between Afridun's defeat of Dahak and the Afshin's defeat of Babak.

294 Babak's fortress-capital in the mountains of north-west Iran, near Ardabil.

295 From NP bālā, 'high, exalted'. For most Muslim historians the kings Mas'udi lists here still belong to the first Persian dynasty, the Pishdadids.

296 Mas'udi is one of the first Muslim authors to give detailed information about the Kurds.

297 This is one of many genealogies ascribed to the Kurds. See EI, 'Kurds, Kurdistan, iii. History, A. Origins and Pre-Islamic History'.

to them (the Kurds) are (the tribes of) the Bazanjan, Shuhjan, Shadhnajan, [89] Nashawira, Budhikan, Lurriyya, Jurqan, Jawaniyya, Barisiyan, Jalaliyya, Mustakan, Jabariqa, Jurughan, Kikan, Majurdan, Hadhbaniyya and others among those who reside among the (Kurdish) bands[298] of Fars, Kirman, Sijistan, Khurasan, Isfahan and the Median lands of Jibal, namely the Mahs of Kufa and Basra,[299] and Masabadhan, as well as the two concessions[300] of Burj and Karaj Abi Dulaf. (They are also found in) Hamadan, Shahrazur, Darabadh, Samghan, Azerbaijan, Armenia, Arran, Baylaqan and Bab al-Abwab, and some are in northern Mesopotamia,[301] Syria and the borderlands.[302]

Some of the modern well-informed Kurds whom we met personally in the regions we have just mentioned believe that they are the descendants of Kurd b. Murad b. Saʿsaʿa b. Harb b. Hawazin, while others think that they are the progeny of Subayʿ b. Hawazin. Yet according to the genealogists of Mudar, Harb and Subayʿ sired no offspring, so they had no descendants; Hawazin[303] continues only through the line of Bakr b. Hawazin. Some Kurds are of the opinion that they hail from Rabiʿa via Bakr b. Waʾil.[304] Long ago, because of warring among them, they settled in the land of the Persians.[305] They dispersed among them, their language changed and they became (different) peoples and tribes.

298 Arabic: *zumūm*, the root of which means to bind or fasten. Minorsky suggests linking it instead to the Persian word *ram*, meaning 'crowd, herd'; see his article in *EI* mentioned in the previous footnote.

299 These were the official designations in the early Islamic period for the cities of Dinawar and Nihawand and their hinterlands, which were associated with the two main Iraqi garrison cities of Kufa and Basra.

300 Arabic: *al-īghārayn*. The term designates an exemption or concession with respect to taxes, namely the privilege of paying a single tax payment direct to the treasury, and by extension it refers to the area covered by such an exemption. The concession of Burj is modern Borujerd, south of Hamadan.

301 Arabic: *al-Jazīra*, literally 'the island', a reference to the land almost enclosed by the Euphrates and Tigris rivers in their upper reaches (modern south-east Turkey and north-east Iraq).

302 Arabic: *al-thughūr*, which is the name for the border territories on the south-eastern edges of the Byzantine Empire and the north-western edges of the Islamic Empire in what is now southern Turkey.

303 A large north Arabian tribal confederation.

304 A tribal confederation of east central Arabia.

305 Arabic: *al-aʿājim*, a term for non-Arabs in general, but very commonly applied to Persians in particular. This story of wars that drove them out of Arabia is evidently told to explain how the Kurds could be descended from Arab tribes and yet live in the east and speak an Iranian language.

In our previous works we mentioned the various peoples who live in the deserts and mountains, in the east [90] and the west, in the north and the south, from among the Arabs, Kurds, Jat,[306] the Baluch and Kuch, who are the Qufṣ[307] of the land of Kirman, the Berbers in the land of Africa and the Maghreb, including (the tribes of the) Kutama, Zawila, Mazata,[308] Luwata, Hawwara, Sanhaja, Awraba, Lamṭa and other Berber clans and tribes, and the Fīra, Beja[309] and other nomadic nations.

It is said that the king who succeeded Manushihr was Sahm b. Aman b. Athfiyan b. Nudhar b. Manushihr, and he reigned for 60 years. After him came Afrasiyab the Turk, who reigned for 12 years and was overthrown by Zaw. The latter ruled for three years, and then Karshasb three years too.

Mention of the third order of the kings of the first Persians, the Kayanids, meaning 'The Powerful'[310]

The first was Kay Qubad, and he ruled for 120 years. After him came Kay Kawus, who ruled for 150 years, Kay Khusraw, who ruled for 60 years, Kay Luhrasb, 120 years, and Kay Bishtasb, also 120 years. After 30 years of the latter's reign had passed, Zoroaster b. Burshasb b. Asbiman[311] brought him the Magian religion,[312] which he embraced. He converted the people of his kingdom to it and he fought on behalf of it until it triumphed. Before that the Persians had followed the doctrine of the ḥanīfs, who are the Sabians.[313]

---

306 A pastoralist people of the Indus valley; see n. 223 above.

307 Arabic: al-balūj wa-l-kūj wa-hum al-qufṣ. The Baluch are a well-known people living in the mountainous areas of south-east Iran (east Kirman) and western Pakistan. Kūj is presumably an attempt to represent the Persian word Kufichī, meaning 'mountain dweller', which is often applied to the Baluch. Qufṣ is an Arabicised form of Kufichī.

308 Possibly this should read Zanata, which, like the others listed here, was a well-known Berber tribe.

309 The Beja are a nomadic people of Eastern Egypt. It is unclear who are meant by the Fīra; the editor suggests the Nuba, which makes sense in terms of geographical proximity, but it is a major emendation.

310 Kay, or rather Kavi, is an old Indo-Iranian word for 'poet', though with the functions of priest and seer, not just of versifier, and therefore powerful in their society. In Manichaean Persian, written kaw, it means 'giant'. See EIr, 'Kayānīān i'.

311 Mas'udi conveys Zoroaster's full name quite well here: his father was Pourushaspa and he belonged to the Spitāma family.

312 Arabic: dīn al-majūsiyya. The word majūsiyya is an abstract term formed from majūs, which refers either narrowly to the Zoroastrian clergy (from OP: magu, Latin: magus, plural magi, whence the English word 'Magi') or more generally to all Zoroastrians. So 'the religion of majūsiyya' or 'the religion of the majūs' conveys our term Zoroastrianism.

313 The Arabic word ḥanīf is related to the Syriac word ḥanpā, meaning 'pagan', but in the

This was the religion that **[91]** Budasf³¹⁴ brought to Tahmurath. *Ḥanīf* is a Syriac word that has been Arabised, and really it should be *ḥanīfwā*; some say that it is pronounced with a letter that is between *ba'* and *fa'*, as Syriac does not have a *fa'*.³¹⁵ It is noted that the Sabians go back to Sabi b. Matushalakh b. Idris, who belonged to the original *ḥanīf* religion, though others say that they go back to Sabi b. Mari, who was a contemporary of Abraham, God's Friend, peace be upon him. (They also recount) other sayings for which we have proposed explanations in our earlier works.

Zoroaster brought him (Kay Bishtasb) the book of the Avesta, which in Arabic was given a final *qaf* and so it was pronounced *al-Abastaq*.³¹⁶ The number of its suras³¹⁷ is 21, each sura comprising 200 pages. And the number of the consonants and vowels (of the script in which it is written) are 60, each consonant and vowel being represented by its own individual character, some of which are in frequent use whereas others have fallen into disuse, for this writing is not specific to the language of the Avesta. Zoroaster devised this form of writing, which the Zoroastrians called *dīn dabīrah*, meaning 'religious script'. It was inscribed on 12,000 skins of oxen with quills of gold in the ancient Persian language,³¹⁸ though there is no one known today who is acquainted with the meaning of that language.³¹⁹ Only some of the suras have been translated for them into this

---

Qur'an it has positive connotations, applied to Abraham with the sense of a monotheist who is neither a Jew nor a Christian. The Sabians are also mentioned in the Qur'an, again with a positive sense, listed among those who have the possibility of entering Paradise, though no details about them are given.

314 Here written Budhasb, but Budasf is more common in Arabic; see n. 112 above.

315 This is a little confused, but has some truth to it. The final 'ā' of Mas'udi's *ḥanīfwā* presumably reflects the definite ending of the noun in a number of Aramaic dialects; the penultimate 'w' may mean that he obtained this information from the speaker of an Aramaic dialect that had wawation (as, for example, does Nabataean Aramaic). The third root letter in the Aramaic word is a 'p' (*ḥanpā*), which could be said to be between a *ba'* and a *fa'*.

316 The final *-aq* reflects the MP ending.

317 This is the word used for the different sections/chapters of the Qur'an, and so it is interesting that Mas'udi uses it to describe the divisions of the Zoroastrian scripture.

318 Arabic: *kutiba fī ithnay 'ashar alf jild thawr bi-quḍbān al-dhahab ḥafran bi-l-lughat al-fārisīya al-ūlā*; cf. Tabari, 1.676: *kutiba fī jild ithnay 'asharat alf baqara ḥafran fī l-julūd wa-naqshan bi-l-dhahab*. On this legend see Nyberg, 'Sassanid Mazdaism', 20–21, and Van Bladel, 'Zoroaster's Many Languages', 193–94. A version of this legend is already found in the late Sasanid text *Shahristan-i Iranshahr*, §4: 'Then Zoroaster brought the religion; by the order of King Bishtasb 1200 chapters in the religious script (*dēn dibīrīh*) were engraved on golden tablets.'

319 Since he is aware that there were some who understood Pahlavi/MP, Mas'udi

Persian (language),[320] and these are the ones they read in their prayers, such as the yashts,[321] the *Vendidad*, [92] the *Bagan-yasht* and the *Hadokht*.[322] In the *Vendidad* is the account of the beginning and end of the world, and in the *Hadokht* there are sermons. Zoroaster made a commentary on the Avesta, which he called the *Zand* and which for them (the Zoroastrians) is the speech of the Lord sent down to Zoroaster. He then translated it from the Pahlavi language into Persian.[323] Thereafter he made a commentary on the *Zand* and called it the *Pazand*.[324] In turn, the scholars from among the priests and clerics produced a commentary on this commentary, which they called the *yasna*, though some called it the *akridah*.[325] It was burned by Alexander (the Great) when he conquered the Persian Empire and killed Dara b. Dara.

Zoroaster devised another script; the Zoroastrians call it *kashan dabīrah*, the meaning of which (in Persian) is 'universal script'.[326] One can write in it all the languages of the nations, as well as the cries of animals

presumably means here either Old Persian or Avestan Persian; see Van Bladel, 'Zoroaster's Many Languages', 190–92.

320 Presumably meaning New Persian, i.e. the Persian widely used in Mas'udi's day, especially in the lands of the Samanid dynasty (892–999), which ruled from Bukhara.

321 Yashts are the hymns that Zoroastrians recite in praise of their deities and that are collected within the Avesta.

322 These titles are garbled in the manuscripts (the editor settles on: *ashtād, jitrasht, bānyast, hādūkht*). My translation is based on the observation of a correspondence between the titles of Mas'udi's four texts and the titles of four texts studied by the youth in the MP tale of Khusraw and Retak (Bailey, *Problems*, 160). On these texts see *EIr*, 'Yašhts', 'Vendīdād', 'Bagān Yašt', 'Hādōkht nask'.

323 Arabic: *min lughat al-fahlawīya ilā l-fārisīya*. Mas'udi obviously does not mean here that the ancient prophet Zoroaster translated the *Zand* into New Persian. Possibly he is thinking about people here; i.e. Zoroaster translated it from the language of the Parthian people (originally from north-east Iran) to the language of the people of Fars (in south-west Iran).

324 *Zand* is the MP word for commentary and is used particularly of commentaries on the Avesta. *Pazand* (Arabic: *bāzand*) refers to the version of the Avestan script used for writing down that commentary and translations of the Avesta in MP.

325 The first word, *yāzdah* (though there are no diacritical marks, so other readings are possible), could plausibly indicate the Yasna, the primary Zoroastrian liturgical text, which is not a commentary, but was put together by priests and is recited by them. The reading and meaning of the second word, a-k/l-r-d-h, are uncertain; Darmester suggested to de Goeje to read *Denkard*, the title of a Zoroastrian religious anthology compiled in the early Islamic period, though such an encyclopaedic text does not seem what is intended. Possibly meant here is the Khordeh Avesta (*EIr*, s.v.), which is a collection of devotional texts used by the laity.

326 Or more exactly 'language of the people', reading *kasan* (MP *kas* = person).

and birds and the like. The number of its consonants and vowels is 160, each consonant and vowel having a different character.[327] None of the other scripts of peoples have as many letters as these two scripts (of Zoroaster). Thus the letters of the Greek script, which today is called the Roman, number just 24, for it has no *ḥaʾ, khaʾ, ʿayn, baʾ* or *haʾ*. The Syriac script has 22 letters; the Hebrew script [93] is the same as the Syriac except that its letters are not joined together and the form of some of them do not resemble their Syriac counterparts. The Himyarite script, which is the writing of Himyar,[328] known as the *musnad*, is close to Syriac.[329] The letters of the Arabic script, in its two calligraphic styles,[330] number 29. Apart from these, the scripts of the various nations are very similar to one another. As for the Persians, besides the two writings that Zoroaster created for them, they have five more, some of which have been affected by the Nabaṭi language and some not.[331] We adduced an explanation of all of this in our books that we have previously cited. (We also set out there) the miracles, indications and signs of Zoroaster that they recount and their belief in the five ancient ones, namely Ohrmazd,[332] who is God the Mighty and Glorious, Ahriman, who is Satan the Evil One, *kāh*, which is time,[333] *jāy*, which is place,[334] and *hūm*, which is a pure intoxicant.[335] (We also set out) their arguments for these beliefs, the reason for their veneration of the two lights and of the other lights, the distinction they make between fire and light, their discussion

---

327 This is close to the description of the religious script, except for 160 instead of 60 characters, and it may be that Masʿudi has mistakenly made two scripts out of one.

328 A south Arabian people that ruled much of what is now Yemen *ca.* 280–525.

329 This is not true; the Himyarite language was written in the Sabaic script, which represents a different branch of the alphabet to the Phoenician–Aramaic one, having 29 letters rather than 22. The word *musnad*, which means 'supported, propped up' in Arabic, is used to refer to the Sabaic script.

330 Possibly intending the Kufic/angular and Naskhi/cursive styles.

331 Probably what Masʿudi is alluding to here is that some scripts, such as Pahlavi, use Aramaic heterograms, whereas some, such as Pazand, do not.

332 Arabic: *ūrmazd*, which is pretty much the same as the MP and NP forms of the name. In English the name is often given in the OP form: Ahuramazda, literally 'wise lord' or 'lord of wisdom' (depending whether one takes *mazda* to be a noun or an adjective).

333 Persian *gāh*; it does not mean abstract time, but a period of time, in particular the five periods into which the day is divided, each devoted to a different prayer.

334 This is the NP form; MP = *gyāg*.

335 *Hūm*, Avestan *haoma* (*EIr*, s.v.), refers to a plant with stimulative properties and to the drink made from it that was used in certain Zoroastrian rituals. The Arabic terms here, *ṭība* and *khamīr*, are usually translated as 'very sweet/clear wine' and 'ferment' (in the sense of a fermentation agent).

of the beginning of procreation, the story of Maysha, who is Mahla son of Gayumart, and Mayshana, who is Mahlina daughter of Gayumart, and of how the Persians trace their ancestry back to these two persons,[336] and other aspects of their rituals, their ways of worship and the locations of their fire-temples.

The theologians of Islam who have authored books on sects and sought to refute Zoroastrians[337] of the past relate from them that they claim that God pondered and from his pondering arose evil, namely the devil, and that God initially reached a compromise with him and allowed him some time to win him over. However, some of these statements about their beliefs (in the writings of these theologians) are rejected by the Zoroastians, who do not accept them or profess them. It is my opinion [94] that they (the theologians) heard such accounts from their common people (of the Zoroastrians) and attributed them to the whole community.

(Returning to the account of the Persian kings:) Bahman reigned for 112 years and Khumani, his daughter, reigned for 30 years. Dara the Elder b. Bahman reigned for 12 years and Dara b. Dara reigned for 14 years. Then Alexander (the Great) prevailed over the Persian realm for six years.

At the end of the seventh part of our book 'The Meadows of Gold and Mines of Gems' we mentioned for what reason the Persians exaggerated the years of reign of these kings and their hidden motives for doing that, as well as their wars with the kings of the Turks – which they called *baykār*,[338] meaning 'battles' – and with other nations. (We also mentioned there) the campaigns of Rustam b. Dastan against Isfandiyar[339] in the lands of Khurasan, Sijistan and Zabulistan, as well as other happenings and events from their days. In our book 'Accounts of former times, past nations, bygone generations and vanished realms that fate has extinguished', we noted the dispute over whether the first Persians were Chaldaeans

---

336 These two are evidently the same as Hamza's Masha and Mashyana (see Hamza, 24 and 65 above).

337 The text just has 'these people', but since he has been talking about Zoroastrians one assumes that they are meant, although Muslim authors tended to lump all dualists together as *Majūs*/Zoroastrian or, more pejoratively, as *zindīqs*/dualist heretics (especially Manichaeans).

338 Representing Persian *paygār*. Mas'udi, *Murūj*, 2.44, says that Ibn al-Muqaffa' translated a *Kitāb al-Baykār*, which dealt with the wars of Isfandiyar against the Turks and other peoples.

339 This Isfandiyar is the son of the Kayanid Bishtasb and Rustam is a great warrior of that time. Their titanic combat is recounted in Firdawsi's *Shāh-nāmah* and numerous illustrations of their encounters survive.

or whether kingship had passed to them from the Chaldaeans and the opinion of those who say that the rule of the Chaldeans passed to the Assyrians, kings of Mosul,[340] only following a period of internal divisions and strife which wiped them out. (We also noted there) those who say that the first kingdom established in the clime of Babel after the Flood was that of Nimrod the Tyrant and of the Nimrodites,[341] his successors, in agreement with what the Torah says, and other controversies over peoples whose eras are far removed from ours and whose histories have not come down to us. God the Mighty and Glorious has forbidden research into the conditions of past centuries and ancient peoples to anyone besides Him because of the antiquity of their times and the remoteness of their days. Thus God said: 'Did there not come to them the report of those [95] who were before them: the people of Noah, 'Ad and Thamud,[342] and those who came after? No one knows them but God.'

Mention of what has been ascertained of the enumeration of the Petty Kings, the fourth order of the kings of the Persians, and the total of years that they reigned
The Petty Kings numbered about 100, of Persian, Nabaṭ and Arab origin (whose empire stretched) from the border of the land of Athur, which is Mosul, to the (eastern) extremity of the territory of the Persians. The greatest of them and those whom the rest obeyed were the Arsacids, descendants of Ashaghan b. Ash the Tyrant b. Siyawukhsh b. Kay Kawus the king. In winter they resided in Iraq and in summer in Shiz in the land of Azerbaijan. There, still today, are the wondrous remains of buildings and paintings in various amazing hues depicting the planets, the stars and the world with its lands and seas, humans, plants, animals and other marvels. There they had a fire-temple, which was venerated by all the other Persian dynasties, and it was called Ādharkhush, *ādhar* being one of the names for fire in Persian and *khush* meaning 'good'.[343] On his

340 Or rather Niniveh, the ruins of which lay only a short distance from the Muslim settlement of Mosul.
341 Nimrod (*namrūd*) is portrayed as the archetypal tyrant in Muslim tradition. His descendants are collectively referred to as the Nimrods (*al-Namārida*). Muslim historians draw their information from the Bible, where Nimrod is a great-grandson of Noah and a 'mighty one in the land', a great king of Mesopotamia.
342 Two of the original Arabian tribes that were wiped out before Islam; the quotation here is from Qur'an 9:70 and 14:9.
343 Mas'udi is referring to the archaeological site known as Takht-i Sulayman in north-west Iran, which has very substantial pre-Islamic ruins. It is considered to be the location of the

accession, every king of Persia would visit it, on foot, in veneration of it, and he would make vows and bring valuable presents and money. (They also ruled)[344] other countries besides, such as the Mahat and the land of Jibal.

Among the Petty Kings only the Arsacids are taken account of in the histories and biographies because of the strength of their authority and the continuity of their rule, as we have just mentioned. The first who is reckoned to belong to them is Ashak b. Ashak b. Ardawan b. Ashaghan b. Ash the Tyrant b. Siyawukhsh b. Kay Kawus the king, and he reigned for 10 years. [96] Then followed Shabur b. Ashak, who was king for 60 years; Gudarz (b. Shabur) b. Ashak, who reigned for 10 years; Bizan b. Shabur, 21 years; Gudarz b. Bizan, 19 years; Narsi b. Bizan, 40 years; Hurmuz b. Bizan, 19 years; Ardawan the Elder, 12 years; Khusraw b. Ardawan, 40 years; Balash b. Khusraw, 24 years; and Ardawan the Younger, 13 years.[345] This is the sum of what is known of the enumeration of the Petty Kings and the years of their reigns; they number 11 and ruled for a total of 268 years. There were other kings that belonged to this category, but their names and the duration of their reigns are unknown and are not recorded in any books of the Persians or any biographical histories of kings,[346] because of the troubled state of government in those times, the contention arising from disagreement and disunity, the predominance acquired by each king in his region and lastly because of something that Ardashir son of Babak did, which we will mention at the end of this chapter.

According to those who are concerned with the histories of ancient nations and their kings, the correct figure for the duration of the era of the Petty Kings from the killing of Dara, that is Dara b. Dara, and the rise of Ardashir b. Babak is 513 years. Here is how we arrive at that. From the beginning of the year in which Alexander, son of Philip, the king of Macedonia, became king, up to our time, which is the year 345 AH (956 CE), is 1267 years.[347] If we subtract from that the difference between the

---

sanctuary of Adur Gushnasp, one of the most revered fire-temples of the Sasanid period; see *EIr*, 'Ādur Gušnasp' and Wiesehöfer, 'Takht-i Sulayman'. Mas'udi's analysis of the Persian meaning of the name is correct: *ādhar*/fire (see n. 215 above) plus *khush*/good.

344 Some words would appear to be missing here or the following words are misplaced.

345 Mas'udi has the same number of Arsacid kings as Hamza, but his fourth and eighth kings are named Bizan and Ardawan (the Elder) respectively, as also in Tabari (1.707), whereas Hamza has Wanhan and Firuz.

346 Arabic: *siyar al-mulūk*.

347 AD 956 = 1267 according to the Seleucid era, which began not when Alexander

years 345 and 32 AH[348] – the year in which King Yazdagird b. Shahriyar was killed – which is 313 years, and (if we also subtract) the number of years that the Sasanid Persians ruled, which was [97] 439 years, that which remains after that is the number of years from the killing of Dara, who was Dara b. Dara, by Alexander and the rise of Ardashir b. Babak, namely 513 years. This is therefore the duration of the rule of the Petty Kings.[349]

We have reported all that has been said about that, with explanation and elucidation, in our book 'Accounts of Former Times' and in our sequel to that, 'The Intermediate Book', and then also in the seventh part of the 'Meadows of Gold and Mines of Gems' in its recent edition, which we have just finalised at this time. It has many necessary additions, alterations of sense and changes of expressions, and is double the size of the first edition, which we composed in the year 332 (AD 943–44). We only mention this because of the prevalence of that (first) edition, which is found in the hands of many people. (We also discussed this subject) in our book 'The Categories of Knowledge and the Events of Past Times', in the book 'Treasures of the Sciences and Events of Past Times', and then in the book 'Remembrance of the Events of Past Ages', which this present book follows and is based upon, and it is the seventh in this series (of historiographical works). Each one of these books follows on from the one before it and is based upon it. Moreover, we have made each book distinct in its teachings and expression from the others, except for certain things that had to be included (in more than one of the books).

As regards the era of Alexander (the Great) there exists a substantial difference between the Persians and other nations that has been neglected by many people. It is one of the religious and state secrets of the Persians scarcely known to any except the priests and clerics and to men of learning and knowledge, as we witnessed in the provinces of Fars, Kirman and

became king but when Seleucus Nicator reconquered Babylon, marking the beginning of the Seleucid Empire (312–311 BC).

348 32 AH = AD 652–53. The more commonly accepted date is 31 AH; e.g. Hamza, 63, above, and Tabari, 1.2872.

349 This figure of 513 years for the duration of Arsacid rule is a lot closer to the real figure (approximately 475 years) than the one he gives in the previous paragraph of 268 years, which is the usual estimate found in Muslim sources, give or take a couple of years (i.e. 266–70 years; see n. 71 above), and it is a shame that Mas'udi is not more explicit about his source for it. He does, however, make a couple of errors: the Seleucid era is a solar one, whereas the Hijra era is a lunar one; the Sasanids ruled for 427 years, not 439; Darius III was killed by Alexander in 330 BC, but the Arsacids did not come to power until around 250 BC.

elsewhere in the lands of the Persians. It is not found in any of the books composed about the history of the Persians or in books of biographies and chronologies. It resides in the fact that Zoroaster b. Burshasb b. Isbiman [98] stated in the Avesta, which is in their view the book sent down (by God) to him, that their rule would be shaken after 300 years but that their religion would survive. However, at the end of 1000 years their rule and their religion would disappear altogether. Now between Zoroaster and Alexander there were about 300 years, for Zoroaster appeared in the reign of Kay Bishtasb b. Kay Luhrasb, according to the report of him that we presented above in the earlier part of this book, and Ardashir b. Babak seized power and reunited the kingdoms 510 years or so after Alexander. He (Ardashir) observed that the time left before the completion of the millennium was only about 200 years and so he sought to extend the (life of the) empire by a further 200 years, for he feared that after 200 years had passed the people would cease to support the empire and defend it, trusting in the report of their prophet about its demise. He therefore deducted about half of the 510 years or so that were between him and Alexander, and he recorded only the Petty Kings who ruled in these years (that he acknowledged) and omitted the rest. He thereafter proclaimed in his realm that his emergence and subjugation of the Petty Kings and killing of Ardawan, who was the most powerful of them and had the greatest army, occurred only in the year 260 after Alexander. Thus he instigated this chronology and it became widespread among the people. This is why the disagreement arose between the Persians and other nations and why the chronology of the years of the Petty Kings became so confused.[350]

Ardashir b. Babak recalled this at the end of the testament on the conduct of religion and government that he bequeathed to the sons that succeeded him as king.[351] He said: 'Were it not for the certainty of the destruction that will befall (the empire) at the end of the millennium, I would have supposed that I were leaving you in my will what, if you held fast to it, would ensure your posterity as long as night and day endured. However, when the days of destruction arrive, you will have heeded your

---

350 Mas'udi's analysis of the problem is correct – the Persians (followed by the Muslims) reckon only about 260–70 years between Alexander and Ardashir, whereas the true figure is about twice that. We do not really know why that is; Mas'udi's solution is ingenious, though rather far-fetched. See *EIr*, 'Arsacids vi: Arsacid chronology'.

351 This refers to a text that survives only in Arabic versions, but which purports to derive from Ardashir himself and which offers political advice to his son and/or his successors. See Grignaschi, 'Les règles d'Ardashir' and 'Quelques Spécimens', 2–4.

passions, cast aside your own judgements, empowered the worst of you and humiliated **[99]** the best of you.'

This was mentioned also by Tansar, the priest of Ardashir, propagandist for him and herald of his rise, who, at the end of his letter to Majushnas,[352] lord of the mountainous regions of Dabawand, Rayy, Tabaristan, Daylam and Jilan, said: 'If we did not know that tribulations will befall (the empire) at the end of the millennium, we would say that the King of Kings has consolidated the rule in perpetuity. However, we do know that tribulations are due at the end of the millennium, and the reason for it is the neglect of royal authority, the constraining of what was free and the freeing of what was constrained. This is the destruction from which there is no escape. Yet, although we are among those who are condemned to perish, we must strive for the survival (of the empire) and plan for it until the onset of the destruction. So be one of those people, do not aid perdition against yourself and your fellows, for it is strong enough to need no aid. Rather, you need to help yourself in whatever way will present you favourably in the abode of perdition and will benefit you in the house of posterity. We ask God that He will give you a place at the most elevated rank and the highest degree.'

Mention of the kings of the second Persians, who are the Sasanids: the fifth order of their kings

The first of them was Ardashir [I] b. Babak b. Sasan b. Babak, a descendant of Bahman b. Isfandiyar b. Kay Bishtasb b. Kay Luhrasb. It is he who put an end to the Petty Kings and therefore his rule was called the reign of unification. He was king for 14 years and a few months, **[100]** and then he renounced the rule and handed it to his son Shabur [I] in order to devote himself to religious worship. His reign is reckoned from the killing of King Ardawan, who was one of the greatest of the Petty Kings of Iraq. We have already mentioned[353] the reason for the rise to

---

352 'The Letter of Tansar' is a political tract ostensibly written by Tansar to Gushtasb (Mas'udi's Majushnas), a ruler in northern Iran, encouraging him to submit to Ardashir and, more generally, justifying Sasanid rule and political conduct. It is preserved in the 'History of Tabaristan' by Ibn Isfandiyar (d. *ca.* 1220), who translated it into New Persian from an Arabic version allegedly rendered from MP by Ibn al-Muqaffa'. See Boyce, *Tansar*, who discusses both Tansar and the 'Letter' in her introduction.

353 Unusually, he does not specify where he mentioned it, unless he is just referring to his remarks in the previous paragraph; in his *Muruj*, 2.151–62 (ch. 24), he talks at length about Ardashir, but does not allude to Tansar.

prominence of Ardashir and given an account of his propagandist, Tansar the Ascetic, whom many people called Dawshar and who was a Platonist and one of the sons of the Petty Kings.[354] (We also recounted how) his father's kingdom in Fars had passed to him, but he had given it up and become an advocate for Ardashir, spreading news of his rise, sending out propagandists throughout the land for that purpose and paving the way for the kingdom to be united under him. Thus Ardashir vanquished all the Petty Kings. Tansar wrote beautiful epistles on the ways of conducting royal and religious affairs, giving information about Ardashir and his circumstances and excusing his innovations in matters of religion and state that were not known to any of the kings before him, but which were right and necessary given the conditions of that time. Among these epistles is the one to the aforementioned Majushnas and his epistle to the king of India, and more besides.

The second (of these kings) was Shabur [I] b. Ardashir, who reigned for 31 years and six months. It was in his days that Mani lived, to whom the Manichaean dualists[355] were affiliated. The third (king) was Hurmuz [I] b. Shabur, who reigned for a year and 10 months. The fourth was Bahram [I] b. Hurmuz, who reigned three years and three months, and who put Mani to death, together with a large number of his followers, in the city of Shabur in Fars. The fifth was Bahram [II] b. Bahram, who reigned for 17 years, or 18 according to others. The sixth was Bahram [III] b. Bahram [II], who reigned for four years and four months. The seventh was Narsi b. Bahram b. Bahram, who reigned for nine years and six months. The eighth was Hurmuz [II] b. Narsi, who reigned for seven years and five months. The ninth was Shabur [II], the Lord of the Shoulders, b. Hurmuz, who reigned for four years. The tenth was Ardashir [II] b. Hurmuz, who reigned four years. The eleventh was Shabur [III] b. Shabur, the Lord of the

---

354 We know very little about Tansar, so it is not possible to say whether Mas'udi's biographical information about him here is correct. The earliest source to mention him, the ninth-century Zoroastrian anthology known as the *Denkard*, simply says that he was a religious authority (*hirbadh*) and was close to Ardashir, helping him collect and collate the Zoroastrian texts that had become dispersed (see Boyce, *Tansar*, 5–7). Dawshar is evidently just a corruption of Tansar (in Book Pahlavi the letter for w is the same as that for n; a shift between d and t is common in Persian; and s and sh are distinguished in Arabic only by dots).

355 Arabic: *aṣḥāb al-ithnayn*. Dualism refers to any doctrine that stresses the existence of two independent principles/gods in the universe. Manichaeans, followers of the prophet Mani, are just one among many who fall into this category. For an account of Mani see Ya'qubi, 180–82, below.

Shoulders, who reigned for five years [101] and four months. The twelfth was Bahram [IV] b. Shabur, who reigned for 11 years. The thirteenth was Yazdagird [I] the Sinner b. Shabur, who reigned for 21 years. The fourteenth was Bahram [V] Gur b. Yazdagird, who reigned for 23 years. He is the one who grew up with the king of Hira and (subsequently) built for him the castle of Khawarnaq[356] in circumstances that we have already mentioned in our earlier works. He was fluent in Arabic and composed in it some good poems. The fifteenth was Yazdagird [II] b. Bahram Gur, who reigned for 18 years, four months and seven days. The sixteenth was Firuz [I] b. Yazdagird, who reigned for 27 years and who was killed by Akhshunwar, king of the Hephthalites.[357] The seventeenth was Balash b. Firuz, who reigned for four years.

The eighteenth was Qubad [I] b. Firuz, who reigned for 43 years. In his time, there lived the priest Mazdak, who interpreted the book of Zoroaster called the Avesta, giving it a hidden meaning opposed to its external one. He is considered the first of the adepts of esoteric interpretation, hidden truths and abandonment of external meanings in the religion of Zoroaster, and to him are attributed the Mazdakites.[358] The nineteenth was (Khusraw I) Anusharwan b. Qubad, who reigned for 48 years and who killed Mazdak and his followers. In our book 'The Treasuries of Religion and the Secret of the Worlds' we set out the difference between the belief of Mazdak and his sect concerning esoteric interpretation and that of Mani, and the difference between Mani and the dualists who preceded him, such as Ibn Daysan, Marcion and others.[359] (And we set out) what all (dualists) believe concerning the two active principles, namely that one of them is good, praiseworthy and desirable, whereas the other is malevolent, reprehensible and to be feared, and the difference between these (pre-Islamic dualists)

---

356 Hira was a capital of the Lakhmid tribe, Arab allies of Persia; Bahram Gur's upbringing with this tribe is narrated at length in a number of Arabic sources (e.g. Tabari, 1.850–58). The palace of Khawarnaq apparently lay a little to the east of Hira, near modern Najaf, and was celebrated for its grandeur in many Arabic poems, both before and after the rise of Islam.

357 See Tabari, 1.874–80, and Appendix 2 below for discussion of this episode.

358 For the idea that Mazdak gave 'an esoteric explanation to the Avesta' see Daryaee, *Sasanian Persia*, 86–88. In general, it is the socio-political aspect of Mazdak's revolt that is emphasised; see Crone, 'Kavad's Heresy'.

359 Ibn Daysan, better known by the Syriac form of his name: Bardaisan (d. 222), believed in one God, but also accorded a role to celestial bodies and spoke of the mixing of light/good and darkness/evil; Marcion (d. 160) made a distinction between the creator god of the Old Testament and the transcendent compassionate god of the Gospel.

and the beliefs of the *Bāṭiniyya*, the practitioners of esoteric interpretation at this time.[360] Anusharwan was the first to lay down the principles of the land tax and clarify its rules; **[102]** before this there was share-cropping.[361] His father Qubad had initiated this change in his last days, but had not completed it. We commented on this in our book 'Remembrance of the Events of Past Ages' in the chapter 'Mention of the Sawad, its surface area, description of its cantons and its divisions, and of Iraq, the limits of its territory and its dimensions in length and breadth from end to end'.

The twentieth (king) was Hurmuz [IV] b. Anusharwan, who reigned for 12 years. Bahram Chobin al-Razi[362] rose up against him and this ended up with Hurmuz's eyes being gouged out. No other king of the Persians either before or after him ever suffered this fate. The twenty-first was Khusraw [II] Abarwiz b. Hurmuz, who reigned for 38 years and who was killed by his son Shirawayh b. Abarwiz. The twenty-second was Shirawayh b. Abarwiz, murderer of his father; his (regnal) name was Qubad [II] and he reigned for six months. The twenty-third was Ardashir [III] b. Shirawayh, who reigned for a year and six months. The twenty-fourth was Shahrbaraz, who reigned for 40 days. We gave the history of him and his death and the death of other Persian knights and braves according to their generations, both kings and other figures whose preeminence, superiority and courage are agreed upon, in our book entitled 'The Book of the Deaths of the Persian Knights', which is a reply to 'Abu 'Ubayda Ma'mar b. al-Muthanna's[363] book 'Deaths of the Arab Knights'.

The twenty-fifth (king) was Khusraw [III] b. Qubad, who reigned for three months. The twenty-sixth was Buran, daughter of Khusraw Abarwiz, who reigned for a year and six months. Her reign began in the second year of the Hijra.[364] Concerning her the Messenger of God, may God pray for

---

360   The Arabic word *bāṭin* means 'inner', and the term *Bāṭiniyya* can refer generically to all who seek to discern the inner/hidden truths behind the external/apparent meaning of Scripture and the Law, but it came to be applied in particular to the Isma'ili Shi'ites, who were gaining adherents across the Islamic world in the tenth century.

361   The word for land-tax here is *kharāj* and for share-cropping *muqāsama* (= payment of a share of the harvest to the landlord). On this topic see Rubin, 'Reforms of Khusro'.

362   Bahram Chobin of Rayy (= al-Razi) was a very successful military commander, scoring major victories against the Turks and Byzantines, and so when slighted by Hurmuz IV he led a revolt against the Sasanid family and for a year (590–91) held power himself, minting coins in his own name. A detailed account of him and his fate is given by Ya'qubi, 188–90, below.

363   On the antiquarian Abu 'Ubayda (d. 825) see the Introduction above.

364   This would be 623–24, whereas Buran ruled 630–31.

him and grant him peace, said, when he heard of her accession and of the disunity and civil strife among them: 'A people does not flourish **[103]** whose affairs are managed by a woman.' The twenty-seventh was Firuz [II] Jushnasbandah, who reigned for six months. The twenty-eighth was Azarmidukht, daughter of Khusraw [II] Abarwiz, who reigned for six months. Khurra Hurmuz the Azeri, the military commander of Khurasan and the father of the Rustam who was in charge of (the battle of) Qadisiyya, attended her court and became enamoured of her and wrote asking to meet with her. She agreed upon a night, but ordered the chief of her guard to assassinate him, and this was done.[365] Rustam deputised for his father in Khurasan, or some say Azerbaijan and Armenia, and when he heard of her murder of his father he marched against the queen and killed her.[366] This happened in the tenth year of the Hijra (631–32 CE). The twenty-ninth (king) was Farrukhzad Khusraw b. Abarwiz,[367] who reigned for a year. The thirtieth was Yazdagird [III] b. Shahriyar b. Khusraw Abarwiz b. Hurmuz b. Anusharwan b. Qubad b. Firuz b. Yazdagird b. Bahram Gur b. Yazdagird the Sinner b. Shabur the Younger b. Shabur the Elder, Lord of the Shoulders, b. Hurmuz b. Narsi b. Bahram b. Bahram b. Bahram b. Hurmuz b. Shabur b. Ardashir b. Babak, who reigned for 20 years and is the last of their kings. He was killed at Merv in the land of Khurasan, in the year 32,[368] during the caliphate of 'Uthman b. 'Affan.

[Miscellaneous Information about the Persians]

The Persians had many offices, the most senior of which were five in number, ranking between the king and his subjects.[369] The first and highest of them was the *mūbadh*, meaning 'custodian of religion', because 'religion' in their

---

365 Sebeos, 130, has the same storyline, but applies it to Buran, not Azarmidukht; given Sebeos' nearness in time to the event, he is more likely to be correct. He also recounts the assassination of Khurra Hurmuz (Armenian: Khorokh Ormizd), whom he calls 'prince of the region of Azerbaijan' (Armenian: Atrpatakan), confirming the surname (al-Ādharī) that Mas'udi gives him.

366 Sebeos, 132, confirms that the son of Khurra Hurmuz was called Rustam and that he took over control of Azerbaijan from his father, but his statement regarding Buran that 'she held the throne for two years and then died' casts doubt on the account of Rustam's revenge.

367 Also called Khurrazad Khusraw; see n. 86 above.

368 That is, 652–53. Usually 31 AH is given as the year of Yazadagird's death (see n. 348 above).

369 On the administration of the Sasanid Empire see Daryaee, *Sasanian Persia*, ch. 5.

language is *mū* and *badh* means 'custodian'.[370] The *mūbadhān mūbadh* is the chief of the priests and the chief judge; whose rank was very high in their estimation, close to that of prophets.[371] The *hirbadhs*[372] are below the *mūbadhs* in the hierarchy. The second (senior office) was the vizier, whose title was *buzurg framadār,* which means 'the greatest officer'.[373] The third was the *iṣbahbadh,* who was the commander-in-chief, and the term means 'custodian of the army', because 'army' [104] is *iṣbah* and *badh* means 'custodian', as we have said before.[374] The fourth was the *dibīrbadh,* which means 'custodian of the scribes'. The fifth was the *hūtukhshah badh,*[375] which means 'custodian of all those who work with their hands', such as craftsmen, peasants, merchants and others. Their chief, who was from among them, was called *wāstaryūsh.*[376] These (five groups of officials) were managers on behalf of the king, executors of his affairs and intermediaries between the king and his subjects. As for the *marzbān,* he oversaw the borders, for *marz* means 'border' in their language and *bān* 'guard'. There were four *marzbāns,* one each for the east, the west, the north and the south, each in charge of one quarter of the empire.[377]

The Persians have a book called 'The Book of the Throne',[378] in which (are listed) all the offices of the Persian Empire, which amount to 600

---

370 Arabic: *ḥāfiẓ.* Given that MP (and NP) *bad* or *badh* means 'lord, master', one would have expected Mas'udi to translate it by the Arabic word *ṣāḥib.*

371 See n. 17 above, especially the comments of Agathias on the high status of the *mūbadh.*

372 Often translated by a term such as teacher-priest, as the office seems to have had an instructional element to it.

373 Arabic: *akbar ma'mūr. Buzurg* does mean 'great, grand' in Persian; *framan* means 'order, command', and *framadār* means something like 'giver of orders'. Mas'udi equates it here with the vizier, the post of chief minister which developed under the Abbasids in the late eighth/early ninth century.

374 MP: *spāhbed* = general, commander, and MP: *spāh* = army (probably from OP: *spada* = group of people).

375 MP: *hūtūkhsh* = 'artisan'. It should be noted that this reading is an emendation of the editor, albeit a reasonable one; the manuscripts have *'sthsh.*

376 This word just means 'cultivator' or 'husbandman', who belonged to a different social group to the artisan. Possibly Mas'udi has missed a few words, and he meant to speak of the chief of the cultivators (given as *wāstaryūshan sālār* in Tabari, 1.869) separately from the chief of the artisans.

377 Mas'udi is correct in his explanation of both the meaning of *marzbān* (border + guard) and its function. The point about there being four *marzbāns* is a confused reflection of Khusraw I's breaking up of the single office of commander-in-chief of the army into four posts, each responsible for a specific region of the empire; the usual title of this office was *spāhbad,* as we know from late Sasanid seals (Gyselen, *Four Generals*).

378 *Kah-nāmāh*; this conveys MP-NP *gāh* ('throne') + NP *nāmah* ('book'). It was probably

according to their classification of them. This book is from the complete work the *Ā'īn-Nāmāh*, the meaning of which is 'The Book of Protocols'.[379] It is a huge text of several thousands of pages, and it is rare to find a complete copy except with the priests or others in positions of authority. At the time of the writing of this history, in the year 345, the (chief) priest of the Persians for the province of Jibal, Iraq and the rest of the lands of the Persians is Anmādh b. Asharhisht.[380] The (chief) priest before him was Isfandiyar b. Adharbad b. Anmīdh,[381] **[105]** who was put to death by (the caliph) Radi in Baghdad in the year 325.[382] We presented an account of him and the tale of his death and the reasons given for it together with (an account of) the Carmathian Sulayman b. Hasan b. Bahram al-Jannabi, sovereign of Bahrain,[383] in the section on Radi in our book 'Meadows of Gold and Mines of Gems'.

Those who have studied the histories of kings and nations disagree about the genealogies of the Persians, the names of their kings and the lengths of their reigns. We only record what the Persians themselves say on these matters, disregarding (the information supplied by) other nations, such as the Israelites, the Greeks or the Romans, since what they profess is contrary to what the Persians relate. And it is more sound to take this data from the Persians, even though their histories have been effaced, their glorious deeds forgotten and their traditions disrupted on account of the passage of time and the flow of events. In any case, we recount only a small portion of it. The Persians were men of great power and high nobility, men of authority and government, chivalrous in battle and

something like the Arabic 'Book of the Crown' (*Kitāb al-Tāj*) attributed to the author Jahiz (d. 868), which deals with court etiquette.

379 Arabic: *kitāb al-rusūm*. The NP word *āyīn* (MP: *ēwēn*) means the proper way to do things, so dictionaries define it with words such as rites, rules, customs, manners etc. Ibn Qutayba cites the *Āyīn* 12 times in his 'Choice Narratives' (*'Uyūn al-akhbār*) for observations about social etiquette, rules of polo, archery and war, and the correct way to prognosticate. See *EIr*, 'Āīn-nāma'; Askari, *Shāhnāma*, 133–37 (on Ardashir's *āyīn*).

380 This must be Emed son of Asharwahist, who composed a well-known question-and-answer collection (*riwāyat*) for the use of the Zoroastrian clergy in the early tenth century; see *EIr*, 'Ēmēd ī Ašawahištān'.

381 Isfandiyar was the son of Adharbad (or Adurbad) son of Emed, who was the final redactor of the Zoroastrian anthology known as the *Denkard*. See *EIr*, 'Ādurbād Ēmēdān'.

382 325 AH = AD 937. Al-Radi (billah) was the twentieth Abbasid caliph (934–40). Baghdad is here referred to by its nickname 'city of peace' (*madīnat al-salām*).

383 The Carmathians (*qarāmiṭa*) were a branch of the Isma'ili Shi'a found mainly in south Iraq and east Arabia. Sulayman al-Jannabi was an early leader of theirs who gained notoriety when in 930 he attacked Mecca and carried off the black stone from its sanctuary.

steadfast in combat. Nations paid them tribute and were led to pay them obeisance out of fear of their power and the size of their army.

We presented the disagreement of people over the genealogies of the Persians and the divergence of their reports in the seventh part of our book 'The Meadows of Gold and Mines of Gems'. The Babylonians had kings who are mentioned in many books and astronomical tables, such as Nimrod, the Nimrodites who succeeded him, Sennacherib, Nebuchadnezzar and his sons who succeeded him, and others.[384] We will not bother to comment on them in this book owing to the disputes concerning their number, their names, [106] the years of their reigns and the order of precedence of their days. The Persians state that these Babylonian kings were only deputies of their ancient kings and governors over Iraq and the neighbouring lands in the west, whilst the capital of their empire was in Balkh until they left it to live in Mada'in in the land of Iraq. The first to do this was Khumani, daughter of Bahman b. Isfandiyar.

Mas'udi said: I saw in a house in Istakhr, in the province of Fars, in the year 303 (AD 915–16), in the house of one of the noblest Persian families, an impressive book. It contained much about their sciences and accounts of their kings, their buildings and their government that I have not found in any of the Persian books like the 'Book of Lords', the 'Book of Ceremonies' or the 'Book of the Throne' or the like.[385] In it were portraits of the kings of Persia from the family of Sasan, 27 kings in all, 25 men and two women. Each one of them had been painted on the day he died, whether he had died young or old, with his finery, his crown, the streaks of his beard and the features of his face.[386] They (the Sasanids) reigned over the land for 433 years, one month and seven days. When one of their kings died, they drew him according to his likeness and hung up the portrait in the treasury so that the image of the dead might not be hidden from the living. Every king who had been in battle (was represented) standing, and all those engaged in government (were represented) sitting. A biography (was written) of each one of them concerning (his relation to) his nobles and commoners and the important events and major occurrences that took place during his reign.

The history of this book is that it was copied from (a text) found in the treasury of the kings of Persia in the middle of (the month of) Jumada II

---

384 These kings are rendered in Arabic as: Nimrūd, Sanḥārīb and Bukht Naṣṣar.
385 Arabic: *Khudāy-nāmāh, Ā'īn-nāmāh, Kah-nāmāh*.
386 This would appear to be the same book as is used by Hamza for his description of the portraits of Sasanid rulers (see above).

of the year 113 (August 731). It was translated from Persian into Arabic for Hisham b. 'Abd al-Malik b. Marwan.[387] The first of their kings (to be represented) in it was Ardashir [I];[388] his vest in his portrait is red and speckled, his trousers sky-blue and his crown green on gold, in his hand is a lance and he is standing. The last of them was Yazdagird [III] b. [107] Shahriyar b. Khusraw Abarwiz; his vest is green and embroidered, his trousers sky-blue and embroidered, his crown dark red, he has a lance in one hand and is resting on his sword.[389] (These portraits were made) with all kinds of foreign dyes the like of which are not found at this time (involving) dissolved gold and silver and scraped copper. The folios were purple in colour, of an amazing dye; because of its fineness and the mastery of its production I do not know whether it was paper or parchment.

We presented all of this in the seventh part of our book 'The Meadows of Gold and Mines of Gems', which comprises the history of the first Persians, who are the Kayanids and the Petty Kings – the Arsacids, the Ardawanids[390] and others – and of the Sasanids, their dynasties, lineages and kings up to Yazdagird [III] b. Shahriyar, the last of them, who had offspring and who did not, their biographies, their campaigns and the ploys and stratagems they employed during them.[391] (It recounts also) the nature of their rule over Iraq, the end of the kingdom of the Nabat, both the Ardawanid and Armenian branches, the ways in which they managed religion and state in its public and private aspects, their testaments, speeches and letters, the number of years of their reigns, their banners

387 The tenth Umayyad caliph, who reigned 724–43. He is the first caliph to take an interest in matters Persian, and appointed a chief secretary, 'Abd al-Hamid al-Katib, of Persian ancestry.

388 Ardashir is the first king for whom Hamza includes descriptions; see the previous note but one above.

389 The description of the regalia of these two rulers matches fairly exactly that given by Hamza, 62, above, reinforcing the point made in n. 386 above.

390 Presumably Mas'udi is referring here to the four Arsacid kings who bore the name Ardawan/Artabanus (EIr, 'Artabanus: Arsacid Kings'), beginning with Ardawan/Artabanus I (ca. 127–123 BC). However, Mas'udi seems to regard them as distinct from the Arsacids, and below and in his Muruj (2.134) he describes them as 'kings of the Nabat', who ruled in Iraq.

391 Mas'udi does indeed include a long section on the Persians in his work 'The Meadows of Gold' (Muruj, 2.105–241 = chs 21–24), but it still gives only historical information, proceeding king by king and dynasty by dynasty (it is longer because it is padded with speeches, letters and anecdotes). For the cultural and material aspects of their civilisation we have to consult, he says there, 'our earlier works' (ibid., 2.239).

and the events and incidents that took place in their times. (It recounts also) the beginning and rise of the religion of Zoroastrianism, the history of their prophet Zoroaster and his revelation, the seven scripts in which they wrote, including the letters and specific uses of each one of them, the festivals of Nawruz and Mihrajan,[392] the reason (behind the dating) of each Nawruz and other things to do with festivals and the pretext for their lighting of fires, pouring of waters and wearing a *kustīj* around their waist, just as the Christians wear a *zunnār*.[393] (It recounts also) the foundations of kingship and people's need of kings and government, the events announcing the passing of the rule of the Persians to the Arabs, the indications and signs of this that they transmitted and came to expect on the authority of their ancestors and the precautions of their kings against its occurrence, their various customs in regard to food, drink, **[108]** dress, riding animals,[394] residences and the like, their laws for nobles and commoners, the cities they built, the provinces they constituted, the water canals they dug, the marvellous buildings that they have left traces of all over the land. (It recounts also) the temples of fire and the reason they venerate it, their beliefs about the degrees of light, the difference between light and fire, and the opposites of light and their degrees, the ranks of royal and religious offices, such as the *marzbāns, isbahbadhs, hirbadhs, mūbadhs* and what is below them, the flags and standards of the Persians, the subdivision of their lineages and what people say about that, their noble houses both from the royal family and outside it, the *shahārija* and the *dihqāns* and the differences between them[395] and those of them who settled in the Sawad and elsewhere before and after the emergence of Islam until now. (Finally it recounts) what the Persians relate about their future time and the return that they expect in the coming days of their kingdom

---

392 The two most popular festivals of the Zoroastrian calendar, which have continued to be celebrated in Iran until the present day. For details about them see *EIr*, 'Nowruz', 'Mehragān'.

393 Both are types of belt that mark adherence to the respective faiths of Zoroastrianism and Christianity.

394 Arabic: *marākib*, which could also mean boats or anything on which one rides, but riding animals seems the most likely.

395 These are two types of rural aristocracy. The *shahārija* (sg. *shahrīj*; Persian: *shahrig/ shahrigān*) seem to be principally in northern Iraq (or at least we encounter them mainly in north Mesopotamian Christian sources), whereas the *dihqāns* are found everywhere (possibly because the term became used in Arabic sources to signify rural landlords/notables in general right across the eastern Islamic lands). See Robinson, *Empires and Elites*, 91–108 (on *shahārija*) and *EIr*, 'Dehqān'.

and its ascendancy and about the indications and warnings of that in the actions of the stars and other signs and signals, such as the appearance of anticipated persons like Bahram Hamawand, Sashiyawus and others,[396] what is told about them and about what will then happen on earth, such as miraculous signs and the stopping of the sun for three days and the like, which will take place for a period they have determined and at times they have ascertained, all things which we decided to omit mention of in this book ...[397] **[110]** ... (In our book we related) very many other things concerning the history of the Persians and of their great achievements, which we took from their learned men, such as the priests and clerics and others acquainted with their past in the land of Iraq, Khuzistan, Fars, Kirman, Sijistan, Jibal-Mahat and other parts of the Persian realm. (All this) we copied from their most accurate and famous books.

396 Bahram Barjawand (or Wahram Warjawand) and the Saoshyant, the former a warrior-king and the latter a saviour figure, are two important characters of Zoroastrian eschatology. See Hoyland, *Seeing Islam*, 321–30, and *EIr*, 'Eschatology i. In Zoroastrianism'.

397 Mas'udi now discusses the fact that 'since the advent of Islam there are Persians who have claimed that their nation belonged to the descendants of Isaac son of Abraham', that Manushihr was a son of Isaac, that the Islamic Empire will pass from the sons of Ishmael to the sons of Isaac, and that the pre-Islamic Persians used to visit the Ka'ba because of its connection with Abraham.

Ahmad al-Yaʿqubi (d. *ca.* 910)

Yaʿqubi wrote the first Arabic universal chronicle that we possess.[398] He has often been confused with an Egyptian scholar by the name of Ahmad ibn Wadih al-ʿAssal, who died in 897, and this death date has come to be applied to Yaʿqubi too. However, since the latter wrote poetry on the death of the caliph Muktafi (902–08), this is certainly too early. In general, though, we know too little about him to give accurate dates for his lifetime. Even his career is unclear. In a geographical text that he wrote, the 'Book of Countries', he tells us that he liked travelling and that he had an ancestor who had worked in the Abbasid government, who is assumed to be the Abbasid client named Wadih who served his masters as a steward. Since he is sometimes called 'Ahmad the scribe' and is said to have worked for the bureau of land-tax in Barqa (modern al-Marj in north-east Libya) in the 870s, we can assume that he followed his ancestor and joined the secretarial class. His universal history certainly displays the receptivity towards foreign learning that is a hallmark of that profession, but that would be much less common among religious scholars. In his pre-Islamic section, for example, he deals with numerous peoples, not just the compulsory three (Israelites, Persians and Arabians), and he evidently has familiarity with their cultures, giving us detailed information about such matters as law, society and cultural achievements. In the section on the Greeks, for example, he gives a detailed summary of the most famous works of Aristotle and Ptolemy.[399]

As regards the Persians, Yaʿqubi is rather dismissive of the first three dynasties, disliking the unscientific feel of the information about them, but his account of the Sasanids is quite full. Of particular interest to us, as I have noted in the introduction above, is the substantial space he allots to the careers of the prophet Mani and the noble warrior and mutineer Bahram Chobin, which he would appear to have drawn from biographies of these two men. Finally, his excursus on the customs of the Persians is

---

398 Dinawari's 'Extended Narratives' is earlier, but he is so focused on Persian material that one should call it a History of Persia rather than a universal chronicle. For a recent discussion of Yaʿqubi's life and works see Anthony, 'Al-Yaʿqūbī'.

399 See Klamroth, 'Auszüge'. Freudenthal and Zonta, 'Ḥabīb ibn Bahrīz', 71–72, show how Yaʿqubi makes direct use of a translation of Nichomachus of Gerasa's *Introduction to Arithmetic* for his summary of that work.

evidently well informed and a useful indication of the extent of knowledge about pre-Islamic Iranian culture in the Muslim world at the turn of the tenth century. In contrast to Hamza and Mas'udi, Ya'qubi does not put the Persians first in his treatment of ancient peoples, which might seem odd for one who opens his 'Book of Countries' by saying: 'I begin with Iraq because it is the centre of the world and the navel of the earth, and I mention (first) Baghdad, because it is in the middle of Iraq and the greatest city with no equal anywhere in the world.' However, he does put them seventh out of the thirteen peoples,[400] nicely in the middle, so perhaps also indicating, very subtly, his Persian propensity.[401]

Translation

[178] The Persian nation claims many things for its kings, the excessive nature of which makes them unacceptable, such as that one of them had many mouths and eyes, another a face of bronze, and that on the shoulders of one were two serpents that fed off human brains. It also claims for them great longevity, the power to drive away death from people, and things like this that are contrary to reason, that are somewhat ludicrous and laughable, and that have no truth to them. However, rational and knowledgeable Persians, including their princes and nobles endowed with honour, pedigree and breeding, will not accept such things as true nor profess them themselves.

We have found that they calculate[402] the (years of) rule of Persia only from the time of Ardashir son of Babak. As for the first of their kings, pertaining to their first kingdom before Ardashir, they are: Gayumart, 70 years; Hushang Pishdad, 40 years; Tahmurath, 30 years; Jamshid, 700 years; Dahak, 1000 years; Afridun, 500 years; Manushihr, 120 years; Afrasiyab, king of the Turks, 120 years; Zaw b. Tahmasb, five years; Kay Qubad, 100 years; Kay Kawus, 120 years; Kay Khusraw, 60 years; Kay Luhrasb, 120 [179] years; Kay Bishtasb, 112 years; Kay Ardashir, 112 years; Khumani daughter of Shahrazad, 30 years; Dara son of Shahrazad, 12 years. Then

---

400 If we take the Israelites at the beginning and the Arabs at the end to be one group each.
401 I translate from the edition of M.T. Houtsma (Leiden, 1883). This is the first translation into English, though Matthew Gordon informs me that the Ya'qubi Translation Project, begun in 1994, will shortly come to fruition, making all of Ya'qubi's extant works available in English (published by Brill).
402 Perhaps understand that they calculate realistically or accurately only from the time of Ardashir.

Alexander, who is called 'Lord of the Two Horns',[403] killed him (Dara) and Persian kingship became fragmented. Kings referred to as the Petty Kings now reigned and their rule was based at Balkh. Genealogists assert that they were the descendants of Gomer son of Japhet son of Noah. They followed the Sabian religion, magnifying the sun, moon, fire and the seven planets; they were not Zoroastrians, but adhered to the prescriptions of the Sabians. Their language was Syriac, which they spoke and which they wrote, and here is an example of the Syriac script.[404] They have a history that has been set down, but since we see that most people dislike it and consider it repugnant, we have omitted it, for our principle is to excise everything offensive.

(We now move on to) the second kingdom from Ardashir son of Babak:

[Ardashir I][405]

Ardashir was crowned as the first of the Persian Zoroastrian kings[406] and his rule was based in Istakhr. Some districts of Persia held out against him and he fought them until he had conquered them. Then he proceeded to Isfahan, and on to Ahwaz and Maysan, before returning to Fars, where he fought a king called Ardawan and killed him. Ardashir was called 'king of kings' and he built a fire-temple at Ardashir Khurra. Next he travelled to northern Mesopotamia, Armenia and Azerbaijan, and on to southern Iraq, which he pacified. He continued on to Khurasan and conquered some of its districts. When he had subjugated the country, he contracted to his son Shabur the rule after him; he crowned him and called him king. Ardashir died after ruling for 14 years.

[Shabur I]

[180] Shabur, son of Ardashir, became king and he raided the land of the Romans. He conquered a number of their cities and enslaved a multitude of Romans. He built the city of Jundishabur and settled in it the Roman prisoners-of-war. The chief of the Romans engineered for him the

---

403 Arabic: *Dhū l-Qarnayn*. This epithet, without mention of Alexander, features in chapter 18 of the Qur'an, applied to a person who travels and erects a wall to keep out Gog and Magog. This sounds like Alexander the Great and this identification has become the standard one in Muslim histories. It is usually assumed that the epithet refers to his portrayal on some coins with the horns of the deity Ammon on his head.

404 Omitted in the mss. Ya'qubi seems to have conflated the Petty Kings with the Chaldeans, who are said to be Syriac-speaking Sabians (see Hamza, 30–31, above; cf. Mas'udi, 90–91).

405 These subheadings are not in the text, but I add them for clarity.

406 Arabic: *mulūk al-furs al-mutamajjisa*, oddly making a verb of the term Majūs, literally: 'Magianising, becoming (of the religion of the) Majūs'.

bridge[407] which is over the river of Tustar and which is a thousand cubits wide. In the days of Shabur son of Ardashir there appeared Mani son of Hammad, the heretic,[408] who denounced Shabur's creed and summoned him to dualism, and Shabur heeded him.

[Mani]

Mani[409] explained that there were two directors of the world, and they were two ancient entities: light and darkness, both of them creators: the creator of good and the creator of evil. Each of the two, light and darkness, contains within itself a name for the five senses: colour, taste, smell, touch and sound, and both of them are seeing, hearing, knowing. Whatever is good and beneficial comes from light and whatever is harmful and distressing comes from darkness. They had been separate, but then they became mixed; the evidence for this is that there was (in the beginning) no material form, but then it came into existence. Darkness was the one that initiated the mixing with the light and they interacted with each other in the same way as the shade and the sun. The proof for the initiatory role of darkness in this mixing is the impossibility of something coming into being from nothing and the fact that the blending of the darkness with the light corrupted the latter. It is, therefore, inconceivable that it was the light that began the process because the light is by its nature good. The proof that both good and evil are ancient entities is that two contradictory actions cannot arise from one substance. Thus cooling can never result from a hot burning fire and that which cools can never give rise to warming; similarly, that which issues from good will not also give rise to evil or vice versa. And the evidence that they are both living active entities is that both can determine [181] action.

Shabur accepted this creed from him and imposed it upon the people of his kingdom. This distressed them and wise men of the kingdom came together to dissuade him from that, but he would not do (as they wished). Mani wrote books in which he demonstrated the (existence of the) two entities. Among his compositions is the book that he entitled

---

407 Tabari, 1.827, and Dinawari, 49, specify the Emperor Valerian and the dam of Tustar (see n. 195 above).

408 Arabic: *zindīq*. It possibly derives ultimately from Aramaic: *zaddīq*, 'righteous', which the Manichaeans then applied to themselves. Used by outsiders opposed to them, the term gained the sense of 'heretic' in MP and Arabic. See *EI*, 'zindīk'.

409 For discussion of this and other Muslim accounts of the prophet Mani see Reeves, *Islamicate Manichaeism*. Mani's experiences at the Persian court are treated in depth in Gardner, *Mani at the Court of the Persian Kings*.

'The Treasure of Life', which describes how the soul embraces both the salvation[410] that comes from light and the corruption that comes from darkness and which ascribes base actions to darkness. Then there is the book that he called *Shāburagān*,[411] in which he describes the pure soul and the soul adulterated by demons and defects, and in which he represents the heavens as laid out flat and says that the world rests on a sloping mountain around which the uppermost heavens revolve. In addition, he composed: a work that he called 'The Book of Guidance and Direction', twenty-two 'Gospels',[412] each one named after a letter of the alphabet and giving instruction in prayer and what should be used to liberate the soul, the book 'The Revelation[413] of Mysteries', in which he contests the signs of the prophets, the book 'The Revelation of the Giants', and many other books and treatises.[414]

Shabur remained in this creed for some ten years. Then the (chief) priest[415] came to him and said: 'This man has corrupted your religion, so bring me and him together so that I can dispute with him.' Shabur convened a meeting between them and the priest defeated Mani with his arguments, and so Shabur reverted from dualism to Zoroastrianism. He intended to kill Mani, but the latter escaped to the land of India and resided there until Shabur died.

[Hurmuz I]

After Shabur his son Hurmuz, who was a courageous man, became king. He was the one who built the city of Ramhurmuz.[416] His days were few and his reign lasted only one year.

---

410 *Khalāṣ*, which one could also translate as 'liberation' or 'purification'.

411 I.e. the book which Mani wrote 'for Shabur' and which gives a summary of his teachings. See *EIr*, 'Šābuhragān'.

412 Arabic: *injīl*. Yaʿqubi writes 12, but since he specifies that there is one gospel for each letter of the (Syriac) alphabet, evidently 22 is meant (corroborated by Biruni, 207).

413 *Sifr*. The root of this word signifies writing in Hebrew and Syriac, but in Arabic it mostly refers to travelling and unveiling, though the Hebrew/Syriac sense exists in Qurʾan 62:5 ('a donkey carrying books/*asfār*'). Since *kitāb*, the standard Arabic word for book, is here placed next to *sifr*, I assume a difference in meaning is intended (i.e. not 'the book of the book'), and so I have chosen to translate it as 'revelation' based on the meaning of unveiling that is present in the Arabic root.

414 On the writings of Mani and his followers see the Brepol series *Corpus Fontiorum Manichaeorum*.

415 Arabic: *mūbadh*, usually assumed to be Kartir; see Russell, 'Kartīr and Mānī'.

416 Though Hamza, 46–47, above, attributes it to Ardashir.

[Bahram I]

[182] Next Bahram son of Hurmuz, who was infatuated with slaves and amusements, became king. The disciples of Mani wrote to him that a young king now ruled, who was much distracted (by earthly pursuits). Mani therefore came to the land of Persia, where his teaching became well known and his whereabouts apparent. So Bahram summoned him and questioned him about his teaching and Mani set out his case. Bahram convened a meeting between him and the priest,[417] who then disputed with him. The priest said to him: 'Let lead be melted for you and for me and let it be poured onto our stomachs and whichever of us is not harmed by that is the one who follows the truth.' 'This is a deed of darkness', exclaimed Mani, whereupon Bahram ordered him to be imprisoned and told him: 'When morning comes, I shall summon you and have you killed in a manner that no one before you has been killed.'[418] Mani was flayed throughout the night with the result that his soul expired. Bahram came in the morning to summon him, but they found him already dead; he ordered his head to be cut off and his body to be stuffed with straw.[419] He pursued Mani's followers and killed a great number of them. The reign of Bahram son of Hurmuz lasted for three years.

[Bahram II and III]

Then Bahram son of Bahram became king and his reign lasted for 17 years. After him, his son, Bahram son of Bahram son of Bahram, became king and reigned for four years.

[Narsi and Hurmuz II]

He was followed by his brother, Narsi son of Bahram, who reigned for nine years. Narsi's son Hurmuz also reigned for nine years; he had a son called Shabur, to whom he contracted the kingship.

[Shabur II]

Hurmuz died when Shabur was still a baby in the cradle; the people of his kingdom remained waiting for him until he had grown up and become an

---

417 The implication being that this is the same priest who had disputed with Mani under Shabur.

418 Zoroaster allegedly demonstrated the truth of his doctrine by the trial of molten lead (see n. 216 above) and so Mani's exclamation amounted to a slight against Zoroaster, which might explain Bahram's extreme reaction.

419 Dinawari, 49, mentions that Mani was flayed and stuffed with straw, but attributes it to Hurmuz son of Shabur.

adult. At that point he displayed arrogance and pride, raiding the land of the Arabs and blocking up their water sources. Julian, king of the Romans, led a campaign against him with the support of all the Arab tribes, who hastened to confront Shabur and attacked him in the very home of his rule, with the result that he fled and abandoned his kingdom, and his city and treasuries were plundered. [183] Then an Arab's[420] arrow struck and killed Julian, king of the Romans. The Romans subsequently crowned Jovian, who made a peace agreement with Shabur.[421] The latter remained in such a state of enmity with the Arabs that he would dislocate the shoulder of anyone he vanquished, earning him the sobriquet of 'lord of the shoulders'. Shabur reigned for 72 years.

[Ardashir II and Shabur III]
Shabur was succeeded by Ardashir son of Hurmuz, brother of Shabur. He behaved abominably, killing nobles and magnates, and so he was deposed after four years. The Persians then placed on the throne Shabur son of Shabur; the deposed Ardashir submitted to him and gave him obedience, but a tent collapsed on top of Shabur and killed him after a reign of five years.[422]

[Bahram IV and Yazdagird I]
After Shabur his son Bahram ruled and he wrote to the four corners of his realm promising justice, equity and fair treatment, but after he had been in power for eleven years the people rose up against him and killed him. Then Yazdagird son of Shabur reigned; he was boorish, crude, presumptuous, ill-behaved and endowed with little good and much evil.[423] He imposed on the Persians harsh punishment, but then a horse kicked him violently and killed him. His reign lasted 21 years.

---

420 The text has *gharb* (West), but it seems more plausible to read *'arab* (Arab); note that the early fourth-century author Philostorgius (7.15) mentions an Arab ally of Persia striking Julian a mortal blow with his spear. Tabari, 1.842, and Dinawari, 52, have 'stray arrow' (*sahm 'ā'ir*). It is likely that the brief reference here to Julian's campaign and death in Mesopotamia derives ultimately from the Syriac *Julian Romance* (Wood, *No King but Christ*, 133–40).

421 This is the so-called Peace of Jovian made in July 363 (Greatrex and Lieu, *Wars*, ch. 1). In the Arabic text Jovian is written Yūbinyānūs.

422 Cf. Tabari, 1.846 (Ardashir obeys Shabur, Shabur killed by collapsing tent).

423 Hence he is often referred to as 'the sinner'; see Hamza, 54, above, Dinawari, 53, and Tabari, 1.847.

[Bahram V Gur]

Then Bahram Gur son of Yazdagird came to power. He had grown up in the land of the Arabs, for his father had dispatched him to Nu'man and he had been suckled by an Arab woman and raised with fine manners.[424] When Yazdagird died, the Persians did not want any son of his to take charge given the father's wicked ways, and, they said, since Bahram had grown up in the land of the Arabs he had no knowledge of government. They therefore agreed to make another man king. Bahram set out with (an army of) the Arabs and so when he encountered the Persians they were afraid of him. They took the crown of kingship and the regalia that the kings wore, placed them between two lions and said to Bahram and (the other contender whose name was) Khusraw[425] that whichever of them wrested the crown and regalia from between these two lions would be (the rightful) king. Once they had spoken thus **[184]** to Bahram he took a club, advanced, struck the two lions dead and seized the crown and regalia. They submitted to him and gave him obedience, and he for his part promised them (to act) well and he wrote to the four corners of his realm promising that and informing them of his justice and he paid attention to the prosperity of the land. Mundhir son of Nu'man came to him and he raised him in rank. Bahram was a man given to diversions, distracted from his subjects. Once he went out in search of hunting and amusement and appointed his brother Narsi as deputy over the kingdom. When the Khagan, king of the Turks,[426] learned of Bahram's nature, he hoped to overcome him and sought to march against him. That reached Bahram and he marched on the Khagan, killed him and wrote to his subjects about the victory. One day he went out hunting and strove to catch an onager, but then his horse threw him in a marshy place and he died. He had reigned for 19 years.[427]

---

424 Tabari, 1.850–58, has Bahram raised by Nu'man I (*ca.* 400–418) and/or his son Mundhir I (*ca.* 418–62), both kings of the tribe of Lakhm, based at Hira in southern Iraq.

425 Tabari, who gives a very full account of this episode (1.858–63), explains that this man was a descendant of Ardashir ibn Babak; cf. Dinawari, 57. Ya'qubi evidently has a longer account before him and in trying to abridge it occasionally omits details like this one, i.e. mentioning Khusraw without any prior introduction.

426 The Turks would not begin to challenge the Persian Empire until the second half of the sixth century, so some other people must be meant, probably the Hephthalites, as Ya'qubi specifies below. Khagan (or Kagan, Qagan, Khaqan etc.) was a title used for a supreme leader by various Central Asian tribal peoples from at least the third century AD. Again, Tabari, 1.863–65, gives a longer version of this incident.

427 Cf. Dinawari, 53, 57–60 (brought up with Arabs, wrested power with Arab help, liked

[Yazdagird II and Hurmuz III]

Then Yazdagird son of Bahram assumed the kingship and reigned for 17 years. This Yazdagird had two sons, one called Hurmuz and the other Firuz. Hurmuz seized the rule after his father and Firuz fled. He reached the land of the Hephthalites[428] and informed their king of his plight and the tyrannical actions of his brother. He (the Hephthalite king) provided him with soldiers; Firuz advanced with them and fought his brother, killing him and dispersing his troops.

[Firuz I]

So Firuz became king, but drought, scarcity and severe famine afflicted the people in his days, rivers and springs diminished, and this situation endured for three years. After that the land became fertile once more and Firuz journeyed to the land of the Turks to make war on their king; before this there had been a peace agreement between the Persians and Turks.[429] When Firuz drew near to the latter's country, their king issued a request for him to withdraw, impressing upon him the grievousness of abandoning faithful observance (of a peace treaty), but Firuz did not accept this. So he (the Turkish king) dug a deep trench and then camouflaged it. As Firuz approached it, he (the Turkish king) mobilised his troops, who rushed at Firuz. The latter fell into the trench along with the whole **[185]** of his army and died. The king of the Turks appropriated his possessions and captured a sister of his. Firuz had reigned for 27 years. When the Persians learned of the killing of Firuz, they were distraught, and one of their commanders, called Sukhra,[430] marched with numerous troops to engage the king of the Turks. Sukhra fought him and won some success against him. The king of the Turks called upon him to make peace on the condition that he would hand over to him all that he had appropriated from the treasuries of Firuz

amusements, fought Turks and died in a marsh). Tabari, 1.865, and Mas'udi, *Murūj*, 2.190, also recount Bahram's death in a marsh.

428 Here Ya'qubi speaks of Hephthalites (*al-Hayātila*).

429 Presumably Hephthalites are again meant (see previous note). Their king bore the name or title of Akhshunwar, according to Mas'udi, 101, above, and other historians, who say that Firuz had already been defeated before by Akhshunwar and had pledged not to attack the Hephthalites again (see Appendix 1 below).

430 Arabic: *Sūkhrā*. Tabari, 1.877–78, gives him an extensive genealogy going back to the Pishdadid king Manushihr and assigns him to the noble Karin family. Muslim authors make him the father of Zarmihr, who was apparently a major force in Sasanid politics in the late fifth century and who presumably corresponds to the Zarmihr of the contemporary Armenian historian Lazar Parpetsi (Bonner, *Historiographical Study*, 157–63).

and return his sister and companions. This he did and Sukhra departed from him.[431]

[Balash I and Qubad I]

Balash ruled for a period of four years and then his brother,[432] Qubad son of Firuz, ascended the throne. He was young and he left to Sukhra the administration of the realm. When he reached maturity and came to the brink of manhood, he no longer approved of the administration of Sukhra and had him killed. He promoted Mihran,[433] but then the Persians removed Qubad from power and imprisoned him.[434] They crowned his brother, Jamasb son of Firuz, so Qubad remained in prison and his brother in power. Then a sister of Qubad entered the prison; when the prison guard confronted her, she made him desirous of her and told him that she was menstruating.[435] She entered (the prison) and remained with Qubad for a day, then she wrapped him in a carpet and had him brought out on the back of a sturdy youth. Qubad fled, heading for the king of the Hephthalites.[436] When he came to Abarshahr, he stopped at (the house of) a certain man and stayed with him; he asked him to seek out for him a woman and he brought him a young maiden. Qubad had intercourse with her and her beauty and grace pleased him. He then proceeded to the king of the Hephthalites,

431 Cf. Dinawari, 60–62, and Tabari, 1.873–80 (Firuz gained power with Hephthalite support, drought/famine, Firuz dies in a Hephthalite ambush and Sukhra forces Hephthalites to make peace).

432 Actually his nephew, since Balash is the brother of Firuz; see n. 54 above.

433 Dinawari, 66, calls him Shabur of the noble Mihran family; Tabari, 1.877–78, says that Sukhra was of the Karin family, so these events may reflect a struggle between these two powerful families (Bonner, *Historiographical Study*, 163–64).

434 Because of his support for the Zoroastrian heresy of Mazdak; see Appendix 2 below.

435 Ya'qubi has excessively abridged the text here; Tabari, 1.887, makes it clear that she makes the guard desirous of her so that he lets her into the prison, and she speaks of her menstruation so that he will stay away from the bedding in which Qubad is wrapped (see Appendix 2 below). Procopius, 1.4.3–9, and Theophylact, 4.6.7–9, say that it was Qubad's wife who seduced the prison guard and that Qubad escaped by dressing up as his wife, who remained in the prison in her husband's clothes. It is possible that both traditions are correct and that Qubad had married his sister, a practice deemed laudable among nobles in Zoroastrianism.

436 *Dakhalat fa-aqāmat 'inda Qubād yawman thumma laffathu fī bisāṭ wa-akhrajathu 'alā 'unq ghulām jald fa-haraba Qubād yurīdu malik al-hayāṭila;* cf. Tabari, 1.887: *dakhalat al-sijn fa-aqāmat 'inda Qubād yawman wa-amarat fa-luffa Qubād fī bisāṭ ... wa-ḥumila 'alā ghulām min ghilmānihi qawī ... wa-haraba Qubād fa-laḥiqa bi-arḍ al-hayāṭila li-yastamidda malikahā.* Evidently the two authors have a common source here.

staying with him for a year, and he sent him off with an army. When Qubad got back to Abarshahr, he asked the man whom he had stayed with: 'What happened to the maiden?' She was brought to him and she had borne a child, who was the most beautiful of children, and he named him Khusraw Anusharwan.[437] **[186]** Qubad marched (with the Hephthalite army) to his country and seized the kingship. His position strengthened and his power increased. He raided the land of the Romans and organised the districts and cantons. He contracted the rule to his son Anusharwan and summoned him, bequeathing to him the best counsel and acquainting him with everything that he needed (to rule). The reign of Qubad lasted 43 years.

[Khusraw I Anusharwan]

Then Anusharwan son of Qubad ascended the throne and he wrote to the people of his realm notifying them of the death of Qubad, promising them justice on his part, instructing them to strive for good fortune and recommending to them obedience and sincerity. He forgave a people who had been attacking him and he killed Mazdak, who had ordered people to share goods and women equally, and Zaradusht Khurrakan for the innovations he had introduced into Zoroastrianism and also their followers.[438] He gave precedence to men of state and nobility and he raided numerous countries that were not part of the Persian realm and brought them under his rule. There arose (enmity) between him and Justinian and so Anusharwan raided the land of the Romans, killing, enslaving and seizing many cities of northern Mesopotamia and Syria, such as Edessa, Qinnasrin, the frontier towns, Aleppo, Antioch, Apamea, Homs and others. Antioch pleased him and he built a city like it (in his own realm), not omitting anything from it; he enslaved many in Antioch and sent them to it (his copy of Antioch) and they recognised everything there (so similar was it to their own Antioch).[439]

---

437 The same story is related in Dinawari, 67–68, who makes the maiden a noblewoman and also in Tabari, 1.883–84, except that he places it before the accession of Qubad, when he was seeking support from the Hephthalites to oust Balash. Both Dinawari and Tabari say that Qubad had obtained the maiden by the intercession of his companion Zarmihr son of Sukhra.

438 In Tabari, 1.893, Zaradusht *son of* Khurrakan. Both Ya'qubi and Tabari imply he is a contemporary of Mazdak, whereas Christian chroniclers place him in the third century (Crone, 'Kavad's Heresy', 24).

439 Khusraw's campaign began in the early summer of 540 and ended with a truce in 545 (Greatrex and Lieu, *Wars*, ch. 7). His construction of a replica of Antioch in Persia is recorded by Procopius, 2.14; John of Ephesus, 3.6.19; Sebeos, 69; *Chronicle of Siirt*, 105; Dinawari, 70.

Anusharwan conducted a survey of the country, imposed a land tax and on every hectare (*jarīb*) of agricultural produce he exacted (taxes) proportional to what could be borne. This remained the established practice while the land flourished. He appointed a man in charge of the military bureau whose prudence and resolution he approved of, and he had his soldiers take whatever weapons they needed. **[187]** He also established a bureau of military stipends with registers of names, equipment and distinguishing features of riding animals, and a bureau of military review according to the same format. Anusharwan was magnanimous, generous and openly fair; nobody asked him anything without receiving a proper answer.[440]

Sayf ibn Dhi Yazan travelled to him and informed him that the Abyssinians had advanced upon the land of Yemen and overwhelmed it. He had gone to Heraclius,[441] king of the Romans, but had not found with him what he sought. Khusraw dispatched across the sea with him men from his prisons and he put in charge of them one of his most venerable commanders, a man named Wahriz, who was courageous and experienced (in warfare). He went to the land of Yemen, fought the Abyssinians and annihilated them; he threw (a spear) at their king, Abraha,[442] and killed him. Wahriz stayed in the country and made Sayf ibn Dhi Yazan king.

Anusharwan contracted the rule after him to his son Hurmuz, whose mother was the daughter of the Khagan, king of the Turks.[443] He (Khusraw) wrote for him (Hurmuz) a covenant in which he gave him instructions appropriate to the like of him, gave him the best of advice, tested him and found him just as he wanted. Hurmuz gave apposite answers to whatever he asked of him, expressed his gratitude[444] and conveyed to him only fine and agreeable sentiments. Anusharwan perished after a reign of 48 years.[445]

440 On Khusraw's fiscal and administrative changes see Rubin, 'Reforms of Khusro'.
441 Heraclius (610–41) was Roman emperor at the time of Khusraw II (591–628), not of Khusraw I (531–79), though the term is perhaps just being used as a general word here for the leader of the Romans.
442 Abraha ruled Yemen for thirty years (*ca.* 535–65), but most Muslim sources say that it was not he, but his son, Masruq, who fought Wahriz. For a longer version of this story see Hamza, 58–60, above.
443 Sebeos, 73, says that Hurmuz's mother was 'the daughter of the great Khagan, king of the T'etals', a term that originally referred to Hephthalites but came to be used of various groups on Iran's eastern flank, including Turks.
444 The editor gives *tanakkara*, 'disguise oneself', but notes an alternative reading of *tashakkara*, 'be grateful', which seems more appropriate here.
445 The same topics of Mazdak, administrative reforms, war against Rome and Sayf's

[Hurmuz IV]

Then Hurmuz son of Anusharwan came to power and he read out to the people a public statement in which he promised justice and fairness, benevolence and right conduct and instructed them to do what is beneficial.[446] He attained victory and glory and conquered a number of cities. Then his enemies grew bold and attacked his country,[447] and the toughest of his enemies was Shabah, the king of the Turks.[448] He marched **[188]** with a great multitude, entered the land of Khurasan and almost captured it. Also, the king of the Khazars advanced with his troops and encamped in Azerbaijan.[449] That weighed heavily on Hurmuz and he feared that he would not have the power to deal with the lord of the Turks.

[The revolt of Bahram Chobin][450]

One of Hurmuz's commanders, named Bihzad, came to him and informed him that in his company was a man called Mihran Sitad, who

reconquest of Yemen (though Dinawari places this at the end of Firuz's reign even though attributing it to Khusraw) dominate Khusraw's reign in the accounts of Dinawari, 69–76, and Tabari, 1.892–900.

446 Dinawari, 77–80, gives the text of a very long speech in this vein that he ascribes to Hurmuz. *Chronicle of Siirt*, 104, has Hurmuz preach about the importance of protecting the Christians of his realm. Anecdotes about Hurmuz's concern for the weak are found in a number of sources (e.g. Dinawari, 80, and Tabari, 1.989–90: Hurmuz punishes the young Khusraw for trampling the crops of a farmer); Wood, 'Christian Reception', argues that this reflects Christian influence on Persian historical writing that began with the reign of Hurmuz.

447 The idea that Hurmuz faced a threat on multiple fronts later in his reign is found in a number of Muslim sources (e.g. Dinawari, 1.81, Tabari, 1.991, and Tha'alibi, 642). Cf. Howard-Johnson, 'Strategic Dilemma', who, however, wants to redate the threat to the reign of Khusraw I.

448 Arabic: *Shābah*. Sebeos, 73, says that Bahram fought 'the great king of the Mazk'ut'k'', and Tabari, 1.991, speaks of 'the supreme ruler of the Turks', so it seems that the Khagan himself is intended. For most of Hurmuz's reign this was Ishbara Khagan (581–87), referred to in Chinese sources as Shiboluo Khagan. On his death rule passed to his brother Chuluohou, who took the title Magha Khagan. The latter was probably the one who fought Bahram Chobin (in Hormuz's 11th year, i.e. 588–89, according to Tabari, 1.991), but the Shabah of the Arabic/Persian sources may well reflect the name Ishbara/Shiboluo, the better-known and longer-serving brother. See Stark, 'Türk Khaganate', 2131.

449 The Khazars become a major force in the Caucasus only in the mid seventh century, so the reference here is anachronistic (Zuckerman, 'Khazars and Byzantium').

450 The narrative about the revolt of Bahram Chobin and his sister/wife Kurdiya takes up about one-third of Ya'qubi's section on the Sasanids. Mas'udi, *Murūj*, 2.223, mentions that 'the Persians have a book devoted to the history of Bahram Chobin and his stratagems in the country of the Turks' and Ibn al-Nadim, 305, lists a 'Book of Bahram Chobin' translated

was knowledgeable (about the king of the Turks, whose)[451] wife was the Khatun.[452] She had asked him about their future and he had informed her that her daughter would bear a son from a Persian king, that he would take charge of the kingdom after his father and that the king of the Turks would march against him with a great multitude, but then a person named Bahram Chobin, who was not of the royal family, would be sent to him with an army squadron and would kill that king and extirpate his kingdom.

When Hurmuz heard that (prophecy), he was pleased by it, and he searched for Bahram Chobin. He was told: 'We do not know any such person except for a man of the people of Rayy who is in Azerbaijan. Hurmuz sent for him and he came to him, and Hurmuz dispatched him to Shabah, king of the Turks, with twelve thousand soldiers. The chief of priests said to Hurmuz: 'How well suited he is to obtain a victory; however, in the corner of his eyebrow (one can discern) the sign of a breach in your rule that he will widen'; and a diviner of his said to him much the same thing. Consequently, Hurmuz wrote to Bahram that he should return, but he did not do so. At Herat Bahram encountered Shabah, who had been duped (to go there), for with him was a man called Hurmuz Jarabzin, whom (King) Hurmuz had sent to deceive Shabah. Then he (Hurmuz Jarabzin) fled from him and took his leave.[453]

Shabah dispatched someone who was acquainted [189] with Bahram, and he went to him and then informed him (Shabah) about his (Bahram's) situation. Shabah sent word to Bahram that he should withdraw, but Bahram gave him a rude and vehement reply. Then he engaged him, having already prepared his army. With Shabah were diviners and sorcerers who were casting confusion on Bahram's men. They joined in close battle and there was extensive killing of Shabah's men until a great many of them had been slain. They turned away in defeat and Bahram inflicted great slaughter on them. He caught up with Shabah, threw a long spear at him and killed him.[454] He then captured a sorcerer who was with the lord of

from Persian into Arabic by Jabala ibn Salim (fl. 740s) – plausibly such a work underlies all the Muslim accounts of Bahram.

451 Lacuna in the text. The words in parentheses are conjecture on my part based on the context.

452 Khatun is a title for a female noble or ruler in Central Asia.

453 Ya'qubi is unclear here, probably abbreviating his source again, but cf. Dinawari, 83 (*wajadūhu qad haraba*), who also reports Hurmuz Jarabzin's double-agent activities, noting that he was one of Hurmuz's *marzbāns*. Firdawsi, 732–34 and 760–62 (Davis), gives his name as Kharrad son of Barzin.

454 Bahram's defeat of the Turks and killing of their king is reported by Sebeos, 73, and

the Turks; Bahram wanted to spare him so that he might be an aide to preparedness in his campaigns, but then he thought it better to kill him.

He wrote of his victory to Hurmuz, who was pleased by it and sent word of it to the outlying regions. Then Barmudhah[455] son of Shabah went to meet Bahram, fought and resisted him, and an intense battle ensued between them, but Bahram held firm and defeated him, pursuing him and besieging him in a fortress.[456] Barmudhah son of Shabah sued for a guarantee of safety on the condition that it be issued by King Hurmuz. So Bahram wrote to Hurmuz, who accepted, sent a written guarantee of safety and instructed Bahram to let him come to him. So Barmudhah son of Shabah left the fortress – for Hurmuz had already dispatched people to Bahram Chobin (to escort Barmudhah) – and travelled to Hurmuz, who treated him with honour and kindness and seated him on the throne next to him. Barmudhah told him about the great wealth and treasures that had accrued to Bahram (from the spoils of war) and that he had concealed that from his confidants; the latter confirmed that (to Hurmuz) and said that what Bahram had sent to Hurmuz was just a little from a lot.[457] So Hurmuz wrote to Bahram ordering him to convey to him what wealth he had acquired. That annoyed Bahram and he informed his soldiers about it and they spoke [190] most vilely about Hurmuz, and Bahram and all his soldiers threw off their allegiance to him.[458]

Theophylact, 3.6.7–10, who says that Bahram campaigned in the Caucasus in the eighth year of Emperor Maurice (589–90) after winning a victory against the Turks.

455 Dinawari, 84, gives his name as Yaltikin, which is Turkish, but Nöldeke, *Sasaniden*, 272 n. 2, argued, plausibly, that this was inserted by Dinawari, writing when Turks dominated the politics of the caliphate. Possibly meant is Rangan, son of Chuluohou/Magha.

456 Tha'alabi, 648, says he shut himself up in the city of Paykand, near Bukhara.

457 Cf. Sebeos, 74: 'He (Bahram) sent (to Hurmuz) … a small part of the booty from the enormous treasures acquired from the plunder of the expedition … (But Hurmuz said to himself) "The feast is exceedingly grand and I acknowledge the token of this portion. From such great treasures it was not right to send to court merely this much".' Hurmuz's sentiment is echoed by the vizier Yazdan Jushnas in Dinawari, 85: 'How grand was the feast whence came this morsel.'

458 That Bahram's revolt against Hurmuz began because of an argument over allocation of plunder is reported by numerous sources, though whereas here it is the Turkish prince who accuses Bahram before Hurmuz, in *Chronicle of Siirt*, 123, it is nameless 'courtiers', and in Dinawari, 85, it is Hurmuz's vizier Yazdan Jushnas (presumably = Ya'qubi's Ādhīn Jushnas). Sebeos, 74, mentions only messengers. Theophylact, 3.8.1–3, says that it was Hurmuz's ridiculing and dismissal of Bahram following the latter's humiliating defeat in battle against the Romans in the Caucasus in 589 that prompted Bahram to revolt.

When news of that reached Hurmuz, he became worried and wrote to Bahram apologising to him and his soldiers for that. However, neither Bahram nor his soldiers accepted Hurmuz's word and Bahram sent to Hurmuz a basket containing knives with bent heads. When Hurmuz saw them, he knew that Bahram had rebelled. He cut off the tips of the knives and returned them to Bahram, who realised what he meant. He therefore sent word to the Khagan, king of the Turks,[459] seeking a peace treaty with him on the basis that he would return to him all the territory that he had seized from his country. Bahram then travelled until he came to Rayy, where he arranged to sow dissension between Hurmuz and his son Khusraw Abarwiz. Now Hurmuz had doubts about his son, for he had heard that some people had encouraged him to make an assault upon his father. He (Bahram) struck many dirhams, placing on them the name of Khusraw Abarwiz, and circulated them in the city of Hurmuz, where many got into the hands of the population. When news of this reached Hurmuz, his anxiety intensified and he wanted to imprison his son Khusraw Abarwiz.

When the latter heard this report, he fled to Azerbaijan. The generals and leaders who were there joined with him, made a compact with him and pledged allegiance to him. Hurmuz dispatched an army against Bahram with a man called Ādhīn Jushnas. When he had gone a part of the way, Ādhīn Jushnas was killed by an aide whom he had released from prison and drawn close to himself, and the latter's companions scattered. The death of Ādhīn Jushnas weakened Hurmuz's hand and his army became emboldened against him, for they were angry with him and hated his rule. They wrote to his son Abarwiz, who advanced with an army from Azerbaijan; they then repudiated Hurmuz and crowned Abarwiz. Hurmuz was seized, imprisoned and blinded. He remained in jail for a few days, after which his son Abarwiz came to see him. [191] He spoke to him and Hurmuz told him: 'Kill those who did this to me', namely Bindawayh and Bistam, maternal uncles of Abarwiz, who had taken over the running of the kingdom.[460] The reign of Hurmuz had lasted for 12 years.

---

459 This is presumably Yongyulu, son of Ishbara, who became head of the eastern Turks after the death of Chuluohou/Magha, bearing the title Dulan Khagan (Stark, 'Türk Khaganate', 2131–32).

460 Coins issued by Bahram suggest that he sought the rule for himself and was not behind the enthronement of Khusraw Abarwiz, which seems to have been orchestrated by Bindawayh and Bistam, who, Ya'qubi implies, are the object of Hurmuz's ire here. *Chronicle of Khuzistan*, 16, says they 'greatly assisted Khusraw for they were of his mother's family'; cf. Sebeos, 75, Dinawari, 86–91, and Tabari, 1.993–96.

[Khusraw II Abarwiz]

When Khusraw's situation had stabilised and he learned of Bahram Chobin's advance towards him, he set out with an army, accompanied by Bindawayh and Bistam, until he encountered Bahram at Nahrawan. He spoke with Bahram and he stressed the gravity of the situation, but Bahram replied coarsely and harshly. Kurdi, brother of Bahram, sided with Khusraw Abarwiz, but Bahram won him over and Khusraw's army left him and his followers deserted him, and so he fled away. When he had gone part of the way, his uncles Bindawayh and Bistam returned (to Mada'in), killed his father Hurmuz and then caught up with him on the way. Khusraw continued his flight until his situation worsened and his suffering and distress intensified. He searched for food, but only found barley bread. The cavalry of Bahram pursued him, but his uncle Bindawayh saved him by a stratagem, and so he went on until he came to Edessa. Bindawayh was captured and brought before Bahram, who imprisoned him, but he escaped from jail and went to Azerbaijan.

Khusraw had come to Edessa intending (to contact) Maurice, king of the Romans, but the governor of Edessa imprisoned him. Khusraw wrote to Maurice, king of the Romans, informing him that he had come to seek his aid. The king of the Romans consulted his companions about the matter of Khusraw; some said he should not respond positively and some said he should. In the end, the king of the Romans gave Khusraw an affirmative answer and married him to his daughter.[461] He sent him off (back to his own kingdom) with a huge army and set conditions on him for when he had obtained victory. Khusraw sent to him three men from among his companions and stipulated that they should (give Maurice) whatever he wanted. Maurice sent his daughter and army in the charge of a brother of his named Theodosius together with a man [192] who was equal to a thousand soldiers.[462]

After consummating the marriage with the daughter of the king of the Romans, Khusraw set off with his army to the province of Azerbaijan to which his uncle Bindawayh had already repaired. When Bindawayh

---

461 Khusraw's flight westwards to seek aid from Maurice and the latter's deliberations and final agreement is reported by Sebeos, 75–76, and Theophylact, 4.12–13. *Chronicle of Khuzistan*, 17, names Maria the Roman as one of Khusraw's wives; Dinawari, 96, and Tabari, 1.999, confirm that she was Maurice's daughter.

462 Theodosius was not the brother of Maurice (thus also Tabari, 1.999), but his son (thus Dinawari, 96; cf. Theophylact, 8.1.4). Note that Dinawari gives the original Persian word for the man 'equal to a thousand soldiers', namely *hazārmard*.

learned of Khusraw's location, he joined him with a large army. On finding out how things had come together for Khusraw, Bahram wrote to the chiefs of his followers informing them of the evil ways of the family of Sasan, describing the (wicked) behaviour of their kings and calling on them to support him. The letter fell into the hands of Khusraw before reaching the (intended) people, and he wrote to Bahram a very rude reply (as though) from the people. The messenger returned to Bahram, who marched out to them until he reached Azerbaijan. He engaged him (Khusraw) in battle and war engulfed both parties. The Roman who was equal to a thousand soldiers came out and said to Khusraw: '(Tell me) where is this slave of yours who has robbed you of your kingdom so that I may kill him.' Khusraw replied: 'He is the one with the piebald horse.' He (the Roman) attacked and Bahram withdrew, but then returned to him, hit him (the Roman) with his sword and cut him in two. Khusraw laughed and said 'Bravo'. The brother of the king of the Romans became angry and said: 'Are you pleased that he has killed one of our men and our comrade?' 'No', he said, 'but your comrade said to me: "Where is the slave who has robbed and seized your kingdom?" and I want you to know that this slave will mete out many such blows every day'. The battle intensified until Khusraw was defeated when he climbed a hill and was almost killed.[463] Then his army rallied and Bahram Chobin was defeated and he went away, not paying heed to anything, heading for the kingdom of the Turks.[464]

Khusraw Abarwiz's situation now became stable and he wrote of that to the lord of the Romans, who presented him with two robes inscribed with the cross. Khusraw put them on and so the Persians said that he had become Christian. Khusraw wrote concerning the Christians that they should enjoy honour, advancement and eminence and he recounted [193] the protection, kinship and affection that he had shared with the Roman (emperor), something no Shahanshah[465] had said before. Bindawayh, uncle of Abarwiz, attacked Theodosius, brother of the king of the Romans, struck him hard and caused him injury. The brother of the king of the Romans said

---

463 Cf. Theophylact, 5.9.11: 'Khusraw urged the Romans to advance towards the hillsides (but they refused) ... . The barbarians (i.e. Persians) were compelled by their own king to grapple with the foolish risks and were soundly routed by their opponents when they dared to climb the mountain.' Dinawari, 97: 'Khusraw went towards a mountain.'

464 The battle between Khusraw and Bahram, which took place south-east of Lake Urmiah, in north-west Iran, in the spring of 591, is narrated in detail by Sebeos, 77–80 (who says Bahram subsequently fled to Balkh), and Theophylact, book 5.

465 King of kings, the title of the Persian emperor.

(to Khusraw): 'Hand over Bindawayh to me or else disaster will ensue', so Khusraw appeased him.

Bahram Chobin arrived in the land of the Turks and the Khagan treated him with generosity and honour. This Khagan had a brother called Nafāris[466] whom he overindulged. Bahram saw him and said to the Khagan: 'How does he venture such insolence towards you?' The brother of the Khagan heard these words and challenged him (to a duel); Bahram said: 'Whenever you want, come out!' The Khagan, king of the Turks, handed to his brother an arrow and to Bahram an arrow, and then he took them out to the desert. The brother of the Khagan shot at Bahram and hit him, but only pierced his armour, whereas Bahram shot at him and killed him. The Khagan was pleased at the slaying of his brother on account of his obduracy towards him and what he feared he might do.

Khusraw became nervous of the standing of Bahram Chobin with the Khagan and did not feel secure from him carrying out some harm against him. So he dispatched one of the nobles of Persia called Bahram Jarabzin,[467] who was a senior figure in Persia, and sent gifts with him to the Khagan, asking him to forward Bahram Chobin to him. He ordered Jarabzin to be subtle in (handling) the task, and so he brought the Khagan the gifts and mentioned to him the matter of Bahram, but he did not find with him what he wanted. So he made a friendly approach to the Khatun, the wife of the Khagan, presenting her with jewels and fine objects, and he asked her about the matter of Bahram. She dispatched one of her attendants who possessed boldness and a daring spirit and told him: 'Go to Bahram Chobin and kill him.' So he went off and asked Bahram permission to enter, but it was his sleep time [194] and so he did not give him permission. He said: 'The royal Khagan has sent me on an important matter', so Bahram let him in. After entering, the attendant said: 'The king had me convey a message by which I might inform you of a secret without anyone else present.' He (Bahram) got up from his seat; the attendant approached him as though he was going to confide in him, and then he smote him with a dagger he had with him under his armpit. Next the Turk hurried out and mounted his riding animal, while Bahram's companions entered and saw the situation. They exclaimed: 'Oh lion of lions, who has struck you; oh lofty mountain, who has destroyed you?'

---

466 The editor gives the name without diacritical marks, so it could be read in different ways. Dinawari, 100–102, who relates this incident at great length, calls the brother Baghawīr; Tha'alabi, 645, gives Faghfūra.

467 Dinawari, 102, calls him Hurmuz Jarabzin, i.e. the double agent that Bahram had dealt with before.

He (Bahram) related to them the tale and wrote to the Khagan informing him that there was no loyalty nor gratitude with him. Then Bahram died and he was placed in a sarcophagus. When Jarabzin learned of his death, he travelled to Khusraw and let him know. He was pleased and announced it throughout his realm and wrote of it to the outlying regions.[468]

Upon Bahram's death, the king of the Turks sent word to Kurdiya, Bahram's wife,[469] and to his companions informing them that he was grieved and that he had killed everyone who had participated in his murder. Also, he sent his brother Niṭrā to them and notified Kurdiya that he (the Khagan) wished her well and he instructed her to marry him (Niṭrā). Kurdiya, wife of Bahram, took charge of her brother's army and set off with her companions and retinue making for the country of the Persians. Niṭrā, brother of the Khagan, caught up with her, whereupon she appeared before him fully armed and said: 'I will not marry anyone who is not as brave and strong as Bahram, so come out to fight me.' Accordingly, the brother of the Khagan came forth to oppose her, but she killed him and continued on her way.[470]

Khusraw became angry at his uncle Bindawayh, so he gouged out his eyes, cut off his hands and feet and crucified him alive on account of what he had done to his (Khusraw's) father.[471] When Bistam, brother of Bindawayh, learned of what Khusraw had done to his brother, he repudiated Khusraw, went [195] to Rayy and mustered (an army). It reached him that Kurdiya, sister and wife of Bahram, had arrived from the land of the Turks. He went out to meet her and her retinue and criticised Khusraw before her and informed her of his treachery and iniquity. He asked that she and

---

468 Sebeos, 80, simply says that Bahram 'went and took refuge in Balkh, where by Khusraw's order he was put to death by its people'. The account of Dinawari, 102–04, is very close to that of Yaʿqubi, whereas Tabari, 1.1001, gives a condensed version and calls Khusraw's agent Hurmuz.

469 Further on Yaʿqubi calls her 'sister and wife of Bahram'; other Muslim sources refer to her only as Bahram's sister (e.g. Dinawari, 105), but Tabari, 1.998, specifically states that she was his sister and he had married her, an admissible and virtuous practice among Zoroastrian nobles.

470 This episode is omitted by Dinawari, but recounted along similar lines by Tabari, 1.1001.

471 Cf. Sebeos, 94: 'Khusraw decided to seek vengeance for the death of his father from those nobles who had killed him. First he wished to condemn his maternal uncles. He commanded Bindawayh ... to be arrested, bound and killed'; Dinawari, 105: 'Khusraw's only concern was to seek vengeance for his father Hurmuz and he wished to begin with his maternal uncles Bindawayh and Bistam.'

her retinue stay with him and that she marry him. She did so and wrote to her brother Kurdi informing him of that and requesting him to obtain for her and her retinue a guarantee of safe conduct from Khusraw. The latter was informed of the arrival at Rayy of Kurdiya and of the troops and companions of Bahram that accompanied her, of her marriage to his uncle Bistam and residence with him. On learning this, he summoned Kurdi, her brother, and asked him to treat her well so that she might kill Bistam and then come to him (Khusraw) so that he might marry her. Kurdi, therefore, dispatched his wife Abrakha to Kurdiya, his sister, with (news of) what the king had told him and conveyed to her letters of guarantee for her and those with her endorsed with the most binding of oaths. Her companions accepted that and so attacked Bistam and killed him, while she made her way to Khusraw so that he might marry her. He granted her an exalted position, and matters became settled for Khusraw and his realm bowed to his will.[472]

Then the Romans rose up against Maurice, their king, killed him and crowned another.[473] The son of Maurice came to Khusraw and he sent him off with an army, but he was killed and Heraclius became king.[474] He attacked the troops of Khusraw, and he (Heraclius) killed them, routed them and advanced against them until Shahrbaraz, Khusraw's commander-in-chief,[475] was defeated.[476] As Khusraw's rule had solidified, he had become

472 Dinawari, 106–10, gives a much expanded account of this episode, making it clear that Bistam mounted a full-scale revolt against Khusraw, as does Sebeos, 95. But whereas Dinawari and Ya'qubi have Kurdiya or her companions kill Bistam, Sebeos, 97, attributes his death to the treachery of the king of the Kushans. *Chronicle of Khuzistan*, 16, says 'a Turk tricked him and killed him'. Tabari, 1.1001, notes that Khusraw married Kurdiya, but does not mention the connection with Bistam.

473 Namely Phocas (602–10).

474 The story of how Maurice's son Theodosius escaped Phocas' henchmen and went to seek support in the east is narrated by Theophylact, 8.13.3–6 and 8.15.8, and *Chronicle of Khuzistan*, 20–21. The latter has him crowned by the head of the church in Mada'in and sent off with an army to fight Phocas. Sebeos, 107, says that a Roman general in Edessa dressed up a youth and sent him to Khusraw, who was attacking Edessa, with the message: 'This is Theodosius, son of Maurice; have pity on him just as his father did on you.' Heraclius became emperor in 610 after defeating Phocas.

475 Arabic: *ṣāḥib Khusraw*, which means friend/companion or lord/master of Khusraw; neither seems appropriate, so I am reading it as short for *ṣāḥib jaysh Khusraw*, 'commander of the army of Khusraw'.

476 This is a massively compressed account of a quarter of a century of warfare that began with the overthrow of Maurice by Phocas in 602 and ended with the defeat of the Persian army by Heraclius in 628. No Muslim history of Persia gives a detailed account

tyrannical and oppressive, seizing people's wealth and shedding their blood. So people hated him for his appropriation of their possessions and for his contempt towards them.

[Shirawayh]

The Persian magnates, when they saw [196] the humiliation, affliction and detestation that they had suffered from Khusraw, deposed him, brought out a son of his called Shirawayh, made him king and brought him to the (capital) city. They hailed him as Shahanshah and they released from the prisons those whom Khusraw had intended to execute. Khusraw himself fled to an orchard of his where they captured him and then imprisoned him.[477] They said to Shirawayh: 'The kingship will not remain firm while Abarwiz is alive, so kill him or else we will depose you.' Shirawayh sent a harsh letter to his father, rebuking him for what he had done and reminding him of what he had appropriated from his subjects and of the wickedness of his conduct, but Khusraw responded with a rebuttal and accusation of ignorance. So Shirawayh sent to Khusraw Abarwiz a man whose hand he had cut off for no cause or crime except that he had been told that the son of this man will kill you, and so he had cut off his hand even though he was one of his chosen few.[478] When he entered, Khusraw asked him his name ...[479] He (Khusraw) said to him: 'Please do as you have been ordered', and so he struck him dead and Shirawayh bore him to his sarcophagus and executed his killer. The reign of Khusraw Abarwiz lasted 38 years. When Shirawayh came to power, he released prisoners, married his father's women and wrongfully and unjustly killed 17 of his brothers.[480] His rule did not go well and his situation did not prosper. His illness got worse and he died after eight months.

of the Persian–Roman war of 603–28, perhaps reflecting the fact that the subject was very unappealing to Persian historiographers.

477 Cf. *Chronicle of Khuzistan*, 28, and Sebeos, 127: Khusraw captured while hiding in the royal gardens.

478 *Chronicle of Khuzistan*, 28, has Khusraw killed by a nobleman named Nihormizd in retaliation for Khusraw's murder of his father. Tabari, 1.1059–60, and Dinawari, 115, also say that Khusraw was killed by a man whose father had been killed by Khusraw, but name him as Mihr Hurmuz and Yazdak respectively. Sebeos, 127, just says that Shirawayh ordered his troops to kill him.

479 For an account of their conversation see Tabari, 1.1060.

480 Sebeos, 127, puts their number at 40; Dinawari, 116, says 25. Tabari, 1.1060, agrees on 17. Hamza, 61, above says 18 and gives their names.

[Ardashir and Shahrbaraz]

The Persians crowned a young son of Shirawayh, named Ardashir, and they chose (as regent) for him a man called Mih-Ādhar Jushnas.[481] They had him care for him (Ardashir) so that he could undertake the running of the kingdom and he did that well and managed things in a praiseworthy manner, and the affairs of the realm proceeded well. However, Shahrbaraz, who had commanded the war against the Romans, had grown powerful and he disliked the position of [197] Mih-Ādhar Jushnas. He wrote to the Persians that they should send him certain men whom he named or else he would come to them to make war on them. They did not comply and he advanced with 6000 men to one side of the capital city and he besieged and fought those who were in it. Then he reflected and used a stratagem to enter the city. He seized the Persian nobles, killed them and violated their women, and he killed King Ardashir, who had reigned for one year and six months.[482] Shahrbaraz sat on the royal throne and called himself king. When the Persians saw what Shahrbaraz had done, they found it distressing and said: 'Such a one as this should not rule over us.' They attacked and killed him and dragged him along by the leg.[483]

[Buran and Azarmidukht]

After killing Shahrbaraz the Persians looked for a man from the royal family, but they did not find one,[484] and so they crowned Buran, daughter of Khusraw. She conducted herself well, spread justice and benevolence, and she wrote a letter to the four corners of her realm in which she promised justice and good conduct and instructed them in proper practice and intention and right action. She effected reconciliation with the king of the Romans and she reigned for a year and four months. Then Azarmidukht, daughter of Khusraw, came to power and her rule was upright. Farrukh Hurmuz, governor of Khurasan, said (to her): 'Today I am the greatest of men and the support of the Persian realm, so marry me to you.' She said:

---

481 Tabari, 1.1061, confirms this, specifying that he held the office of chief steward.

482 Sebeos, 129–30, says that Shahrbaraz was prompted to do this by Heraclius, who promised him military support to subdue any opposition in return for Shahrbaraz's loyalty and the return of the fragment of the Cross of Christ taken by the Persians during their sacking of Jerusalem. See Mango, 'Deux études', 111.

483 Tabari, 1.1063, makes clearer both why the Persians disliked Shahrbaraz's usurpation – 'because he was not of the royal house' – and how they killed him – 'they tied a rope round his leg and dragged him forwards and backwards'.

484 In particular, because Shirawayh had killed all the male rival claimants he could find.

'It is not right for the queen to marry off herself, but if you want to see me come to me at night.' He accepted that and she ordered the chief of her guard to watch out for his entry and then to kill him. When it was night he came and entered; the chief of the guard spotted him and said: 'Who are you?', to which he replied: 'I am Farrukh Hurmuz.' The chief of the guard said: 'What are you doing at this time of night in a place that the likes of you may not enter?' [198] and he struck him dead and tossed him into the courtyard. When people came by in the morning, they saw him dead and spread news of him. His son Rustam, the one who engaged Sa'd ibn Abi Waqqas at (the battle of) Qadisiyya, was in Khurasan, and he came and killed Azarmidukht, whose reign only lasted six months.[485]

[Mihr Jushnas, Firuz and Farrukhzad Khusraw]

Then a descendant of Ardashir ibn Babak, called Khusraw b. Mihr Jushnas,[486] came to power. He had been called to rule before that, but had refused; his residence was in Ahwaz. When he was made king, he put on the crown and sat on the throne, but they killed him after only a few days – he did not even complete a month. The Persian grandees lacked any member of the royal family whom they could make king, but then they found a man called Firuz, whom Anusharwan had sired by his mother, and they crowned him out of necessity. However, when he was seated to receive the crown, he, having a large head, said: 'How tight this crown is', which the Persian nobles took as a bad sign and killed him.[487] Then a

---

485 Sebeos, 130, relates this story to Buran not Azarmidukht and calls her first minister Khurra Hurmuz (Armenian: Khorokh-Ormizd). Mas'udi, 103 (above), follows Sebeos in calling the minister Khurra Hurmuz, but follows Ya'qubi in attributing the story to Azarmidukht. Tabari, 1.1065, also assigns the story to Azarmidukht, but calls her minister Farrukh Hurmuz; he also notes that the latter's son Rustam killed Azarmidukht. Regarding Buran, *Chronicle of Siirt*, 259, says that a Persian general named Firuz strangled her, but gives no explanation; *Chronicle of Khuzistan*, 30, just says that she was strangled without naming the perpetrator.

486 Tabari, 1.1065, agrees with Ya'qubi regarding his name and career. Hamza, 22, above (citing Musa b. 'Isa), and Mas'udi, 102, speak of Khusraw son of Qubad. Whether one of these two, and if so which one, should be identified with the Khusraw of Sebeos, 130, who was 'from the family of Sasan', is unclear; or possibly they are the same person, whose genealogy has become confused. Coins have been found that appear to be issued by a Khusraw IIII (Mochiri, 'Khusraw III').

487 Tabari, 1.1066, says he was the son of 'Mihran Jushnas, who was also called Jushnasdih'. One might assume that it was Mihran Jushnas who was also called Jushnasdih, but since Tabari, 1.1064, gives the name of an earlier ruler called Jushnasdih, it perhaps makes more sense to assume that it was Firuz who was also called Jushnasdih. One might

son of Khusraw, who had fled to Nisibis at the time when Shirawayh had killed (his brothers), came forward, by the name of Farrukhzad Khusraw, and he was crowned and began to rule. He was of noble blood and reigned for a year.[488]

[Yazdagird III]

Then they found Yazdagird son of Khusraw;[489] his mother was a cupper[490] whom Khusraw had had intercourse with. She brought forward Yazdagird; (initially) they considered him inauspicious and concealed him, but necessity obliged them to accept him, even though their affairs remained in a state of turbulence and members of the regime boldly challenged him. After four years of his reign Sa'd ibn Abi Waqqas advanced to Qadisiyya and Yazdagird sent Rustam against him (but Sa'd defeated him). Then the Muslims came to Mada'in, which was the royal city, on the day of Nawruz, and the Persians had prepared various kinds of foods and their best clothes. The Persians were again defeated and Yazdagird fled, but the Muslims kept on pursuing him until they reached Merv. He entered a mill, whose owner killed him; his rule up to his death lasted 20 years.

[Customs of the Persians]

[199] The Persians worship fires and they do not purify themselves (after excretion) with water, but only with oil.[491] They do not use doors in their palaces, but hang curtains over the openings, which the guard will defend from (incoming) men. Their eating is accompanied by *zamzama*, that is, hidden speech.[492] They marry their mothers, sisters and daughters,

then identify him with the ruler called Firuz Jushnasbandah by Hamza, 28 (citing Bahram b. Mardanshah), and Mas'udi, 103.

488 Hamza, 16 and 28, calls him Khurrazad Khusraw, but *ibid.*, 22 (citing Musa b. 'Isa), has Farrukh b. Khusraw; Tabari, 1.1065–66, mentions a Khurrazad Khusraw and a Farrukhzad Kusraw as rulers, both being sons of Khusraw II and both discovered hiding in a fort near Nisibis, but they are presumably the same person.

489 Usually called Yazdagird son of Shahriyar; perhaps Ya'qubi or a copyist made a slip, confused by the three mentions of the name Khusraw just before and after Yazdagird.

490 Cupping is an ancient and widespread medical therapy which involves placing heated cups on the skin to achieve suction, with a number of alleged benefits, such as improved bloodflow. Presumably those who practised it, since they worked with their hands on people's bodies, would have been deemed unclean in Zoroastrianism, hence the doubt about Yazdagird's fitness to rule.

491 I.e. so as not to pollute the pure water with bad matter.

492 This refers to the Zoroastrian practice of ritual intoning of religious texts during eating.

and they believe that it is a gift for them (the women), a pious act by which they are brought closer to God.[493] They do not have public baths or toilets.[494] They glorify water and fire, sun and moon, and all the forms of light. They calculate time according to their months and feast days. Autumn for them is (the months of) Shahriwar, Mihr and Aban; winter is (the months of) Adhar, Day and Bahman; spring is (the months of) Asfandarmad, Frawardin and Ardbahisht; and summer is (the months of) Khurdadh, Tir and Murdadh.[495] There is an extra five days in autumn, which they call *andarkāh*,[496] for the year is 365 days and their months are 30 days long.

The beginning of their year is the day of Nawruz, which is the first day of Frawardin, and this falls in (the Near Eastern months of) Nisan and Adhar (= April and May) when the sun has passed into Aries, and it is their most venerated feast day. The day of Mihrajan (which honours the deity Mihr)[497] falls on the sixteenth day of the month of Mihr. Between Nawruz and Mihrajan there are one 175 days, that is, five months and 25 days. Mihrajan falls in (the Near Eastern month of) Tishrin II (= November). The Persians assign to every day of their months a name, and they are (known collectively as) the *rūzāt*:[498] the first is Hurmuz (and then comes) Bahman, Ardbahisht, Shahriwar, Isfandarmadh, Khurdadh, Murdadh, Day-ba-Adhar, Adhar, Aban, Khur, Mah, Tir, [200] Jush, Day-ba-Mihr, Mihr, Surush, Rashna, Frawardin, Bahram, Ram, Badh, Day-ba-Din, Din, Ard, Ashtadh, Asman, Zamyadh, Marasfand and Aniran.

The doctrine of the community, which they cite from Zoroaster, whom they claim as their prophet, is that light is ancient and eternal, and they call it Zurvan. He thought of evil as a lapse on his part, something which

---

493 On consanguineous marriage in Zoroastrianism see *EIr*, 'Marriage, ii. Next-of-kin marriage'.

494 Or at least not of the Roman–Islamic sort; the later Sasanid rulers did introduce them, but it angered many of their religious authorities because of the Zoroastrian laws about purity and use of water.

495 These are very close to the NP names of the months, except that Murdadh would be Amurdad. The names of the months and days reflect divinities and things important to Zoroastrianism: e.g. fire (*ādur/ādhar*), waters (*ābān*), (the star) Sirius (*tīr*), (the deity) Mithra (*mihr*, also = bond/covenant), and the Creator (*day*, i.e. Ohrmazd).

496 Persian: *andargāh*, literally meaning 'inbetween time'.

497 I insert this because it seems like some such short explanatory phrase has dropped out of the text. On these two important Persian festivals see *EIr*, 'Nowruz', 'Mehragān'.

498 *Rūz* is the Persian word for day. For information about the Zoroastrian calendar and for further reading see *EIr*, 'Calendars, i. pre-Islamic calendars'.

he (Zoroaster) taught them (the community) about.[499] Just as beauty turns to ugliness and sweet smell to stench, so the Ancient One in their view is not precluded from being affected by change and corruption upon part of him, though not all of him. When the Ancient One thought about evil, he sighed and that sorrow emerged from within him and it manifested itself before him. They apply to that sorrow that appeared to the Ancient One the name of Ahriman, and Zurvan they also call Ohrmazd.[500] Ahriman wanted to fight Ohrmazd, but Ohrmzad disliked that lest he do evil. So Ahriman made peace with him on the condition that every noxious and corrupt thing be made over to him. They maintain that these two are two (separate) bodies and two spirits and that there is a gulf between them on account of the resentment (towards each other that cannot be dissipated) because they never meet. They (the Zoroastrians) profess that Ohrmazd is light, the maker of bodies and their (soul) partners, while Ahriman makes only the noxious part in these beings, like the poison in reptiles, as well as the ire, anger, irritableness, wickedness, hostility, rancour and fear in animals. So it is God (Ohrmazd) who is the maker of (essential) substances and the resulting accidents.

The residence of the Persian kings at the beginning of the reign of Ardashir son of Babak was at Istakhr in one of the districts of Fars, but then the kings kept moving around until the reign [201] of Anusharwan son of Qubad, who resided in Mada'in in the land of Iraq. This then became the royal residence, and learned astrologers and physicians are unanimous that there is no city in the realm that is more conducive to health, virtue and moderation than that spot and the clime of Babylon that encompasses it. As for the regions which the Persians used to rule and hold sway in, they are the districts of Khurasan, namely: Nishabur, Herat, Merv, Merv al-Rudh, Faryab, Taliqan, Balkh, Bukhara, Badhghis, Abiward, Gharshastan, Tus, Sarakhs and Gurgan. In charge of these districts was a governor called the *isbahbadh* of Khurasan. As for the districts of Jibal, they are: Tabaristan, Rayy, Qazwin, Zanjan, Qom, Isfahan, Hamadan, Nihawand, Dinawar, Hulwan, Masabadhan, Mihrajan-Qadhaq, Shahrazur, Samaghan

---

499   Reading *'allamahum minhā*; one could also read *'ilmuhum minhā*, 'their knowledge is from it (the lapse)'. Possibly the text is corrupt here and some words are missing.

500   In the Avesta Zurvan is just a minor deity connected with Time, but in Manichaeism he has a much higher status as 'Father of Greatness' and in a number of Christian and Muslim texts he is the supreme deity with Ohrmazd (Ahriman is merely his offspring), and his cult was perceived to be bound up with Time and Fate. See *EIr*, 'Zurvan' and 'Zurvanism'. Note that Ya'qubi writes Ohrmazd as *Hurmuz*.

and Azerbaijan, and for these districts there is an *iṣbahbadh* called the *iṣbahbadh* of Azerbaijan. As for Kirman and Fars, their districts are: Istakhr, Shiraz, Arrajan, Nubandajan, Gur, Kazarun, Fasa, Darabgird, Ardashir Khurra, Shabur and Ahwaz together with its districts of Jundishabur, Susa, Nahr-Tira, Manadhir, Tustar, Idhaj and Ramhurmuz. In charge of all these is the *iṣbahbadh* known as the *iṣbahbadh* of Fars.

The districts of Iraq have 48 cantons along the Euphrates and Tigris. The Euphrates gives water to Baduraya, Anbar, Bahrasir, Rumaqan, the Zab – Upper, Lower and Middle, Zandaward, Maysan, Kutha, Nahr Durqit, Nahr Jawbar, Falluja [202] – Upper and Lower, Babel, Khutarniya, Jubba, Budat, Saylahin, Furat Baduqla, Sura, Barbisma, Nahr al-Malik, Barusma and Nistar. The Tigris gives water to Nahr Buq, Nahr Bin, Buzurg Shabur, Upper and Lower Radhan, Zabiyayn, Daskara, Burazruz, Silsil, Mahrudh, Jalula', Upper, Middle and Lower Nahrawan, Jazur, Mada'in, Bandanijin, Rustaqabad, Abaz Qubadh, Mubarak, Baduraya and Bakusaya. These come under a fourth *iṣbahbadh* called the *iṣbahbadh* of the West. The Persian frontier zone[501] adjoining the Euphrates ends at Anbar, and then you arrive at the frontier zone of the Romans; as for (the Persian frontier zone) adjoining the Tigris ...[502] and then you arrive at the frontier zone of the Romans. However, the matter proceeds by turns, for sometimes the Persians enter Roman territory by stealth and sometimes the Romans enter Persian territory.

Every Persian king always takes the name *Kisrā*,[503] and when they addressed him or mentioned him they would say *Kisrā Shāhanshāh*, meaning 'Caesar King of Kings'. The vizier is called *buzurg-framadār*, which refers to the one who takes on the affairs of state.[504] The religious specialist who is in charge of the laws of their religion is called *mūbadh mūbadhān*, meaning 'chief religious authority',[505] and the first to take

---

501 Arabic: *masāliḥ*, plural of *maslaḥa*, which can mean either the frontier zone itself or the defensive installations (guard posts, lookouts etc) placed along it.

502 Lacuna in the text; it presumably would have said that it ends somewhere in northern Mesopotamia.

503 *Kisrā* is the Arabicised form of the Persian name Khusraw. It is not true that every Persian king took this name, but because Khusraw II was the last major ruler of the Persian Empire before the Arab conquests his name became synonymous with the office, just as *Hiraql* (Heraclius) did for the office of Roman emperor.

504 On this and the following offices see Mas'udi, 103–4, above and the footnotes thereto.

505 Arabic: *'ālim al-'ulamā'*, literally meaning 'scholar of scholars', which is the best Ya'qubi could do given the lack of a concept for priest in Islam. On the meaning of *mūbadh* see n. 17 and Mas'udi, 103, above.

this name was Zoroaster. The custodian of the fire is called *hirbadh* and the scribe is called *dibīrbadh*.[506] The commander[507] is called by them *iṣbahbadh*, which means 'chief', [203] and below them is the *pādūsbān*,[508] which means 'repeller of enemies'. The head of a province is the *marzbān* and the head of a district is the *shahrīj*. Those who conduct battles and lead armies are referred to as *asāwira*.[509] The person responsible for the redress of wrongs is the *shāhrīst* and the head of the treasury is the *mardmār'ad*.[510]

506 This means the supervisor of the scribes (see Mas'udi, 104, above), so presumably Ya'qubi intended to write something like *ṣāḥib al-kuttāb*.

507 Arabic: *'aẓīm*, which means 'mighty, great' and can be applied to any powerful person, but Ya'qubi seems to have in mind the military here and hence my translation of 'commander'.

508 The editor says that the manuscript has f-'-d-y-r/z-'-s-t-'-r; he emends it to f-'-d-w-s-b-'-n without explanation, but probably because the *pādūsbān* became well known as the official responsible for the civil administration of one of the four divisions of the empire created by Khusraw I (e.g. Tabari, 1.892; whereas the *iṣbahbadh* was in charge of the military affairs of the divison). Ya'qubi may have translated it as 'repeller of enemies' because he linked it with MP *padyz*, 'to chase off'.

509 This only means cavalry or cavalrymen, an Arabic plural of Persian *aswār/*'horseman, rider', though they were certainly deemed the most important part of the military.

510 Possibly one should read *dar-āmārghar* here, i.e. court financial manager. The editor recognises that the rendering is corrupt and suggests *mardmānbadh* without explanation.

APPENDIX 1

Ibn al-Muqaffaʿ and
the 'History of the Kings of the Persians'

The first person in Hamza's list of those who translated the 'History of the Kings of the Persians' from Persian into Arabic is Ibn al-Muqaffaʿ (d. 757), a senior bureaucrat in the early Abbasid administration. Nöldeke argues not only that he was the first person to do this but also that later translators of this text 'presumably all used the work of their illustrious predecessor'.[1] Thus, in Nöldeke's view, Ibn al-Muqaffaʿ serves as the main conduit for information about ancient Persia passing to Muslim authors. The hole in this argument is that none of our extant Muslim texts directly cites Ibn al-Muqaffaʿ as a source for Persian history.[2] Nöldeke nevertheless maintained that it was possible to locate 'several individual passages of his book'. He provides what he feels is an example of such a passage, namely the tale of the encounter between Emperor Firuz and Akhshunwar, king of the Hephthalites, which is related at length and with similar wording in the chronicles of the Egyptian physician and patriarch Eutychius (d. 940) and of the Iranian legal scholar Tabari (d. 923) and in a literary anthology of the Iraqi judge and polymath Ibn Qutayba (d. 889).[3] I translate here the first part[4] of this episode in full to give some idea of the closeness of the three versions.[5]

---

1 These and ensuing quotes are taken from Nöldeke, *Sasaniden*, xx–xxii, where he presents his case for Ibn al-Muqaffaʿ.

2 Dinawari, 15, cites him once, but only for a refutation of the view of 'ignorant persons' that King Jamshid was to be identified with King Solomon.

3 Unbeknown to Nöldeke, and also to Rubin, who comments on this tale ('Ibn al-Muqaffaʿ', 67–68), it is also found partially in the 'History' of Maqdisi, 166–67, and fully in the *Nihāyat al-arab*, 184–87.

4 The second part deals with Firuz's surrender to Akhshunwar on condition of never again attacking the Hephthalites, his subsequent violation of that pledge and death, and the successful revenge mission of his minister Sukhra.

5 I translate Eutychius (E), 187–88, and give the versions of Ibn Qutayba (IQ), *ʿUyūn*,

Translation of Firuz-Akhshunwar encounter

Then Firuz marched with his troops to Khurasan[6] to attack Akhshunwar.[7] When Akhshunwar, king of the Hephthalites at Balkh,[8] heard that, he was afraid (*fazi'a*).[9] He assembled his confidants and consulted them.[10] One of them said:[11] 'If you give me a pledge that I can trust to the effect that you will adequately provide for my family and descendants and substitute sufficiently for me regarding them,[12] I will show you a way by which God will give you power over Firuz'.[13] So the king guaranteed that to him and he (the man) said to him (Akhshunwar): 'Cut off my hands and my legs and throw me into the path of Firuz[14] and I will spare you the trouble of (dealing with) him'.[15] He (Akhshunwar) did that to him and he was carried and thrown where he described to them and they then left him.[16] When Firuz passed him, he asked him about his condition, and he (the man) said

1.197–98, and Tabari (T), 1.875–76, in the footnotes. The account is also to be found in MS Sprenger 30, 142–43, but this mostly follows Tabari. The accounts of E + IQ differ from T in some respects in the second part of the story, which led Nöldeke to conclude that their narratives 'in part went back to Ibn al-Muqaffa' and in part to another' (*Sasaniden*, xxii), and led Rubin, 'Ibn al-Muqaffa'', 68–69, to doubt whether Ibn Muqaffa' was a direct source for any of the surviving witnesses.

   6 Same wording in all three texts (*sāra bi-junūdihi naḥwa Khurāsān*).

   7 E + IQ: *li-yaghzū Akhshunwar*; T: *murīdan ḥarb Akhshunwar*.

   8 IQ has this phrase, but places it in the previous sentence, on the first occurrence of Akhshunwar.

   9 IQ: 'When he (Firuz) arrived at his (Akhshunwar's) country, Akhshunwar's fear of him intensified (*ishtadda ru'b minhu*) and wariness towards him (Firuz) intensified'. T: 'When news of him (Firuz) reached Akhshunwar, his fear of him intensified' (*ishtadda ru'buhu minhu*).

   10 IQ: 'He examined his companions and ministers concerning him (Firuz); T omits.

   11 IQ: 'A man from among them said'; T: 'A man from among the companions of Akhshunwar offered up his life for him, saying'.

   12 IQ: 'Give me a covenant and a pledge that I can trust to the effect that you will adequately provide for my family and descendants and act well towards them and substitute for me regarding them'; T: 'act well towards my descendants and my dependents'.

   13 IQ: omits; T: 'He intended by this, so it is reported, to trick Firuz.'

   14 Same wording in all three texts (*iqṭa' yadayya wa-rijlayya wa-lqinī 'alā ṭarīq Fīrūz*); E notes that one version has *ūthiq*/'bind' but he prefers the reading *iqṭa'*/'cut off'.

   15 IQ: 'I will spare you the trouble of (dealing with) them and their might and I will ensnare them in a snare in which will be their perdition'; T omits. IQ now has Akhshunwar ask the man how he will benefit from his action, to which the man replies by extolling the merit and reward of self-sacrifice.

   16 IQ: 'He (Akhshunwar) did that to him and ordered him to be thrown where he described'; T: 'Akhshunwar did that to that man and threw him into the path of Firuz.'

to him:[17] 'I was one of the chiefs of the Hephthalites, but then when he heard of your march to him he consulted me as one of his confidants and I informed him that he would not be able to withstand Firuz because of the strength of his (Firuz's) valour and so it would be better to send him tribute and ransom. He became very angry at me and ordered me (to be put) into the state that you see and said to me: 'Go to the one whom you praise. And he ordered some of his troops, saying to them: "Go carry him to Firuz".[18] May you have compassion and mercy on me and order me to be carried with you so that the wild beasts do not ravage me in this wasteland.[19] I will show you a path that is shorter than this one so that you enter upon Akhshunwar in his place of safety and God will take revenge on him for me. The path that I will show you is only two day's march and you will then attain what you seek.'[20] ... Firuz refused to accept (the warnings) from them (his advisers)[21] and so they all went with that man wherever he took them for two days and they did not get across the desert ....[22] They went separately to the right and to the left searching for water, but most of them died of severe thirst and only a small number of his strongest companions escaped with Firuz, and they continued with him until they drew near to their enemy.[23]

17 IQ: 'When Firuz passed by him he asked about his state, and so he (the man) informed him ...'; T: 'When he passed by him he found his condition terrible and asked about his state, and so he (the man) informed him ...'.

18 T makes the same basic point as E here, though is much shorter: 'Akhshunwar did that to him because he had said to him: you cannot resist Firuz and the Persian army', but IQ takes a different tack: 'Akhshunwar did that to him, but he (the man) had employed a ruse so that he might be carried to that spot to be a guide to him (Firuz) despite his disability and unpreparedness'.

19 IQ omits; T: 'Firuz felt pity and compassion for him and ordered him to be carried with him.'

20 IQ: 'I will show you a path that is shorter than this one that you wish to follow and more hidden, so Akhshunwar will be unaware (of you) and you may take him by surprise and God will take revenge on him for me through you. There is nothing bad about this path except a journey of two days, then you will achieve all that you seek'; T: 'He (the man) let him know by way of advice to him, so it is alleged, that he would show him (Firuz) and his companions a quicker path to the king of the Hephthalites that no one had trodden.'

21 E has Firuz's ministers warn him at length that this was a trap; IQ simply says that 'his ministers advised him to be suspicious and wary of him', and T does not mention the ministers' caution at all, just noting that 'Firuz was deceived by that'.

22 E, IQ and T describe differently how the deceit became clear and the perilous journey in the desert.

23 IQ: 'They separated in the desert to the right and to the left, searching for water; thirst killed most of them and only a small number of them escaped with Firuz, and then they

Discussion

Since none of the three transmitters mentions Ibn al-Muqaffaʿ by name, it is not at first obvious why Nöldeke is so sure that he must be the source of the above account and why he goes so far as to say that 'one would be inclined to derive Eutychius' other reports about the Sasanids from Ibn al-Muqaffaʿ'. His argument would appear to be threefold:

1. Ibn Qutayba says of his version of the Firuz-Akhshunwar encounter that he read it in the 'Book of the Biographical History of the Iranians'.[24] Such a title could only refer, says Nöldeke, to the 'oldest and most famous work' of that genre, i.e. that of Ibn al-Muqaffaʿ.

2. Ibn Qutayba cites other works of Ibn al-Muqaffaʿ in the same text, namely the 'Book of the Crown', the 'Book of Protocols' and the 'Manners' (*ādāb*).

3. Eutychius not only has a similar account to Ibn Qutayba in this one narrative about Firuz but has a number of points of correspondence with the synopsis of Sasanid history in Ibn Qutayba's 'Book of Knowledge' (*Kitāb al-maʿārif*),[25] so 'both must have followed the same source, which can only reasonably be the work of Ibn al-Muqaffaʿ'.

It does seem certain that Eutychius and Ibn Qutayba shared a source for Persian history. Besides the episode of Firuz-Akhshunwar that Nöldeke drew attention to, there is also the tale of how Ardashir conquered Hatra by means of the subterfuge of the daughter of its king, who, in return for marriage to Ardashir, showed him a secret way into the city.[26] Since Ibn Qutayba ascribes both of these narratives to the 'Book of the Biographical History of the Iranians', it is, as Nöldeke says, reasonable to suppose that this work

continued with him until they drew near to their enemy'; T: thirst killed most of them and Firuz went on with those who had made it out safely with him to their enemy'.

24 *Kitāb siyar al-ʿajam*; I translate *ʿajam* as Iranian here rather than Persian so that I can distinguish it in translation from *Furs*. The singular of *siyar*, *sīra*, is the usual word for 'biography' (strongly connected with that of the prophet Muhammad), but in the plural it can mean more broadly '(heroic) deeds/exploits' and also 'military campaigns'.

25 Nöldeke gives no examples, but he may well be right; e.g. Eutychius, 106 = Ibn Qutayba, *Maʿārif*, 653: 'He (Ardashir) wrote to the kings of Fars who were near to him and the petty kings who were far from him … . Some of them professed obedience to him … and some waited for him to come to them' (same wording).

26 Ibn Qutayba, *ʿUyūn*, 4.116; Eutychius, 106. A different version of the Persian capture of Hatra is found in numerous Muslim histories, where it is Ardashir's son Shabur who schemes with the king of Hatra's daughter to enter the city (e.g. Tabari, 1.827–30, on the authority of Hisham ibn al-Kalbi).

is indeed their common source. However, Nöldeke's grounds for attributing it to Ibn al-Muqaffaʿ are very weak, for in the first Abbasid century many authors wrote on Persian history, and we have no indication as to which of them might have produced this particular work. Moreover, the way the source is referred to makes one wonder whether a specific text is meant:

1. The exact title 'the Book of the Biographical History of the Iranians' does not feature in Hamza's list of eight early translations of Persian history.[27]

2. Ibn Qutayba refers to this source in different ways: 'the Book of the Biographical History of the Iranians', 'the books of the Biographical History of the Iranians' and simply 'the Biographical History of the Iranians'.[28]

3. The tenth-century scholar Maqdisi records that he 'read in one of (the books of) the Biographical History of the Iranians' (*fī baʿḍ siyar al-ʿajam*) that Abraham was born during the reign of King Afridun.[29]

4. Some of the material quoted from this source is more edifying in nature than historical, and is not found in Arabic chronicles; e.g. 'I read in the Biographical History of the Iranians that Ardashir, when he was confident of his rule, assembled the people and addressed to them a speech in which he urged upon them friendship and obedience and warned them against disobedience and breaking away from the (righteous) community, and he organised the people into four castes.'[30]

It would appear, then, that many texts circulated with the title 'History of the Iranians'. From the offhand way that Hamza, 29, above, and others refer casually to the *kutub al-siyar* one may even say that we should think of it as a genre, embracing all types of text that treated Persian history, with an evident focus on the lives of their rulers and heroes.

---

27 See Hamza, 8, above, where Ibn al-Muqaffaʿ's translation of Persian history is called 'Biographical History of the Kings of the Persians' (*Siyar mulūk al-Furs*). Ibn al-Nadim, 118, calls it 'Book of Lords' (*khudāy-nāmah*).

28 Ibn Qutayba, *Maʿārif*, 57, 652; Ibn Qutayba, *ʿUyūn*, 1.171, 1.197, 1.273, 4.116.

29 Maqdisi, 3.144. Note that Maqdisi also records two of the three stories that Ibn Qutayba attributes to the 'Biographical History of the Iranians', namely the Firuz-Akhshunwar encounter and a tale about how Bahram Gur demonstrated his prowess at hunting to a slave girl (Ibn Qutayba, *ʿUyūn*, 1.273; Maqdisi, 3.164).

30 Ibn Qutayba, *ʿUyūn*, 1.171. Note that Abu Bakr al-Dinawari al-Maliki (d. 333/994) gives a number of aphorisms quoted from the 'Biographical Histories of the Persians' on the authority of Ibn Qutayba that do not appear in the latter's surviving works; e.g. 'A sign of the free is that being met by what they love and being deprived of what they hoped for is more desirable to them than being met by what they hate and being given beyond what they hoped for' (*al-Mujālasa*, 5.276).

As for the accounts of Firuz's encounter with Akhshunwar, it is noticeable that, even though it is a very long story, they are surprisingly similar, often matching word for word. This is not so common in the Muslim narratives of pre-Islamic Persia. In general, they exhibit a broad likeness and short bursts of closeness in wording, but few examples of sustained close correspondence for a whole episode. One major exception is the report of the exploits of Bahram Chobin (especially as conveyed by Dinawari and Ya'qubi), which existed as an independent text according to a number of tenth-century authors. Possibly, then, the tale of Firuz's campaigns against Akhshunwar also survived as a stand-alone text before being incorporated into the *siyar* literature, the compilations of narratives about ancient Persia that became so popular in early Abbasid times.

There is one last point that I would like to make, which is that, despite Nöldeke's emphasis on Ibn al-Muqaffa''s importance as a bridge between Sasanid historiography and Islamic historiography on the subject of pre-Islamic Persia, he is not later celebrated or commemorated for this role. Jaako Hämeen-Anttila has recently reasserted Nöldeke's view, maintaining that 'all sources agree that he (Ibn al-Muqaffa') translated the *Xwadāynāmag*' and that 'Ibn al-Muqaffa''s translation of the *Xwadāynāmag* was very influential'.[31] But that is simply not true. Only one source, Ibn al-Nadim, makes this claim.[32] One may defend Hämeen-Anttila by saying that by *Xwadāynāmag* he means not the specific title but more generally the official history of Persia that is supposed to have been compiled in late Sasanid times. Yet even widening the definition like this brings us only one other support, namely Hamza al-Isfahani, who says that Ibn al-Muqaffa' translated 'The Biographical History of the Kings of the Persians' (*siyar mulūk al-Furs*). This is repeated by some later authors, but they are clearly just copying from Hamza.[33] One might argue that Muslim authors were disdainful of citing the work of someone suspected of dualist leanings,[34] and yet they are happy to credit Ibn al-Muqaffa' with translating some specific historical texts, such as the book on the wars of the Kayanid prince Isfandiyar,[35] and even more so with translating and expounding upon texts treating Sasanid statecraft, administrative practice, court etiquette

---

31 'Ibn al-Muqaffa'', 171 and 181.

32 Ibn al-Nadim, 118, and even he does not use the MP form, but the NP form: *Khudāy-nāmah*.

33 As shown by Hämeen-Anttila himself in his article 'Al-Kisrawī', 66–74.

34 Thus Savant, *New Muslims*, 45–46.

35 See the introduction above and Mas'udi, 94, above (*Kitāb al-Baykār*).

and Persian wisdom (see below). I do not mean to infer from this that Ibn al-Muqaffa' did not translate a universal history of pre-Islamic Persia, but simply to note the lack of acknowledgement of it by later writers, especially by historians.[36] It perhaps makes more sense to assume that the translation of Ibn al-Muqaffa' was just one of many renderings and reworkings of the Persian historical tradition that circulated in the early Abbasid period with titles such as 'The History of the Kings of the Persians' and 'The Biographical History of the Iranians'. To illustrate my point, I give examples of the recollections of Ibn al-Muqaffa' by some very well-known authors writing in the first two centuries after his death and of the sort of material that they transmitted from him.

Jahiz (d. 868)

'Once he (the novice scribe) has memorised the most eloquent speeches and the most erudite witticisms and has recited the aphorisms of Buzurgmihr, the counsel of Ardashir, the letters of 'Abd al-Hamid, and the etiquette of Ibn al-Muqaffa' and once he has made the "Book of Mazdak" the mine of his knowledge and "Kalila and Dimna"[37] the treasury of his wisdom, he thinks that he is God's gift to administration' ('Dhamm al-kuttāb', 191–92).

'We cannot know whether the treatises attributed to the (pre-Islamic) Persians are genuine and not fabricated, ancient and not newly composed,

---

36 The writers that copy Hamza's list, including Ibn al-Muqaffa', are, except for Ibn al-Nadim, all in the Persian tradition (Bal'ami, Muhammad al-Balkhi and the anonymous authors of the *Mujmal al-tawārīkh* and the older prose preface to Firdawsi's *Shāh-nāmah*). No medieval Arabic chronicle refers to Ibn al-Muqaffa''s translation of a historical work. The only exception is the anonymous *Nihāyat al-arab*, which tells in one of its two prefaces (*ibid.*, 17) how Ibn al-Muqaffa' (born in 720) and two other scholars were commissioned to produce the work at the request of the caliph 'Abd al-Malik (died in 705). Even if we concede that some of its accounts are older than those of Tabari and Dinawari, as Grignaschi claims ('La nihāyatu'), this does not mean, as Hämeen-Anttila states, that 'it has to go back to a ninth- or eighth-century original' ('Ibn al-Muqaffa'', 176), but simply that it draws on ninth- and eighth-century sources (whether directly or indirectly), as do all narrators of pre-Islamic Persian history. In the form that we have it, however, it is unlikely to antedate the eleventh century and its frequent allusions to Ibn al-Muqaffa', the most famous transmitter of Iranian lore, are surely added to enhance the text's claims to genuine ancient knowledge.

37 All sources agree that these two texts were translated from Persian into Arabic by Ibn al-Muqaffa', the first (the 'Book of Mazdak' – the reading of the latter name is uncertain, possibly Marduk) was a piece of wisdom literature and the second ('Kalila and Dimna') a very famous collection of Indian animal fables that offered wisdom and guidance for rulers.

since the likes of Ibn al-Muqaffa', Sahl ibn Harun, Abu 'Ubaydallah, 'Abd al-Hamid and Ghaylan, were able to compose anew such treatises and fabricate biographical histories (*siyar*)' (*Bayān*, 3.29).

Ibn Qutayba (d. 889)

'Ibn al-Muqaffa' translated for him (Caliph Mansur) the books of Aristotle on logic and the book of Kalila and Dimna' (*Ma'ārif*, 31).

'The most famous of those who translated from Persian to Arabic were Ibn al-Muqaffa', Fadl ibn Nawbakht, Moses and Yusuf, sons of Khalid, and many others' (*Ma'ārif*, 54).

'I read in a book of Ibn al-Muqaffa': People are of the (same) religion as the ruler except for a few' (*Uyūn*, 1.54).

'I read in the "Manners" (*ādāb*) of Ibn al-Muqaffa': Do not be in the company of rulers until you have trained yourself to obey them in what is detestable to you, to agree with them in what you find objectionable, and to value things according to their preferences and not yours' (*'Uyūn*, 1.74).

Baladhuri (d. 892)

He gives a long citation from Ibn-al-Muqaffa' on details of administrative procedures involving the king in the Sasanid state, in particular the sealing of documents, the number of royal seals and the recording of tax revenues on parchment (*Futūḥ*, 464).

Dinawari (d. 895)

'Ibn al-Muqaffa' would say: the ignorant and unlearned Persians claim that King Jam was Solomon son of David, but that is wrong, for more than 3000 years separate Solomon and Jam' (p. 15).

Ibn al-Faqih (wr. ca. 903)

'When (the littérateur) Abu l-'Ayna' (d. ca. 896) heard some of the prose of Ibn al-Muqaffa', he said: His diction is pure, his speech eloquent, his mark is true, his expression clear as scattered pearls, as unfurled brocade, as rain-splashed meadows' (p. 194).

'Ibn al-Muqaffa' said: (The region of) Ādharbayjjān is (named after)

Ādharbādh ibn Īrān ibn al-Aswad ibn Shem ibn Noah, or some say Ādharbādh ibn Biyurasb' (p. 284).[38]

'Ibn al-Muqaffaʿ said: The first city wall that was constructed after the Flood was the wall of Susa and of Tustar, and it is not known who built them' (p. 395).[39]

Maqdisi (wr. *ca*. 950)

'Ibn al-Muqaffaʿ reported that the desert of the Hijaz was in ancient times all estates, villages, residences, flowing wells and incessant rivers, then after that it became a brimming sea on which boats sailed, but then it became a dry wasteland, and none knows how its condition changed' (2.150).

'Ibn al-Muqaffaʿ reported that those coffers (of Yazdagird III) held 7000 containers of gold that Qubad had had made, each one of them (weighing) 12,000 mithqals (approx. 56 kgs), not counting what had been made by the rest of the kings and their heirs' (5.195).

Hamza al-Isfahani (d. *ca*. 960s)

'I have read in the book that Ibn al-Muqaffaʿ translated that the surviving vaulted hall (*īwān*) at Mada'in was built by Shabur ibn Ardashir, but the chief priest Emed ibn Ashawahisht said to me: the matter is not as Ibn al-Muqaffaʿ asserted, for (Caliph) Mansur Abu Jaʿfar destroyed that hall (of Shabur) and this surviving one was built by Khusraw Abarwiz.'[40]

'In reporting all that was required for this chapter, I had no recourse but to collect copies (of the history of the Persian kings) that have been differently translated. In all I chanced upon eight copies, which are: "The Biographical History of the Persian Kings" translated by Ibn al-Muqaffaʿ ...' (p. 8, above).

---

38 This is according to the Leiden edition. It is repeated by Yaqut, s.v. 'Ādharbayjān', who counters: 'Rather *ādhar* is the word for fire in Pahlavi and *bāykān* means protector and keeper'. One would have expected Ibn al-Muqaffaʿ to know that as a translator of Persian, so the saying may not be by him.

39 This does not seem to be in the Leiden edition, but it is in the Beirut edition, which uses the Mashhad manuscript. Its presence in the original text is confirmed by Yaqut, s.v. 'Tustar'.

40 Yaqut (s.v. 'Īwān') cites this on the authority of 'Hamza ibn Hasan', which must be Hamza ibn Hasan al-Isfahani, the author of the work from which we have translated the section above. Unfortunately, Yaqut does not specify what book of Hamza's he took it from. I include it here because it is a more concretely historical report than the others.

APPENDIX 2

The *Chronicle of Siirt* and the 'Book of Lords'

It has recently been asserted that the tenth-century Christian Arabic *Chronicle of Siirt* – its name taken from the town in modern southern Turkey where it was discovered – draws directly from the putative 'Book of Lords'.[1] The basis for this assertion is the fact that there are some instances of correspondence between the *Chronicle of Siirt* and Muslim Arabic histories on aspects of pre-Islamic Persian history.[2] Perhaps the most famous example is a speech attributed to Hurmuz IV in which he reprimands some Zoroastrian priests who had urged him to persecute the Christians, counselling them to bolster Zoroastrianism by the practice of virtue rather than by the exercise of coercion. He reminds them that the religions of the empire are like the legs of the royal throne: they are all crucial to the maintenance of equilibrium and balance:[3]

> *Chronicle of Siirt*, 104: 'The throne has four legs and will not stand on the two inner legs without the two outer ones. Likewise, the Zoroastrian religion will not stand without the support (of other religions), so take care ... that none of you oppose my order to protect the Christians.'

---

1 Wood, 'Christian Reception', 9: the author of the *Chronicle of Seert* 'uses material drawn from the Xwadāy-Nāmag tradition'; *id.*, *Chronicle of Seert*, 172: 'the *Chronicle of Seert*'s inclusion of sections from the *Xwadāy-Nāmag*'.

2 Wood, 'Christian Reception', 9, also observes that both Sebeos, 72, and *Chronicle of Siirt*, 123, cite a 'Royal History' at the beginning of their accounts of Hurmuz's reign. This is interesting, though he overeggs the point by translating the Arabic expression *akhbār al-mulūk* as 'the Persian royal annals', whereas it just means 'history/narratives of the kings'.

3 This speech and its significance is analysed by McDonough, 'The Legs of the Throne', and Payne, *State of Mixture*, 166–68. The latter work offers a rich and positive picture of Christian involvement in the Sasanid state. See also Wood, 'Christian Reception', esp. 278–79.

Tabari, 1.991: 'Just as the royal throne cannot stand with only the two front legs and not the two rear legs, so the kingdom cannot stand firm if we antagonise the Christians in our land and the people of the other religions different to ours.'

It is possible that both the *Chronicle of Siirt* and Tabari are drawing here on a Sasanid historical source, but, given that the author of the *Chronicle of Siirt* is writing after Tabari,[4] it should also be considered whether he is using Tabari directly or whether he shares with Tabari (and other Muslim historians) an earlier Muslim source, especially as we can see that the *Chronicle of Siirt* is influenced by Muslim sources elsewhere, as, for example, in the list of Muslim signatories to the peace treaty awarded to the Christians of Najran and in the details of Muhammad's death.[5] In order to probe this question further, I translate here the entry on the emperor Qubad in the *Chronicle of Siirt* and indicate parallels with other sources.

Translation of *Chronicle of Siirt*, 32–36, 40–41, 54:

[32] When the Persians chose Balash[6] son of Firuz[7] and rejected Qubad, the latter became angry and he headed for the king of the Hephthalites and acquainted him with the events of Balash's rise up to his coronation. He (Qubad) remained for three years with him, who treated him honorably and then dispatched him, in his fourth year, with an army to fight his brother.[8] When he (Qubad) arrived at Mada'in, he found that he (Balash) had died[9] and that the people had had enough of war and bloodshed. He (Balash) had reigned for four years. Some say that they (the people) had poked out his eyes and killed him. He had built a city on the (river) Zab in the land

---

4 Hoyland, *Seeing Islam*, 444, gives the time of composition to between 912 and 1020. Wood, *Chronicle of Seert*, offers extensive and useful discussion of this text.

5 *Chronicle of Siirt*, 297–98.

6 The text has Mīlās.

7 The *Chronicle of Siirt* agrees here with the Muslim sources in making Balash son of Firuz, whereas pre-Islamic sources make him the brother of Firuz (see n. 54 above).

8 If this refers to Balash, it may indicate that the author of the *Chronicle of Siirt* also has a non-Muslim source before him. However, he may just be confused by the fact that Qubad later raises an army to fight his brother Jamasb. Note that some sources have Qubad go twice to the Hephthalites, the first time to win the throne from Balash and the second time to win the throne from Jamasb (e.g. Tabari, 1.883 and 887), and some just once, either at the beginning of his reign (Ibn Qutayba, *Ma'ārif*, 662; Maqdisi, 3.167), or after his escape from prison (Procopius, 1.6.10; Agathias, 4.28.3; Ya'qubi, 185).

9 Thus Tabari, 1.884; Maqdisi, 3.167.

of Marga. Qubad then ascended the throne without any trouble. He sent presents to the king of the Hephthalites and acted well towards his subjects and did not punish them for what they had done. He was the greatest of the (Persian) kings in terms of humility and serenity and understanding of Zoroastrianism.[10]

[33] He took an interest at the beginning of his term in building cities and villages.[11] He constructed bridges and dams across rivers and (canals) to bring water to desolate places.[12] He established a number of villages in Mosul and Iraq and transported people there from other places and ordered them to cultivate (crops). He allowed the erection of convents and monasteries and he supported the doctrine of Zaradusht[13] in their belief that there were two major eternal (principles) and that women should be made available to men, no one man possessing any one woman to the exclusion of his fellows.[14] He ordered the construction throughout his kingdom of temples and also of hostels so that the more desirous and fornication-inclined men and women might couple there. This angered the (male) Zoroastrians on account of their (own) women and children.

He reduced culinary expenditure, just as Julian, king of the Romans, had done, deeming that excess in that respect was a form of dissipation.[15] He emulated the Romans in the digging of canals and the cultivation of lands. He disliked warfare and fighting.[16] The Zoroastrians asked him to rescind his order to apply the doctrine of Zaradusht, but he did not heed them, saying that Zoroastrianism requires that a woman not be prohibited

10 Agathias, 4.27.6–7, says he was 'harsh and unyielding, ready to upset the established order'.

11 Ibn Qutayba, Ma'ārif, 663, and Tabari, 1.885, say he built Arrajan, Hulwan and Qubad Khurra.

12 Thus also Tabari, 1.885.

13 Most sources mention Mazdak only in connection with Qubad: Dinawari, 66–67; Tabari, 1.885–86; Mas'udi, 101; Mas'udi, Murūj, 2.195; Hamza, 56; Maqdisi, 3.167. Ya'qubi, 186, and Tabari, 1.893, mention Zaradusht (son of Khurrak) later in connection with Khusraw I. The contemporary Ps-Joshua, 249, says that Qubad restored 'the loathsome Zoroastrian sect called the Zardushtakan, which teaches that women belong in common'.

14 Thus also Procopius, 1.5.1, and Agathias, 4.27.7. Ibn Qutayba, Ma'ārif, 663, Tabari, 1.886, Maqdisi, 3.167–68, and MS Sprenger 30, 148–49, present Mazdak's message, with substantial correspondence in wording, as being about equal access to property as well as women.

15 Emending jāra majrā l-tabdhīr to jarā majrā l-tabdhīr.

16 Dinawari, 66, Ya'qubi, 185, and Tabari, 1.885, have Qubad entrust the running of government for the first part of his reign to Sukhra (see nn. 430–31, above), whom he later has killed.

from pairing secretly with someone other than her husband and that if
she bore a child from another man it should be attributed to him. They
contrived to kill him, but were not able. Then after ten years they found a
way and deposed him from the rule.[17]

... [34: Account of how Qubad ordered all religions in his realm 'to
compose a treatise on their faith and to present it before him', which
was carried out for the Church of the East by Elishe of Nisibis ... [35]
After deposing Qubad, the Zoroastrians elected (his brother) Jamasb,[18]
appointed him in his place and put Qubad in prison.[19] His sister[20] strove
to get to him, but she was not able. She asked Jamasb many times to
allow her to go to him and stay with him.[21] She did not stop scheming to
get her brother out of prison until she on one occasion found a way.[22] She
wrapped him in a mattress and pretended that it was the cloth (that she
used) for her menstruation. She summoned the bleacher to carry it out
and wash it, [36] and those responsible for the prison would not go near it
because of its impurity.[23] Thus Qubad escaped and proceeded to the king
of the Turks[24] on account of the friendship and familiarity that existed
between them due to his stay with him during the time of his father.[25]
He aided him and dispatched him with an army.[26] He returned to his

17 Agathias, 4.28.1; Dinawari, 667; Ya'qubi, 185; Tabari, 1.885.

18 Ps-Joshua, 251; Procopius, 1.5.2 (but confuses Jamasb with Balash); Agathias, 4.28.2;
Dinawari, 667; Ya'qubi, 185; Tabari, 1.886 and 887; Mas'udi, *Murūj*, 2.196: Hamza, 56.

19 Procopius, 1.5.7, and Agathias, 4.28.1, call it the 'prison of oblivion' (*frourion tēs
lēthēs*), 'for if anyone is cast into it the law permits no mention of him to be made thereafter'.

20 Some sources say his sister (Dinawari, 67; Ya'qubi, 185; Tabari, 1.887), and some
say his wife (Procopius, 1.6.1; Agathias, 4.28.3). She could have been both given that
Zoroastrianism approves incestuous marriage, especially for the high-born.

21 Or she seduced the guard who then let her in: thus Procopius, 1.6.1–2, and Tabari,
1.887.

22 Procopius, 1.6.3–4, says that Qubad also had the help of a close companion of his,
named Seosēs.

23 The menstruation stratagem appears also, with some correspondence in wording, in
Ya'qubi, 185, and Tabari, 1.887 (see conclusion below). Procopius, 1.6.6–7, says that Qubad
swapped clothes with his wife/sister and pretended to be her.

24 Or rather Hephthalites, as above. Thus also Procopius, 1.6.10; Agathias, 4.28.3;
Dinawari, 67; Ya'qubi, 185; Ibn Qutayba, *Ma'ārif*, 663; Tabari, 1.887.

25 This may be an allusion to the fact that Firuz handed over his son to the king of the
Hephthalites for a time as a form of IOU since he did not have sufficient funds to make a
tribute payment (Ps-Joshua, 243 and 251).

26 Procopius, 1.6.10, and Agathias, 4.28.4, say that the Hephthalite king also gave Qubad
his daughter in marriage; Ps-Joshua, 251, agrees and specifies that the mother was one of
Qubad's sisters, taken captive by the Hephthalites during the reign of Firuz. Muslims sources

kingdom[27] and removed Jamasb, though he did not kill him.[28] However, he killed a great number of the Zoroastrians and imprisoned a host (of them). He was kind to the Christians because a group of them had served him on his way to the country of the Turks.[29]

[40] When Qubad returned from the country of the Turks, he headed for Amida and besieged it for a time,[30] but was not able to capture it because of the thickness of its walls.[31] He intended to leave it in favour of another city of the Romans, but he dreamed that night of someone telling him not to weaken or depart.[32] Surprised by that, he remained (besieging the city) and it was captured the following night, and he killed in it a great many people.[33] A large number hid in the convents, but when Qubad entered the city they were opened for him. Then he saw an image of Our Lady in (one of) them. He asked about it and was told (what it was), whereupon he prostrated before it, saying to his companions: 'This is the figure that I saw address me in my dream, saying to me: "Return to the city, for I shall surrender it to you on account of the sins [41] of its people"'. He ordered that those who sought refuge in the convents should not be killed and that the people be spared. He seized everything that he found in the city and

narrate how Qubad had intercourse with a woman on his way to the king of the Hephthalites, either at the beginning of his reign (Ibn Qutayba, *Ma'ārif*, 662–62; Tabari, 1.883–84) or after his escape from prison (Dinawari, 67; Ya'qubi, 185; Tabari, 1.887), and that she gave birth to the future Khusraw I.

27 On the border of which he first, according to Procopius, 1.6.12–16, dealt with the matter of who should hold the governorship (with the rank/title of *kanarang*) of Khurasan.

28 Dinawari, 68; Ya'qubi, 186; Tabari, 1.887. Procopius, 1.6.17, says he blinded and imprisoned him, though confusing Jamasb with Balash; Ps-Joshua, 251, says Jamasb fled, and Agathias, 4.28.7, says he gave up the throne voluntarily.

29 Ibn Qutayba, *Ma'ārif*, 663, Tabari, 1.886, Mas'udi, *Murūj*, 2.196, and Maqdisi, 3.168 have an alternative story in which Qubad is restored to the throne by Zarmihr son of Sukhra, without mention of Hephthalites.

30 The siege of Amida (October 502–January 503) is narrated only very briefly in Muslim sources (Dinawari, 68; Ya'qubi, 186; Tabari, 1.887), but in great detail by Ps-Joshua, 276–80, Procopius, 1.7.3–32, and Ps-Zachariah, 7.3.c-7.

31 Procopius, 1.7.12–13, and Ps-Zachariah, 7.3.c, also says that the Persians were unable to breach the walls.

32 Ps-Zacahriah, 7.4.a, says that it was Christ that Qubad saw in a dream, telling him 'he would hand over the inhabitants of the city to him in three days because they had sinned against him'.

33 Procopius, 1.7.16–30, also says that Qubad was about to call off the siege, but the jeers of the Amidans made the Persians want to continue, and then one of them discovered a disused underground passage into the city, allowing the Persians to capture the city by surprise.

transported it to Mada'in, and he left behind in Amida some men to guard it.[34] The Romans were informed of what had happened, and they headed for Amida and fought the Persians who were in it, surrounding them until they had defeated them and ejected them from the city.[35]

[54] Qubad reigned for 42 years[36] and he had many children. Before his death he bequeathed the rule to his son Khusraw Anusharwan, who was born in the land of the Turks at the time of his (Qubad's) flight there.

Conclusion

From the above it would seem that the *Chronicle of Siirt* is using Christian and Muslim sources, but no late Sasanid Persian sources (or at least only indirectly via Muslim texts). The Christian material is evident in the notices about the erection of convents and monasteries, the requirement of religious leaders to compose a treatise on their faith and the siege of Amida. The most obvious indication of Muslim input is the erroneous statement that Balash was a son of Firuz rather than his brother – a mistake made only by Muslim writers, and one that would surely not be made by a Sasanid source. There is also the correspondence with Ya'qubi and Tabari on the ruse of Firuz's sister to get him out of prison:

> *Chronicle of Siirt*, 35–36: 'She (Qubad's sister) wrapped him (*laffathu*) in a mattress (*firāsh*) and pretended that it was the cloth (that she used) for her menstruation. She summoned the bleacher to carry it out (*yahmilahā*) and wash it, and those responsible for the prison would not go near it because of its impurity.'

> Tabari, 1.887 (cf. Ya'qubi, 185, above): 'She (Qubad's sister) ordered that he be wrapped (*luffa*) in a carpet ... and carried out (*humila*) by a servant boy ... . The one in charge of the prison asked what he was carrying ... and the sister of Qubad informed him that it was a mattress (*firāsh*) that she had lain on during her menstruation ... and he would not approach it deeming it dirty.'

This correspondence seems more likely to derive from a common Arabic source than from a shared Sasanid one, in part because of the coincidence in Arabic wording and in part because the late Roman sources speak rather

34 Thus also Procopius, 1.7.33, specifying 1000 men.
35 Procopius, 1.8–9, gives a long account in which he explains that the Romans did not manage to eject the Persians by war, but rather negotiated a payment for them to leave.
36 Agathias, 4.28.8 (41 years). Muslim sources say 43 years: Dinawari, 69; Tabari, 1.888; Mas'udi, 101; Mas'udi, *Murūj*, 2.195.

of Firuz's wife and of a different stratagem: Firuz putting on his wife's clothes to evade the prison guards.

Finally, it is worth pointing out the complexity of transmission that is revealed by the translation above. For example, Tabari shares with Ibn Qutayba and Maqdisi the theme of Mazdakite communism, with Ya'qubi and the *Chronicle of Siirt* the theme of the menstruation cloth of Firuz's sister and with Ibn Qutayba, Mas'udi and Maqdisi the theme of Zarmihr restoring Qubad to power. In each case the clusters of sources share large chunks of text that have similar or identical wording. Presumably our late ninth- and tenth-century authors did a fair amount of cutting and pasting from earlier works, perhaps because many of the latter were relatively short texts treating individual persons or single events. Again, though, I am obliged to emphasise that my conclusions are tentative until more study has been done. Selecting more episodes from Persian history and comparing all the different versions of it in our extant sources, as I have done here with Qubad's reign, may well help to elucidate further the question of the nature and scope of the lost works.

APPENDIX 3

Abu Maʿshar and the Lost Books of Jay

The authority most cited by Hamza al-Isfahani is the astrologer Abu Maʿshar (d. 886), who was a native of Balkh, in modern north Afghanistan. Many of the latter's writings were subsequently translated into Latin and were enormously influential in medieval Europe. The text that caught Hamza's attention was Abu Maʿshar's 'Book of Thousands' (*Kitāb al-ulūf*), which is a work of historical astrology focused on providing an interpretation of history in terms of the movements and conjunctions of heavenly bodies. To achieve this aim chronography was very important for providing dates for key events and phenomena in human history that could then be linked to planetary conjunctions and the like, and it has been shown that Abu Maʿshar was well versed in chronological data of all sorts, such as pre-Islamic Arabian calendars, reign lengths of Greco-Roman kings and Indian world cycles.[1] He also made use of chronological sources from different cultures, including Sanskrit and Greek. It is not surprising, then, that Hamza found this book useful.

The thirteenth-century scientific biographer Ibn al-Qifti observed that Abu Maʿshar was 'the most knowledgeable person in the biographical history of the Persians (*siyar al-Furs*) and the histories of the other nations'.[2] This is illustrated by his efforts to reconcile ancient Persian chronology with Judaeo-Christian models. Hamza gives us evidence of this in the passage from the 'Book of Thousands' that I translated above (Hamza, 9–12), and a particularly fascinating example comes from a later part of Hamza's text, which I translate below. It also appears verbatim in the bibliographical oeuvre of his younger contemporary Ibn al-Nadim (d. 990). It highlights further Abu Maʿshar's acquaintance with the history of pre-Islamic Iran[3]

---

1 Van Bladel, *Arabic Hermes*, 147–54.

2 Ibn al-Qifti, 152.

3 An interest in history, especially its chronological aspect, is common among astrologers, and it suggests that their works might offer new insights, especially for fields

and at the same gives a nice little insight into the survival of texts in medieval Iran and attitudes towards them. It occurs in Hamza (H), 197–201, and Ibn al-Nadim (IN), 240–41.[4]

Translation

[H] In the year 350 one wing of the building called Sarawayh collapsed, which is in the city of Jay. This revealed 50 loads of leather tomes written in a script that the people had never seen the like of before, and it was not known when these had been deposited in this building. I was asked what I knew[5] of the history of this wonderfully constructed[6] edifice. I brought out to the people who were present a book of the astrologer Abu Ma'shar of Balkh, translated as the 'Book of the Differences of Astronomical Tables', in which he says [H + IN] that the kings of the Persians were so concerned to preserve the sciences, so anxious for their long-term survival and so worried about (what might befall) them from atmospheric events and natural disasters, that they chose for (recording) them the writing materials that were the most resistant to accidents and the least likely to rot and decay, namely the bark of the white poplar tree, the bark of which is called *tūz*. The peoples of India, China and neighbouring nations followed them in that. They also picked it for their bows, which they would shoot from, on account of its toughness, smoothness and durability for the bows over time.

When they had obtained the best writing material that they could find in the world for recording their sciences, they desired for them (the place) among all the locales, countries and regions of the world that had the most salubrious ground, the least amount of decay, the greatest distance from earthquakes and eclipses, the richest clay and whatever gave the best

such as pre-Islamic Persia, where literary sources are few. Note the comment of Kennedy, 'Islamic Astronomical Tables', 1: 'Thousands of Byzantine, Greek, Sanskrit, Hebrew, Arabic, Persian and Turkish astronomical and astrological manuscripts exist, many in uncatalogued collections, and most of them untouched by modern scholarship'.

4   The texts have almost exactly the same wording, so either they are both copying from Abu Ma'shar, as they claim, or, as Pourshariati has argued ('Hamza al-Isfahani', 113), Ibn al-Nadim is 'borrowing the material from Hamza without proper citation'. After finishing this appendix I found that the passages had been given in summary form and discussed in Pingree, *Thousands of Abu Ma'shar*, ch. 1 and Appendix I.

5   Hamza wrote a history of Isfahan and so was presumably known for his knowledge of the city's past.

6   The text has *al-'ajība ilaynā*; read *al-'ajība al-binā'*.

chance for durable building. So they sent out scouts[7] throughout the lands and locales of the kingdom and they did not discover under the panoply of heaven any city that better combined these qualities than Isfahan. Then they searched the places of this city and they did not find anywhere better than the encampment of Jay and they did not find in the encampment of Jay anywhere that comprised all that they sought more than the site[8] where the city of Jay would be marked out in the time to come.[9] They came to the citadel which was inside the city and they deposited in it all their (books of) sciences, and this (building) has survived until our time and is called Sarawayh.

As regards this building, people knew who was responsible for its construction,[10] and that is because many years before our time a side of this edifice collapsed, and they discovered within it a chamber that had been sealed by the clay of the broken-off section.[11] They found in it many books of the writings of the ancients, all of them inscribed on white poplar bark and preserving all kinds of the sciences of the ancients in the ancient Persian script. Some of those books fell into (the hands of) a person who took an interest in them and he read them and came upon one book that belonged to one of the early Persian kings. It mentioned that King Tahmurath, the lover of science and its practitioners, received information about an atmospheric event[12] in the west in the form of successive rains of long duration and great intensity beyond the usual bounds. From the first day of the years of his reign to the first day of the onset of this storm in the west (there elapsed) 231 years and 300 days, and from the very beginning of his rule the astrologers made him fearful that this storm would cross from the west to the adjoining eastern regions. He therefore ordered the engineers to arrive at a choice of the soundest place in the realm as to ground and atmosphere, and they selected for him the site of the building known as Sarawayh, which is standing until now in the city of Jay. So he ordered the construction of this secure building. When it had been completed for him, he transferred to it

---

7 H: *intaqaḍū*; IN: *intafaḍū*; I prefer reading *istanfaḍū*.

8 H: sites (*mawāḍi*').

9 *Dahr al-dāhir*. Dodge translates 'in the time of Dāhir', taking the latter to be a reference to a warrior mentioned in Firdawsi's *Shāhnamāh* as a supporter of Kay Khusraw.

10 H: who would come to it (*man kāna ya'tīhā*).

11 This is an oddly worded sentence: *ẓaharū fīhā 'alā azaj ma'qūd min ṭīn al-shaqīq*. Dodge translates: 'They found a vault in the cleft-off side built without mortar'.

12 H: *ḥādith*; IN: *ḥadath*. This is a reference to the Biblical flood and is an example of one of many attempts by Abu Ma'shar to reconcile Persian and Biblical chronology.

from his libraries scientific works of many diverse kinds, and they were copied for him onto white poplar bark. He then deposited them in a side of that building[13] so that they might be preserved for mankind until after the storm had come to an end.

Among them was a book attributed to one of the ancient sages in which (were presented) the years and known cycles for deriving the mean longitudes of the planets and the irregularities of their motions. The people of the time of Tahmurath and the other Persians who preceded them called these the cycles of the thousands.[14] Most of the scholars and kings of India, who were of long standing,[15] the first kings of the Persians and the ancient Chaldaeans, who were tent dwellers among the people of Babel in the earliest times, computed the mean longitudes of the seven planets from these years and cycles. He (Tahmurath) valued it above all the astronomical tables of his time because he, and others of that time, found it on examination to be the most accurate of all them and the most concise. And the astrologers who attended the major kings[16] at that time produced from it tables that they called the Zīj Shahriyār, which means in Arabic 'the king of astronomical tables...'[17] [IN says: This is the end of the statement of Abu Maʿshar] [H continues] ... and the chief of them. They would use this astronomical table rather than any of their own astronomical tables for (ascertaining) what the kings sought to know about future happenings in this world. This title continued (to be used) for the astronomical tables of the Persians in ancient and modern times. And its status among many of the nations of that time until our own day has grown such that (astronomical) judgements are (deemed) valid for planets only if reckoned on the basis of it. As far as here runs the narrative of Abu Maʿshar concerning the description of the building still present in Isfahan. However, Abu Maʿshar only describes a chamber of this building which collapsed more or less a thousand years ago and linked it to (the atmospheric event mentioned in) the Zīj Shahriyār. As for what collapsed in the year 350 of the Hijra, it was

---

13 H: *tilka l-binya*; Ibn al-Nadim: *dhālika l-bayt*.

14 Thus IN; H: 'the years and the cycles of the thousands'.

15 H: *ʿalā wajh al-dahr*; IN: *ʿalā wajh al-arḍ*.

16 This phrase, 'who attended the major kings'/*alladhīna kānū maʿa ruʾasāʾ al-mulūk*, is only in H.

17 'A zīj consists essentially of the numerical tables and accompanying explanation sufficient to enable the practicing astronomer, or astrologer, to solve all the practical problems of his profession, i.e. to measure time and to compute planetary and stellar positions, appearance and eclipses' (Kennedy, 'Islamic Astronomical Tables', 1).

another chamber, the location of which had not been known, because the surface of it (the whole edifice) was judged to be solid (i.e. not hollow) until it collapsed, thereby revealing these many[18] written books, which no one[19] has managed to read since their script does not resemble any of the (known) scripts of the nations. In short, this building is one of the wonders existing in the land of the East just as the building in Egypt called the pyramid is one of the wonders existing in the land of the West.

[IN] A reliable informant[20] told me that in the year 350 of the Hijra another chamber collapsed, the location of which had not been known[21] because the surface of it (the whole edifice) was judged to be solid (not hollow) until it collapsed and revealed these many books, which no one has managed to read and which I have inspected personally.

In the (3)40s Abu l-Fadl ibn al-ʿAmid dispatched here some torn books found in Isfahan, in the wall of the city, in boxes. They were in Greek; people knowledgeable in this field, like John and others, worked out that they were names of troops and the amounts of their rations. The books were extremely foul smelling, as though they had just been tanned. When they had remained in Baghdad for some time, they dried out and changed and the smell disappeared from them. At this time some are with our sheikh Abu Sulayman. It is said that the Sarawayh is one of the sturdy ancient buildings of extraordinary construction, a parallel in the East to the majesty and wonder of the Egyptian pyramids in the land of the West.

The late ninth-century author of 'The Book of the Reasons behind Astronomical Tables', one ʿAli ibn Sulayman al-Hashimi, suggests that Abu Maʿshar benefited from one of these discoveries of books at Jay, finding a work that he could use for his own research, possibly the one described above as belonging to 'one of the ancient sages':

Abu Maʿshar composed a *zīj* based on cycles said to be Persian cycles that he

18 Reading *kathīra* with IN rather than *kabīra*/'large'.

19 A negative seems to have dropped out of H; compare the text of IN below.

20 Ibn al-Nadim says he is no longer citing from Abu Maʿshar and yet the following sentence has almost the same wording as Hamza. Either Ibn al-Nadim's unnamed informant is Hamza, and he is here citing from a communication from the latter to him, or Pourshariati is right that Ibn al-Nadim is copying from Hamza's chronological work without acknowledgement.

21 Dodge translates 'the location (of the books) did not become known', but 'location' must refer to the chamber, since the relative pronoun is masculine (*makānuhu*) and in any case in the Arabic text the books are only mentioned further on.

found in Isfahan in a book (discovered) in an underground room (*sarab*). He said that he had studied most of it[22] and that he had tested them (the cycles) and found them to be accurate. So he made his *zīj* from them according to two dates that he took (from it): the date of the Flood and the other, the date of Yazdagird (III). He noted that atmospheric events are only correct (when determined) by it, and he admits that it is (equivalent to) the 'Astronomical Tables of the King'.[23]

22 Or: 'most of it had been effaced' (*qad darasa aktharuhu*).
23 *Zīj al-Shāh*, which is another name for the *Zīj Shahriyār* mentioned above. This quotation is taken from Ms Bodleian Selden A11, 96r = 98v (96 is written in Arabic form, 98 in English form).

GAZETTEER

I note if a toponym refers to a river, city/village or region (used loosely to refer to any tract of land, whether district, province or country). I indicate if a toponym is included on one of the three maps below, and if not I indicate a place/region that it is near to/inside of and that is to be found on one of the maps. The point of this gazetteer is to help the reader locate a particular place; for information on the place, the reader should look to its first occurrence in the translation section above and this can be found via the general index below.

Ābād Ardashir, city in Sawad (q.v.)
Abarshahr, region of Khurasan (q.v.)
Ahwaz, city in south-west Iran, map 2
Aleppo, city in northern Syria, map 1
Alexandria: name of 12 cities of Alexander the Great
Ānārabād, region near Isfahan (q.v.)
Anbar, city near Baghdad, map 1
Ansha'a Ardashir, city near Basra (q.v.)
Antioch, city in northern Syria, map 1
Ardistān, village near Isfahan (q.v.)
Armenia, region, map 1
Ardashir Khurra, *see* Gur
Arrajan, *see* Bih-Az-Amid Kawad
Arran, region, map 1
Azerbaijan, region, map 1

Bab al-Abwab, *see* Darband
Babylon, city in Iraq, map 2
Badhghis, region of east Iran, map 3
Baghdad, city in Iraq, map 1
Bahman Ardashir, city in Sawad (q.v.)
Balashabad, city near Mada'in (q.v.)

Hamadan, city in north-west Iran, map 1
Hamaniya, *see* Ābād Ardashir
Ḥamhīn, city near Isfahan (q.v.)
Hanbu Shabur, city near Madaʾin (q.v.)
Herat, city in eastern Iran, map 3
Ḥarwān, village near Jay (q.v.)
Hulwan, city in west Iran, map 2
Hurmuz Ardashir, *see* Ahwaz

Idhaj, city near Ahwaz (q.v.)
Indus, river in Sind, map 1
Iran Shad Kawad, city between Hulwan and Shahrazur (q.v.)
Isfahan, city in northern Iran, maps 1+3
Istakhr, city in Fars, map 3
Īzad Qubad Kard, city in Sawad (q.v.)

Jājāh, village near Jay (q.v.)
Janbu Shabur, *see* Hanbu Shabur
Jawastad, city in Khuzistan (q.v.)
Jay, city near Isfahan (q.v.)
Jerusalem, city in Palestine, map 1
Jibal, region of west Iran, map 1
Jundishabur, city of Khuzistan, map 2

Kabul, city in Central Asia, map 1
Karka d-Ledan, city in south-west Iran, map 2
Karkh Maysan, *see* Anshaʾa Ardashir
Karun, river in south-west Iran and Iraq, map 2
Kazarun, city in Fars west of Shiraz (q.v.)
Kermanshah, city in west Iran, map 2
Khabur Kawad, city near Mosul (q.v.)
Khurasan, region of north-east Iran, maps 1+3
Khurrah Shabur, *see* Susa
Khuwār, region near Isfahan (q.v.)
Khuzistan, region of south-west Iran, map 1
Kirman, city and region of south-east Iran, maps 1+3
Kushid, mountain, between Fars and Isfahan (q.v.)

Mada'in, city in Iraq, map 2
Mahat, *see* Jibal
Mahrin, village near Isfahan (q.v.)
Mamnūr, village near Isfahan (q.v.)
Manbij, city east of Aleppo (q.v.)
Maragha, city in north-west Iran, map 2
Masabadhan, city in Jibal (q.v.)
Maysan, region around Basra (q.v.)
Merv, city in Khurasan, maps 1+3
Mosul, city in north Iraq, maps 1+2

Nahrawan, village near Baghdad (q.v.)
Najjān, region near Jay (q.v.)
Nihawand, city in west Iran, map 2
Nishabur, city in Khurasan, maps 1+3
Nisibis, city in northern Mesopotamia, map 2

Palmyra, city east of Damascus (q.v.)

Qazvin, city in northern Iran near Rayy (q.v.)
Qinnasrin, city south of Aleppo (q.v.)
Qom, city in northern Iran near Rayy (q.v.)
Qumis, city in northern Iran, map 3

Ram Ardashir, city in Fars (q.v.)
Ramhurmuz (Ardashir), city in Fars (q.v.)
Rayy, city in northern Iran, maps 1+3
Resh'aina, city in nothern Syria, map 2
Rishahr, *see* Riw Ardashir
Riw Ardashir, city in south-west Iran, map 1
Rustam Kawad, *see* Rustuqabad
Rustuqabad, city in Khuzistan (q.v.)

Samarkand, city in Soghdia, map 1
Sarakhs, city in Khurasan, map 3
Sawad, region in southern Iraq, maps 1+2
Seleucia-Ctesiphon, *see* Mada'in
Shahrabad Kawad (or Shahr Qubad), city in Fars (q.v.)
Shahrazur, city in north-west Iraq, map 2

Shiraz, city in south-west Iran, map 1
Shiz, city south-east of Maragha (q.v.)
Shustar, *see* Tustar
Sijistan, region in south-east Iran, maps 1+3
Soghdia, region in Central Asia, map 1
Susa, city in Khuzistan, map 2

Tabaristan, region in northern Iran, map 1
Taymara, region near Isfahan (q.v.)
Tustar, city in south-west Iran, map 2

'Ukbara, *see* Buzurg Shabur

Wahisht Ardashir: location unknown
Wahisht Hurmuz, region in Khuzistan (q.v.)
Walashgird, city between Kermanshah and Hamadan (q.v.)

Yawān, village, near Jay (q.v.)
Yemen, region in southern Arabia, map 1

Zabulistan, region south-east of Kabul (q.v.)

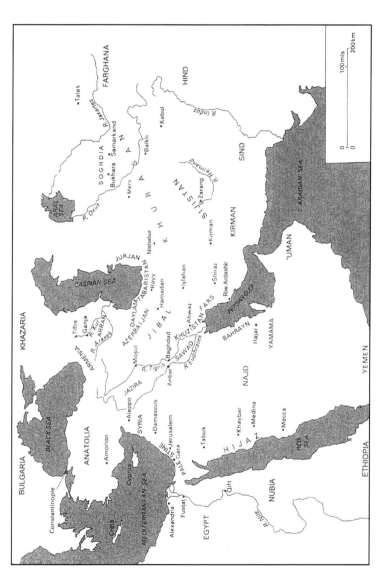

Map 1 Regions of the Early Islamic Middle East

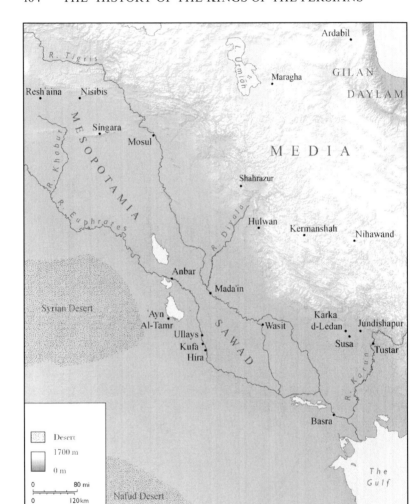

Map 2 Iraq and West Iran

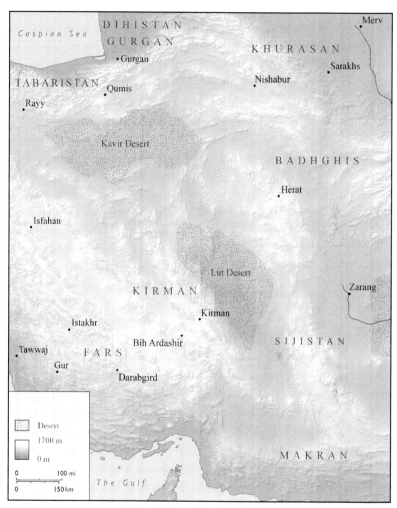

Map 3 Central and East Iran

TABLES

Table 1:
Reign lengths of Pishdadid, Kayanid and Arsacid kings

Kings	Hamza (yrs)	Bahram (yrs)	Mas'udi (yrs)	Ya'qubi (yrs)
Pishdadids				
Hushang Pishdad	40	40	40	40
Tahmurath b. Nawbijahan	30	30	30	30
Jam(shid) b. Nawbijahan	716	716 (616 + 100)	700 + 3 months	700
Biyurasb b. Arwandasb (= Dahak)	1000	1000	1000	1000
Afridun b. Athfiyan	500	500	—	500
Manushihr (Mas'udi adds Sahm b. Aman)	120	120	120 (+ Sahm: 60)	120
Afrasiyab the Turk	12	unspecified	12	120
Zaw b. Tahmasb	3	4	3	5
Karshasb	9	unspecified	3	—
Kayanids				
Kay Qubad	126	100	120	100
Kay Kawus	150	150	150	120
Kay Khusraw	80	60	60	60
Kay Luhrasb	120	120	120	120
Kay Bishtasb	120	120	120	112
Kay (Ardashir) Bahman	112	112	112	112
Khumani Shahrazad	30	30	30	30
Dara b. Bahman	12	12	12	12
Dara b. Dara	14	14	14	—

Kings	Hamza (yrs)	Bahram (yrs)	Mas'udi (yrs)	Ya'qubi (yrs)
Alexander (the Great)	14	14	6	unspecified
Arsacids				
Ashak b. Ashak	52	20	10	—
Shabur b. Ashak	24	60	60	—
Gudarz b. Shabur	50	—*	10	—
Wanhan b. Balash b. Shabur [Mas'udi: Bizan b. Shabur]	21	—	21	—
Gudarz the Younger b. Wanhan	19	—	19	—
Narsi b. Wanhan	30	—	40	—
Hurmuz b. Balash	17	19	19	—
Firuz b. Hurmuz [Mas'udi: Ardawan the Elder]	12	17	12	—
Khusraw b. Firuz	40	—	40	—
Balash b. Firuz	24	12	24	—
Ardawan b. Balash	55	13**	13	—

*Bahram lists here: Bahram b. Shabur, Balash b. Bahram, Narsi b. Balash, Khusraw b. Malad and Balash
** Bahram now lists six sons of the last Arsacid king: Ardawan, Khusraw, Bihafarid, Balash, Gudarz, Narsi, and ends with Ardawan 'Afdam'

Table 2:
Reign lengths of Sasanid kings

Kings	Hamza	Musa	Bahram	Mas'udi	Ya'qubi
Ardashir [I]	14 + 6 Months	19 + 6 M	14 + 10 M	14 + a few M	14
Shabur [I]	30 + 28 Days	32 + 4 M	30 + 15 D	31 + 6 M	unspecified
Hurmuz [I]	1 + 10 M	1 + 10 M	2	1 + 10 M	1
Bahram [I]	3 + 3 M + 3 D	9 + 3 M	3 + 3 M	3 + 3 M	3
Bahram [II]	17	23/17	17	17/18	17
Bahram [III]	13 + 4 M	13 + 4 M	40 + 4 M	4 + 4 M	4
Narsi	9	9	9	9 + 6 M	9
Hurmuz [II]	7 + 5 M	13	7	7 + 5 M	9
Shabur [II]	72	72	72	4	72
Ardashir [II]	4	4	4	4	4
Shabur [III]	5 + 5 M	82	5	5 + 4 M	5
Bahram [IV]	11	12	11	11	11
Yazdagird [I] the Sinner	21 + 5 M + 16 D	82	21 + 5 M + 18 D	21	21
Bahram [V] Gur	23	18 + 5 M	19 + 11 M	23	19
Yazdagird [II]	18 + 4 M + 18 D	26 + 1 M	4 + 4 M + 18 D	18	17
Firuz [I]	27 + 1 D	29 + 1 D	17	27	27
Balash	4	3	4	4	4
Qubad [I]	43	68/43	41	43	43
Khusraw [I] Anushirwan	47 + 7 M	47 + 7 M + some days	48	48	48
Hurmuz	11 + 7 M + 10 D	23/13	12	12	12
Khusraw [II] Abarwiz	38	38	38	38	38
Shirawayh	8 M	8 M	8 M	6 M	8 M
Ardashir [III]	1 + 6 M	1	1 + 6 M	1 + 6 M	1 + 6 M
Shahrbaraz	—	38 D	—	40 days	unspecified

Kings	Hamza	Musa	Bahram	Mas'udi	Ya'qubi
Buran Dukht	1 + 4 M	1 + some days	1 + 4 M	1 + 6 M	1 + 4 M
Firuz II Jushnasbandah	2 M	2 M	some days	6 M	unspecified
Azarmidukht	1 + 4 M	4 M	6 M	6 M	6 M
Khurrazad/ Farrukh(zad) Khusraw	1 M	1 M + some days	1	1	1
Khusraw [III]	—	10 M	—	3 M	—
Yazdagird [III]	20	20	20	20	20

Table 3:
Genealogy of the Sasanid Emperors
(dates of some of the early rulers are tentative)

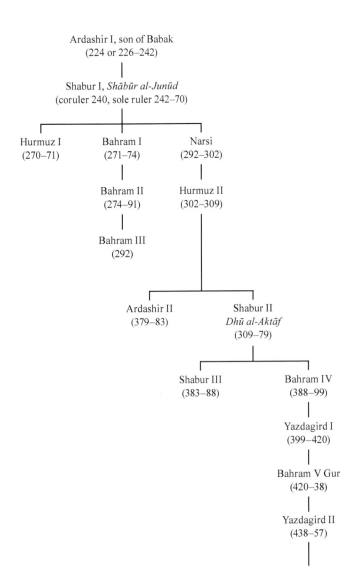

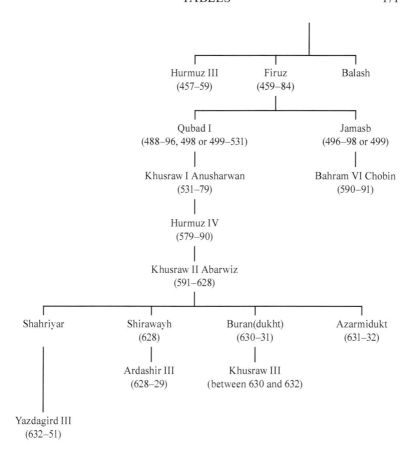

Table 4:
Transmission of key sources cited in this book

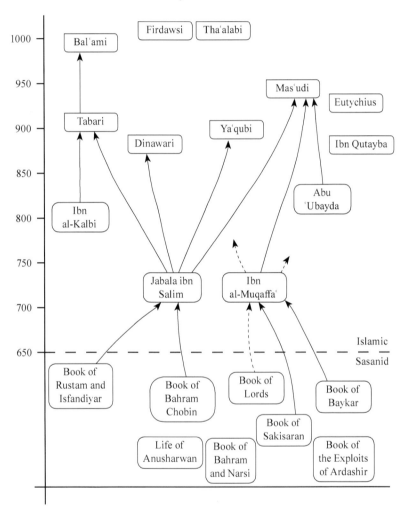

Key:

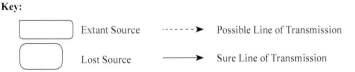

Extant Source   ┈┈┈▶   Possible Line of Transmission

Lost Source   ───▶   Sure Line of Transmission

BIBLIOGRAPHY

Primary sources

Abu Bakr al-Dinawari al-Maliki, *Al-mujālasa wa-jawāhir al-'ilm* (Beirut, 1419).

Agathias, *Histories*, ed. R. Keydell (Berlin, 1967).

Baladhuri, Ahmad ibn Yahya al-, *Futūḥ al-buldān*, ed. M.J. de Goeje (Leiden, 1866).

Bal'ami, Abu 'Ali Muhammad, *Tārīkh*, ed. M.T. Bahar and M.P. Gunabadi (Tehran, 1974).

Biruni, Muhammad ibn Ahmad al-, *Al-āthār al-bāqiya*, ed. E. Sachau (Leipzig, 1878).

Chronicle of Khuzistan = I. Guidi ed./tr. *Chronicon anonymum* (CSCO 1–2 Scr. Syri 1–2; Paris, 1903), 15–39/15–32.

Chronicle of Siirt, ed./tr. Addai Scher, *Patrologia Orientalis* 7 (1911), 1–110; 13 (1919), 111–319.

Dinawari, Abu Hanifa al- (d. 282/895), *Kitāb al-akhbār al-ṭiwāl*, ed. Vladimir Guirgass (Leiden, 1888).

Eutychius, *Annales/al-Ta'rīkh al-majmū'* I, ed. L. Cheikho (CSCO Scr. Arab. iii.6; Paris, 1906).

Firdawsi, Abu l-Qasim, *Shāh-nāmah*, tr. Dick Davis (New York, 2006) with the title *Shahnameh: The Persian Book of Kings*). The manuscript tradition is very complex (Davis, *ibid.*, xxxv, says that he used 'various editions'), and so, since Firdawsi's text is not my main concern, I will just cite Davis' translation.

Hamza al-Isfahani, *Ta'rīkh sinī mulūk al-arḍ wa-l-anbiyā*, ed. J.M. Gottwaldt (St Petersburg and Leiden, 1844).

Hashimi, 'Ali b. Sulayman al-, *The Book of the Reasons behind Astronomical Tables (Kitāb fī 'ilal al-zījāt): A Facsimile Reproduction of the Unique Arabic Text Contained in the Bodleian MS Arch. Seld. A.11.* translation and commentary by Fuad I. Haddad *et al.* (Delmar, NY, 1981).

Ibn al-Faqih al-Hamadhani, *Mukhtaṣar kitāb al-buldān*, ed. M.J. de Goeje (Leiden, 1885); ed. Yusuf al-Hadi (Beirut, 1996).

Ibn Hisham, *Kitāb sīrat rasūl Allāh / Das Leben Muhammed's*, ed. F. Wüstenfeld (Göttingen, 1858).

Ibn al-Nadim, *Kitāb al-Fihrist*, Muhammad ibn Ishaq (d. 380/990), ed. Gustav Flügel (Leipzig, 1871).

Ibn al-Qifti, *Taʾrīkh al-ḥukamāʾ*, ed. Julius Lippert (Leipzig, 1903).

Ibn Qutayba, *ʿUyūn al-akhbār* (Beirut, 1997).

— *Kitāb al-maʿārif*, ed. Tharwat ʿUkasha (Cairo, 1981).

Ibn Taghribirdi, *al-Nujūm al-zāhira fī mulūk Miṣr wa-l-Qāhira* (Cairo, 1963).

Istakhri, Abu Ishaq al-, *Kitāb al-masālik wa-l-mamālik*, ed. M.J. de Goeje (Leiden, 1870).

Jahiz, ʿAmr ibn Bahr al-, *al-Bayān wa-l-tabyīn*, ed. ʿA-S.M. Harun (Cairo, 1960–61).

— ʿKitāb fī dhamm al-kuttābʾ, in ʿA-S.M. Harun, ed., *Rasāʾil al-Jāḥiẓ* (Cairo, 1964), 2.183–209.

Maqdisi, al-Mutahhar ibn Tahir, *Kitāb al-badʾ wa-l-taʾrīkh*, ed./tr. C. Huart (Paris, 1899–1919).

Masʿudi = Masʿudi, ʿAli ibn al-Husayn al-, *Kitāb al-tanbīh wa-l-ishrāf*, ed. M.J. de Goeje (Leiden, 1894); tr. B. Carra de Vaux as *Le livre de l'avertissement et de la revision* (Paris, 1897).

Masʿudi, *Murūj* = Masʿudi, ʿAli ibn al-Husayn al-, *Murūj al-dhahab wa-maʿādin al-jawhar*, ed./tr. C. Barbier de Meynard and J.B. Pavet de Courteille (Paris, 1861–77).

MS Sprenger 30: an Arabic manuscript in the Staatsbibliothek in Berlin which, on its first page, bears the Arabic title *Taʾrīkh ʿaẓīm* ('Great History') and the English title 'Handbook of Chronology and History from Creation to the Hijrah': <http://digital.staatsbibliothek-berlin.de/werkansicht?PPN=PPN78202 6311&PHYSID=PHYS_0116&DMDID=DMDLOG_0001>.

Nihāyat al-arab fī taʾrīkh al-Furs wa-l-ʿArab, ed. M. Taqi Danish-Pazhuh (Tehran, 1954).

Philostorgius = Joseph Bidez ed., *Philostorgius, Kirchengeschichte* (revised by F. Winkelmann, Berlin, 1981); tr. Philip Amidon (Atlanta, 2007).

Procopius, *History of the Wars I–II*, ed./tr. H.B. Dewing (Loeb; London and New York, 1914).

Ps-Joshua = J.B. Chabot ed., *Incerti auctoris chronicon pseudo-Dionysianum vulgo dictum I* (CSCO 91 Scr. Syri 43; Paris and Louvain, 1927); tr. Frank Trombley and John Watts (Translated Texts for Historians 32; Liverpool, 2000).

Ps-Zachariah = Geoffrey Greatrex *et al.*, tr., *The Chronicle of Pseudo-Zachariah Rhetor* (Translated Texts for Historians 55; Liverpool, 2011).

Sebeos = G.V. Abgaryan ed., *Pamutʿiwn Sebeosi* (Erevan, 1979); tr. Robert Thomson and James Howard-Johnston (Translated Texts for Historians 31; Liverpool, 1999).

Shahristan-i Iranshahr, ed. Touraj Daryaee as: *Šahrestānīhā ī Ērānšahr: A Middle Persian Text on Late Antique Geography, Epic and History* (Costa Mesa, 2002).

Tabari, Muhammad ibn Jarir al-, *Ta'rīkh al-rusul wa-l-mulūk/Annales*. ed. M.J. de Goeje *et al.* (Leiden, 1879–1901).

Tha'alabi, 'Abd al-Malik ibn Muhammad al-, *Ghurar akhbār mulūk al-Furs*, ed./tr. H. Zotenberg (Paris, 1900).

Theophylact Simocatta, *History*, ed. C. de Boor (Leipzig, 1887); trans. Michael and Mary Whitby (Oxford, 1986).

Ya'qubi, Ahmad ibn Abi Ya'qub al-, *Ta'rīkh*, ed. M.T. Houtsma (Leiden, 1883).

Yaqut, Abu 'Abdallah, *Mu'jam al-buldān/Jacut's geographischen Wörterbuch*, ed. Ferdinand Wüstenfeld (Göttingen, 1866–73).

Secondary sources

Adang, Camilla, 'The Chronology of the Israelites according to Ḥamza al-Iṣfahānī', *Jerusalem Studies in Arabic and Islam* 32 (2006), 286–310.

Anthony, Sean, 'Was Ibn Wāḍiḥ al-Ya'qūbī a Shi'ite Historian?', *Al-'Uṣūr al-Wusṭā* 24 (2016), 15–41.

Askari, Nasrin, *The Medieval Reception of the Shāhnāma as a Mirror for Princes* (Leiden, 2016).

Bailey, H.W., *Zoroastrian Problems in the Ninth-Century Books* (Oxford, 1943).

Bausani, Alessandro, 'Two Unsuccessful Prophets: Mani and Mazdak', in *id.*, ed., *Religion in Iran from Zoroaster to Baha'ullah* (New York, 2000), chapter 2.

Bonner, Michael J., *Three Neglected Sources of Sasanian History in the Reign of Khusraw Anushirvan* (MPhil thesis; Oxford, 2010; published in the series Cahiers de Studia Iranica, no. 46; Leuven, 2011).

— *A Historiographical Study of Abū Ḥanīfa Aḥmad ibn Dāwūd ibn Wanand al-Dīnawarī's Kitāb al-Akhbār al-Ṭiwāl* (DPhil thesis; Oxford, 2014; published in the series Res Orientales, no. 23; Leuven, 2015).

Bosworth, C.E., *The History of Al-Tabari, Volume 5: The Sasanids, The Byzantines, the Lakhmids and Yemen* (Albany, NY, 1999).

Boyce, Mary, *The Letter of Tansar* (Rome, 1968).

Cameron, Averil, 'Agathias on the Sassanians', *Dumbarton Oaks Papers* 23–24 (1969–70), 67–183.

Christensen, Arthur, *L'Iran sous les Sassanides* (Copenhagen, 1936).

Christensen, Peter, *Decline of Iranshahr: Irrigation and Environments in the History of the Middle East* (Copenhagen, 1993).

Cobb, Paul, 'Al-Mutawakkil's Damascus: A New 'Abbasid Capital?', *Journal of Near Eastern Studies* 58 (1999), 241–57.

Crone, Patricia, 'Kavad's Heresy and Mazdak's Revolt', *Iran* 29 (1991), 21–42.

— 'Buddhism as Ancient Iranian Paganism', in Teresa Bernheimer and Adam Silverstein, eds, *Late Antiquity: Eastern Perspectives* (Oxford, 2012), 25–41.

Daryaee, Touraj, 'Kāve the Blacksmith: an Indo-Iranian Fashioner?', *Studien zur Indologie und Iranistik* 22 (1999), 9–21.

— 'Gayōmard: King of Clay or Mountain: the Epithet of the First Man in the Zoroastrian Tradition', in Siamak Adhami, ed., *Paitimāna. Essays in Iranian, Indo-European and Indian Studies in Honor of Hanns-Petter Schmidt* (Costa Mesa, CA, 2003), 339–49.

— *Sasanian Persia: the rise and fall of an empire* (New York, 2009).

— 'Ardaxšīr and the Sasanian's Rise to Power', *Anabasis* 1 (2010), 236–55.

— 'On the Epithets of Two Iranian Kings in the *Mujmal al-tawarikh wa-l-qisas*', in R. Hillenbrand *et al.*, eds, *Ferdowsi, the Mongols and the History of Iran. Studies in Honour of Charles Melville* (London, 2013), 11–14.

— and Rezakhani, Khodadad, *From Oxus to Euphrates: The World of Late Antique Iran* (London, 2016).

Daudpota, U.M., 'The Annals of Hamzah al-Isfahani', *Journal of the K.R. Cama Oriental Institute* 21–24 (Bombay, 1932), 58–120.

Davidson, Olga, *Poet and Hero in the Persian Book of Kings* (Ithaca, NY, 1994).

Davis, Dick, 'The Problem of Ferdowsi's Sources', *Journal of the American Oriental Society* 116 (1996), 48–57.

Esin, E., 'Tarkhan Nīzak or Tarkhan Tirek. An Enquiry concerning the Prince of Badhghis', *Journal of the American Oriental Society* 97 (1977), 323–32.

Fisher, Greg, *Arabs and Empires before Islam* (Oxford, 2015).

Freudenthal, Gad, and Zonta, Mauro, 'Ḥabīb ibn Bahrīz' Arabic Translation of Nicomachus of Gerasa's Introduction to Arithmetic', in Y. Tzvi Langermann and Josef Stern, eds, *Studies in the Interaction between Islamic and Jewish Thought and Literature* (Paris-Louvain, 2007), 67–82.

Gardner, Iain, *et al.*, *Mani at the Court of the Persian Kings: Studies on the Chester Beatty Kephalaia Codex* (Leiden, 2015).

Greatrex, G., and Lieu, Sam, *The Roman Eastern Frontier and the Persian Wars. Part II: AD 363–630* (London, 2002).

Greenwood, Tim, 'Sasanian Echoes and Apocalyptic Expectations: A Re-evaluation of the Armenian History attributed to Sebeos', *Le Muséon* 115/3–4 (2002), 323–97.

Grenet, Frantz, *La geste d'Ardashir fils de Pâbag: Kārnāmag ī Ardaxšēr ī Pābagān* (Die, 2003).

Grignaschi, Mario, 'Quelques spécimens de la literature sassanide conserves dans les bibliothèques d'Istanbul', *Journal Asiatique* 254 (1966), 1–144.

— 'La nihāyatu l-arab fī akhbār al-Furs wa-l-'Arab', *Bulletin d'Etudes Orientales* 22 (1969), 15–67, and 26 (1974), 83–105.

— 'Les règles d'Ardašīr b. Bābak pour le gouvernement du royaume', in M.T. Gökbilgin, ed., *Islām Tetkikleri Enstitüsü Dergisi* (Istanbul, 1973), 95–112.

Gutas, Dimitri, *Greek Thought, Arabic Culture. The Graeco-Arabic Translation Movement in Baghdad and Early Abbasid Society* (London, 1998).

Gyselen, Rika, 'A propos d'un toponyme Sasanide', *Journal Asiatique* 270 (1982), 271–72.

— *La géographie administrative de l'Empire Sassanide: Les témoignages sigillographiques* (Paris, 1989).

— *The Four Generals of the Sasanian Empire: Some Sigillographic Evidence* (Rome, 2001).

Hämeen-Anttila, Jaakko, 'Al-Maqdisī and his Sources', *Orientalia Lovaniensia Analecta* 207 (2012), 151–63.

— 'Al-Kisrawī and the Arabic Translations of the Khwadāynāmag', in S. Akar *et al.*, eds, *Travelling through Time. Essays in honour of Kaj Öhrnberg* (Helsinki, 2013), 65–92.

— 'Ibn al-Muqaffaʿ and the Middle Persian Book of Kings', *Orientalia Lovaniensa Periodica* 254 (2014), 171–84.

Howard-Johnston, James, *Witnesses to a World Crisis: Historians and Histories of the Middle East in the Seventh Century* (Oxford, 2010).

— 'The Sasanians' Strategic Dilemma', in H. Börm and J. Wieschöfer, eds, *Commutatio et Contentio. Studies on Late Roman, Sasanian and Early Islamic Near East. In Memory of Zeev Rubin* (Düsseldorf, 2010), 37–70.

Hoyland, Robert, *Seeing Islam as Others Saw it* (Princeton, NJ, 1997).

— *Theophilus of Edessa's Chronicle and the Circulation of Historical Knowledge In Late Antiquity and Early Islam* (Liverpool, 2011).

Huyse, Philip, 'Late Sasanian Society between Orality and Literacy', in V.S. Curtis and S. Stewart, eds, *The Sasanian Era. The Idea of Iran III* (London, 2008), 140–53.

Kennedy, E.S., 'A Survey of Islamic Astronomical Tables', *Transactions of the American Philosophical Society* 46 (1956), 123–77, and issued in book form numbered pages 1–55.

— and Pingree, David, *The Astrological History of Masha'allah* (Cambridge, MA, 1971).

Klamroth, M., 'Ueber die Auszüge aus griechischen Schriftstellern bei al-Jaʿqūbī', *Zeitschrift der Deutschen Morgenländischen Gesellschaft* 46 (1886), 415–42.

Klima, Otakar, 'Wie sah die persische Geschichtsschreibung in der vorislamischen Periode aus?', *Archiv Orientalni* 36 (1968), 213–32.

Llewellyn-Jones, L., and Robson, J., *Ctesias' History of Persia* (Abingdon and New York, 2010).

Macdonald, D.B., 'The Earlier History of the Arabian Nights', *Journal of the Royal Asiatic Society* 3 (1924), 353–97.

McDonough, Scott, 'A Question of Faith. Persecution and Political Centralization in the Sasanian Empire of Yazdgard II', in Harold Drake, ed., *Violence in Late Antiquity: Perceptions and Practices* (Aldershot, 2007), 69–81.

— 'A Second Constantine? The Sasanian King Yazdgard in Christian History and Historiography', *Journal of Late Antiquity* 1 (2008), 127–41.

— 'The Legs of the Throne: Kings, Elites and Subjects in Sasanian Iran', in J.P. Arnason and K.A. Raaflaub, eds, *The Roman Empire in Context* (Chichester and Malden, MA, 2011), 290–321.

Macuch, Maria, 'Pahlavi Literature', in Ronald Emmerick and *ead.*, eds, *The Literature of Pre-Islamic Iran* (History of Persian Literature 17; London, 2009), 116–96.

Mango, Cyril, 'Deux études sur Byzance et la Perse Sassanide', *Travaux et Mémoires* 9 (1985), 91–116.

Marsh, Adrian, '... "the strumming of their silken bows": The Firdawsī Legend of Bahram Gūr and Narratives of Origin in Romani Histories', in *id.* and Elin Strand, eds, *Gypsies and the Problem of Identities* (Istanbul, 2006), 39–58.

Melville, Charles, ed., *Persian Historiography* (History of Persian Literature X; London, 2012).

Minorsky, V., 'The Older Preface to the Shāh-nāma', in *id.*, *Iranica: Twenty Articles* (Tehran, 1964), 260–74.

Mittwoch, E., 'Die literarische Tätigkeit Ḥamza al-Iṣbahānīs. Ein Beitrag zur älteren arabischen Literaturgeschichte', *Westasiatische Studien. Mitteilungen des Seminars für orientalische Sprachen* 12 (1909), 109–69.

Mochiri, M.I., 'A Coin of Khusraw IIII's Third Year', *The Numismatic Chronicle* 143 (1983), 221–23.

Nokandeh, J., *et al.*, *Persia's Imperial Power in Late Antiquity: The Great Wall of Gorgan and the Frontier Landscapes of Sasanian Iran* (Oxford, 2013).

Nöldeke, Theodor, 'Ueber den syrischen Roman von Kaiser Julian', *Zeitschrift der deutschen Morgenländischen Gesellschaft* 28 (1874), 263–92.

— *Geschichte der Perser und Araber zur Zeit der Sasaniden* (Leiden, 1879).

— *Das iranische Nationalepos* (Strassburg, 1896; reprinted Berlin and Leipzig, 1920).

— *The Iranian National Epic or the Shahnamah* (Bombay, 1930; reprinted Philadelphia, PA, 1979), translated from *Das iranische Nationalepos* but with minor changes.

Nyberg, H.S., 'Sassanid Mazdaism according to Moslem sources', *Journal of the K.R. Cama Oriental Institute* 39 (1958), 1–63.

Payne, Richard, *A State of Mixture: Christians, Zoroastrians, and Iranian Political Culture in Late Antiquity* (Oakland CA, 2015).

Peacock, Andrew, *Medieval Islamic Historiography and Political Legitimacy: Bal'amī's Tārīkhnāma* (Abingdon, 2007).

— 'Early Persian Historians and the Heritage of Pre-Islamic Iran', in Edmund Herzig and Sarah Stewart, eds, *Early Islamic Iran* (The Idea of Iran 5; London, 2012).

Pingree, David, *The Thousands of Abū Ma'shar* (London, 1968).

Pourshariati, 'Ḥamza al-Iṣfahānī and Sāsānid Historical Geography of Sinī mulūk al-arḍ w'al-anbiyā', *Res Orientales* 177 (2007), 111–41 (this issue of the journal is entitled *Des Indo-Grecs aux Sassanides*).

Reeves, John C., *Prolegomena to a History of Islamicate Manichaeism* (Sheffield, 2011).

Rezakhani, Khodadad, *Reorienting the Sasanians: East Iran in Late Antiquity* (Edinburgh, 2017).

Robinson, Chase, *Empires and Elites after the Muslim Conquest: The Transformation of Northern Mesopotamia* (Cambridge, 2000).

Rosen, Baron K., 'K voprosu ob arabskikh perevodakh Khudây Nâme', *Vostochnie Zametki Imperatorskoy Akademii Nauk* (1985), 167–87.

Rubin, Zeev, 'The Reforms of Khusro Anūshirwān'', in Averil Cameron, ed., *The Byzantine and Early Islamic Near East III: States, Resources and Armies* (Princeton, NJ, 1995), 227–97.

— 'Ibn al-Muqaffa' and the Account of Sasanian History in the Arabic Codex Sprenger 30', *Jerusalem Studies in Arabic and Islam* 30 (2005), 52–93.

— 'Musa ibn ʿIsa al-Kisrāwī and the Other Authors on Sasanian History known to Ḥamza al-Iṣfahānī', paper presented to the workshop *Jahiliyya to Early Islam* (Jerusalem, 2006), 1–31.

Russell, J.R., 'Kartīr and Mānī: a shamanistic model of their conflict', in D. Amin *et al.*, eds, *Iranica Varia: Papers in Honor of Professor Ehsan Yarshater* (Leiden, 1990), 180–93.

Sarre, Friedrich, and Herzfeld, Ernst, *Archäologische Reise im Euphrat- und Tigris-Gebiet* (Berlin, 1911–20).

Savant, Sarah, *The New Muslims of Post-Conquest Iran* (Cambridge, 2013).

Shahbazi, A.S., 'On the Xwadāy-nāmag', in D. Amin *et al.*, eds, *Iranica Varia: Papers in Honor of Professor Ehsan Yarshater* (Leiden, 1990), 208–29.

Shaked, Shaul, 'Administrative functions of priests in the Sasanian period', *Proceedings of the First European Conference of Iranian Studies* (Rome, 1990), Part 1, 261–73.

Shboul, Ahmad, *Al-Masʿūdī and His World* (London, 1979).

Silverstein, Adam, *Veiling Esther, Unveiling her Story: The Reception of a Biblical Book in Muslim Lands* (Oxford, 2018).

Smith, Sidney, 'Events in Arabia in the 6th c. AD', *Bulletin of the School of Oriental and African Studies* 16 (1954), 425–68.

Sprengling, Martin, *Third Century Iran: Sapor and Kartir* (Oriental Institute; Chicago, 1953).

Spuler, Bertold, *Iran in the Early Islamic Period*, ed. Robert Hoyland (Leiden, 2015).

Stark, Soeren, 'Türk Khaganate', in J.M. MacKenzie *et al.*, eds, *The Encyclopedia of Empire* (Malden, Oxford and Chichester, 2016), 2127–42.

Toral-Niehoff, Isabel, 'Die Legende "Barlaam und Josaphat" in der arabisch-Muslimischen Literatur', *Die Welt des Orients* 31 (2000–2001), 110–44.

Van Bladel, K., *The Arabic Hermes: From Pagan Sage to Prophet of Science* (Oxford, 2009).

— 'The Arabic History of Science of Abū Sahl ibn Nawbakht (fl. ca. 770–809) and its Middle Persian Sources', in F. Opwis and D. Reisman, eds, *Islamic Philosophy, Science, Culture and Religion. Studies in Honor of Dimitri Gutas* (Leiden, 2012), 41–62.

— 'Zoroaster's Many Languages', in Joseph Lowry and Shawkat Toorawa, eds, *Arabic Humanities, Islamic Thought. Essays in Honor of Everett K. Rowson* (Leiden, 2017), 190–210.

Wiesehöfer, J., 'The Changing Face of an Iranian Sacred Place: The Takht-i Sulayman', in R. Hillenbrand *et al.*, eds, *Ferdowsi, the Mongols and the History of Iran. Studies in Honour of Charles Melville* (London, 2013), 15–25.

— *Ancient Persia from 550 BC to 650 AD* (London, 1996).

Wood, Philip. *'We Have No King but Christ'. Christian Political Thought in Greater Syria on the Eve of the Arab Conquest* (Oxford, 2010).

— *The Chronicle of Seert: Christian Historical Imagination in Late Antique Iraq* (Oxford, 2013).

— 'The Christian Reception of the Xwāday-Nāmag: Hormizd IV, Khusrau II and their Successors', *Journal of the Royal Asiatic Society* 26 (2016), 407–22.

— 'Al-Hira and its Histories', *Journal of the American Oriental Society* 136 (2016), 785–99.

Yamimoto, Kumiko, *The Oral Background of Persian Epics* (Leiden, 2003).

Zakeri, Mohsen, *Persian Wisdom in Arabic Garb: 'Alī b. 'Ubayda al-Rayḥānī (d. 219/834) and his Jawāhir al-kilam wa-farā'id al-ḥikam* (Leiden, 2007).

Zuckerman, Constantin, 'Heraclius and the Return of the Holy Cross', *Travaux et Mémoires* 17 (2013), 197–218.

— 'The Khazars and Byzantium – First Encounters', in P. Golden *et al.*, eds, *The World of the Khazars* (HdO; Leiden, 2007), 399–432.

INDEX